A BLUE FIRE

A BLUE FIRE

SELECTED WRITINGS BY James Hillman

A BLUE FIRE

INTRODUCED AND EDITED BY Thomas Moore
IN COLLABORATION WITH THE AUTHOR

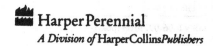
Harper Perennial
A Division of HarperCollins*Publishers*

An audio cassette version of *A Blue Fire* is available from Spring Audio Inc., P.O. Box 365, Gracie Station, New York, NY 10028.

A hardcover edition of this book was published in 1989 by Harper & Row, Publishers.

First HarperPerennial edition published 1991.

Designer: Barbara DuPree Knowles

The Library of Congress has catalogued the hardcover edition as follows:

Hillman, James
     A blue fire: selected writings/by James Hillman; introduced and edited by Thomas Moore in collaboration with James Hillman.—1st ed.
     p. cm.
     ISBN 0-06-016132-9
     I. Archetype (Psychology). 2. Psychoanalysis.   I. Moore, Thomas, 1940-   . II. Title.
     BF175.5.A72H54 1989
     150.19'54—dc20   89-45053

ISBN 0-06-092101-3 (pbk.)

HB 12.04.2017

Joints: whole and not whole,
connected-separate, consonant-dissonant.

—HERACLITUS

As rational metaphysics teaches that man
becomes all things by understanding them,
imaginative metaphysics shows that man
becomes all things by *not* understanding them,
for when . . . he does not understand he . . .
becomes them by transforming himself into them.

—VICO, New Science

CONTENTS

WORLD

EROS

ACKNOWLEDGMENTS

In his book Inter Views, James Hillman remarks that instead of being the founder of a school of thought, he sees himself as the member of a community of people in various fields who are at work re-visioning things. The selections from his writings gathered here, these "pieces," for that is what they are, demonstrate the range of Hillman's re-visioning imagination. From the conception of this book, members of that re-visioning community, obviously inspired by James Hillman's writings and attached to his work, have offered their encouragement and detailed suggestions. For their helpful contributions I would like to thank David Miller, Dan Noel, Lynda Sexson, Shaun McNiff, Edward Casey, Howard McConeghey, Ellen Kaplan-Maxfield, and Lee Robbins. I received constant valuable suggestions and support also from Kathy Zilbermann and Christopher Bamford. I would like to acknowledge Charles Boer's coauthorship with James Hillman of Freud's Own Cookbook. Finally, I would like to express my appreciation to James Hillman, who helped in selecting passages and refining the final text. His passion for ideas and love of language made the editing of this collection a collaborative work filled with learning and pleasure.

—THOMAS MOORE

*A BLUE FIRE

PROLOGUE

James Hillman is an artist of psychology. If it sounds odd to call a psychologist an artist, then you, the reader, know your task as you take up this anthology. You will be challenged all along the way to rethink, to re-vision, and to reimagine. The difficulty in reading Hillman is not to learn a new bag of techniques or a new conceptual system. Hillman demands nothing short of a new way of thinking. He takes psychoanalysis out of the context of medicine and health, not only in the obvious ways, rejecting the medical model, but in subtle ways: asking us to give up fantasies of cure, repair, growth, self-improvement, understanding, and well-being as primary motives for psychological work. He is more a painter than a physician, more a musician than a social scientist, and more an alchemist than a traditional philosopher.

This art of psychology is apparent in the way Hillman writes. For him, to re-vision psychology implies re-visioning writing about psychology. Continually he suggests, insinuates, argues, exaggerates, redefines, and etymologizes. He likes to hold dialogues in his writing. He brings footnotes into the music of his argument. His style may change from one essay to the next. His books often depart from the usual in form. He often collaborates, comments on an old text, and without warning wanders into excursions.

If you were to apply the Renaissance notion of rhetoric, in which various styles of expression correspond to the various gods and goddesses, you would find many classical modes in the writings included here. The polemics of Mars shine through clearly, as Hillman separates (the traditional work of Mars) his version of psychologizing from that of others, both friends and foes. A venusian appreciation for the sensuality of words and ideas, so rare in modern analytical writing, appears in his language and in the tapestry of his thinking. Saturn is there, too, with his incorrigible love of tradition and abstraction. Hillman gives over to Saturn by indulging in detailed footnotes. But the true archon of these writings is Mercury, the god who is always in transit between the precincts of the divine and the concerns of the human.

The elaborate psychological theory sketched in this collection of writings glistens with a strong tincture of Mercury. According to medieval and Renaissance alchemists and philosophers, Mercury is the god who reveals insight in the colors of a thing, in the surprise visages that appear when a thing is turned around and over and upside down. Hillman takes philosophy into his hands and speaks elegantly about it, but his words do not sound like philosophy. He speaks of religion in ways that worry theologians and devotees and yet give religious language new life. He takes up ancient mythology and alchemy and turns them so that they speak to the most recent concerns. Above all, he re-visions psychology, taking it back from those who use it as a science of behavior, to treat it as an art of the soul.

The reader approaching James Hillman for the first time, therefore, might understand that the ideas he presents so freshly are in fact quite ancient. The challenge in reading Hillman, as so many of his readers confess, is not to grasp new ideas as much as to find a new angle on experience and a new way of hearing old wisdom. He engages in conversation with the archaic Greek mythographers, with the pre-Socratic sage Heraclitus, with the Renaissance magus Marsilio Ficino, with the modern philosophers Karl Jaspers and Alfred North Whitehead, and always with Sigmund Freud and Carl Jung, and he finds in that community of departed scholars a vibrant re-visioning of psychology.

Psychologists, therefore, find him more difficult than do people in the arts, theater, film, and dance, who have the necessary metaphorical ear and the appreciation for form. For Hillman, style and imagination *are* method. If the theory holds that imagination is the primary activity of the psyche, then Hillman's own psychological writing will above all reflect imagination. If one wants to learn something about archetypal psychology, it would be helpful to notice not only *what* Hillman says, but also *how* he explores an idea and expresses it.

One aspect of style that strikes some readers is Hillman's way of depersonalizing and deliteralizing himself as author. A third-person sense seems always to qualify his first-person statements. Except for some brief passages in *Inter Views,* one rarely comes across autobiographical details. When he does write in the first person, he is almost always engaged in a passionate debate about ideas. In effect, Hillman fictionalizes himself in his writing, adding one more metaphoric stone to his building of the imaginal.

He regards empirical studies and cases as fantasies elaborated in the genre of objective science and technical formula. Empiricism has its own literary style and need not be taken literally on its own terms. *Cases* and *studies* do not have, in Hillman's view, a privileged place among various rhetorical ways of describing psychological realities. The professional community of psychology at the moment prefers the rhetoric of research and verbatim case study, but other styles are equally valid. Hillman lays out this critique in his book *Healing Fiction,* which radically probes the most fundamental presuppositions of the therapeutic industry.

Hillman's way of writing and his penetrating critiques not only contribute to his definition of psychology, they are also part of his therapeutic purpose. Psychoanalysis, as a theory and a system, needs therapeutic attention. The style of psychoanalysis may work against its aims, especially when it is given to scientific and personalistic modes. Hillman sees his writing not only as a therapeutic resource for his reader, but also as a way to animate psychoanalysis. He reserves the words *psychology* and *psychological* to refer to a genuine sensitivity to the soul. Psychoanalysis, therefore, is itself not always psychological.

Hillman does not sit back and muse about the psychological condition of persons and societies. Rather, like the artist, he seeks to engage. In this, he betrays his background in existentialist thought. He enjoys polemics, persuasion, and controversy. At the heart of an essay he will often plant a bomb that explodes some axiomatic assumption. He turns upside down many ideas people hold dear and unreflected. After an hour with Hillman's writing, a reader might feel himself twisting and turning in the wind.

Another of Hillman's roots is Husserlian phenomenology. As in his first book, *Emotion,* he turns his topic in many directions to let it reveal itself. He does the same with suicide, masturbation, depression, paranoia, betrayal, heart disorders, feeling, death, failure, growth, and love—all standard themes of psychology's discourse. Like an artist painting a still life, he allows phenomena to show themselves for our contemplation. When he thus presents something typically judged evil or unhealthy, such as suicide fantasies, or paranoia, it is revealed more fully. We come to know ourselves, not through dissection and abstraction, but through this particular revelation of the psyche's nature. Again, Hillman's style may change according to the subject under consideration. Each phenomenon, each god, has its own rhetorical style and emotional tone. The subject has a say in the way it is written about.

SENEX AND PUER

Not surprisingly, this very approach of recasting old ideas, of reimagining everything from the occult to art to philosophy, is the embodiment of one of Hillman's key paradigms: senex and puer. Hillman found a nascent psychology of the senex-puer in the writings of Jung, but he developed it and brought it to center stage as an archetypal pairing powerfully influential in modern thought. *Senex* is Latin for "old man," *puer* for "young man." Senex is a style of life and thought characterized by a sense of time and history, a concern for order, a love of tradition, and a tendency toward the abstract and the regulated; it is rather heavy in tone and depressive in mood. Puer, in contrast, focuses on the here and now; prefers experiment and adventure; looks to the future; wants to transcend laws and traditions; and is light, airy, idealistic, charming, and ephemeral. It raises the spirits, but it has a habit of crashing down.

Hillman recommends a paradoxical reconciliation of senex and puer in which one influences the other without domination. His own writing has this unusual quality of intense love of tradition accompanied by liberating turns of imagination. This odd oxymoron, this unsettling juxtaposition of opposites, might also provide a context for understanding Hillman's complex relation to Jung.

Some readers think of Hillman simply as a Jungian. He is an

officer in the Jungian system; he was director of studies at the Jung Institute in Zurich for ten years; he uses Jungian terminology in most of his writings; his book *Anima*, by no means an early work, has Jung's words on one page and Hillman's on the facing page, as though the old sage and the mercurial scion were sitting across from each other deep in conversation. On the other hand, many Jungian psychologists call Hillman a renegade, heretic, or not a Jungian at all. A clue to this apparent puzzle is the fact that he relates to tradition, including Jung, more with passionate engagement than with filial devotion. Through his close, original reworking of Jung's thought, he stands nearer to Jung and more faithful to his spirit than do many of Jung's devotional followers. Hillman has made moves in each of Jung's major areas, from typology, clinical syndromes, theory of complexes, and instinct theory to alchemy and theology. He has also elaborated many of Jung's seed ideas for contemporary civic life and opened sources in the history of ideas, in the manner of Jung, that feed Jungian thought with new material. By turning to Jung with precision and a comprehensive knowledge of Jung's extensive and intricate writings, Hillman engages Jung in a genuine creative dialogue.

THE IMAGINAL METHOD

One of the first things the new reader of Hillman will notice is his frequent use of that odd word Jung returned to psychology—*soul*. Hillman likes the word for a number of reasons. It eludes reductionistic definition; it expresses the mystery of human life; and it connects psychology to religion, love, death, and destiny. It suggests depth, and Hillman sees himself directly in the line of depth psychology, going all the way back to Heraclitus, who observed that one could never discover the extent of the soul, no matter how many paths one traveled, so profound is its nature. Whenever Hillman uses the forms *psychology, psychologizing,* and *psychological,* he intends a reference to depth and mystery.

Hillman also takes seriously Jung's statement that psyche is image. To this radical idea, suggesting that there is nothing that is not imagistic, not poetic, he adds the terminology of Henry Corbin, who learned it from his Islamic studies, of the *mundus imaginalis*. Corbin's "imaginal world" is neither literal nor abstract and yet is utterly real, with its own laws and purposes. This imaginal world is the matrix of all of Hillman's theorizing.

Work with dreams, for example, requires an appreciation for the integrity and self-determination of the dream. Hillman argues strongly against all symbolic and allegorical translations of dream imagery into ideas, concepts, and humanistic applications. We should not lose the dream in the light of day; rather, we should visit the land of dream and be affected by the peculiarities of that world. Hillman sees most modes of interpretation, whether they are brash or subtle, as heroic, herculean efforts to spoil imagination, ultimately to defend against the challenging otherness of the dream or image.

Hillman complains about the "naturalistic fallacy," the tendency to expect dreams to follow the laws of nature as we know them and to find something wrong in dreams when they depart from our upper-world views. Hillman's therapeutic approaches do not favor the ego; in this way his work is a true psychotherapy, or therapy of the soul. When speaking of therapy and life, he recalls the words of the poet John Keats, who called this world "the vale of soul-making." Soul-making is not interpretation, it is not change, and it is not self-improvement—all modern attempts to get the upper hand on fate and therefore to constrain the soul.

THE RHETORIC OF PATHOLOGY

This reverence for what is given leads to Hillman's emphasis on *pathologizing*. He says that of its nature the soul pathologizes. That is to say, it gets us into trouble, it interferes with the smooth running of life, it obstructs attempts to understand, and it seems to make relationships impossible. It also makes us see perversely. The soul also of its own accord presents pathologized images: fantasies that are bizarre, twisted, immoral, painful, and sick. For Hillman, these pathologized experiences and images are special revelations of soulfulness. They allow an entry into life and soul that cannot be had without them. Both in his analytical writings and in his intimations of an archetypal psychotherapy, he searches out all ways possible to preserve these pathologies and to enter more intimately into their meaningfulness.

Hillman's emphasis on pathologizing has striking implications. He has no interest whatsoever in changing dreams for the better or in quickly and heroically getting rid of symptoms. He quotes Wallace Stevens, saying that "the way through the world is more difficult to find than the way beyond it." He criticizes various techniques for avoiding the twistedness, cloudiness, and general mess of the soul. Particularly, Hillman distinguishes soul from spirit. He sees the tendencies of spiritual practice to rise above or move beyond the valley of the soul, preferring the peaks of spirit. Spirit tends to be escapist, literalistic, and single-minded in its detours around soul. In a context in which spirit (religion, strategies for life, and new-age experiments) is widely championed, Hillman speaks strongly for the soul, but at the same time he values spirit highly, stressing the importance of the arts, a religious sensibility, and, especially, ideas.

PSYCHOLOGICAL THINKING

Intellect is a special issue in Hillman's writing. Some readers come away thinking of him as an intellectual psychologist, more a philosopher than a practitioner. Hillman, in fact, writes strongly about the need for ideas, especially psychological ideas. These are ideas that do not work against soul and are not split off from the concerns of the soul. We need to entertain ideas, he says, even if that idea sounds old-fashioned. And, we need a therapy of our ideas. Our problems, he says, are due to sick ideas, ideas that are not reflected and are too rigid and unimaginative.

Tradition places soul midway between intellect and body. In the context of this tradition, Hillman's psychology is not intellectual. He uses intellect to fortify imagination, because it is image, imagination, and the imaginal world that is Hillman's primary ambience. He complains that modern psychology has replaced ideas with nominalistic, allegorical, and disembodied words. We count heads and make classifications and exchange information as if this were thinking. Hillman appeals for an "angelology of words," a return to the ancient notion that words have a life of their own and say more than we mean when we use them. He uses words carefully, always aware of the imaginal history, the etymology, and ancestry of a word. Often he makes the etymology explicit, as a way toward imagination and body.

Modern thought often tries to find body by gathering literal data. But Hillman is after the bodies of ideas and words themselves, the body of an image. When experience is divided dualistically into mind and matter, we tend to look for body in literalism. Hillman seeks the body of images themselves. He recommends that we encounter images as they present themselves, embodied in their own imaginal, yet precise, detail. Surprisingly, he says, imagination itself provides grounding and body. Perhaps because of this move beyond the literalism of premodern tradition and the rejection of modernist attempts to explain away everything, Hillman is sometimes called postmodern and compared with deconstructionists.

We find that Hillman never writes of *the unconscious* as a separated area of the psyche or an objectified field of investigation. He insists that unconsciousness runs through everything, including psychology itself. This is particularly clear in the late essay "Notes on White Supremacy," where he forcefully argues the case for the shadow as being essentially present in "white" consciousness itself and not, as usually claimed, only projected outward into "black." His shift from the unconscious as a self-contained psychic reservoir to the unconsciousness in everything both deconstructs everything yet allows each thing to reveal itself in its fullness. When the shadow is projected away from a thing, all we see is its shell, a distortion shaped by the moralistic motives of projection. When the shadow is given back, as in Hillman's essay on masturbation, where inhibition and compulsion are both given a place, we see something familiar as though for the first time.

Hillman's reliance on myth and alchemy as root metaphors for grounding his perceptions and positions conforms to the idea of keeping the unconscious elements present. Neither myth nor alchemy, he says, can be taken literally. They are fantastic accounts, elaborated tales, symbol systems that ground because they *open*, leading farther into the unknown. Instead of always valuing consciousness or trying to make the unconscious conscious, Hillman looks for routes into the unconscious areas. It is all part of the gravity of his approach, his tendency always to go down, to find holes into the undersphere.

His essay "Psychology: Monotheistic or Polytheistic?" first appeared in 1971. He claimed to find in Greek polytheism, revived in the European Renaissance, an effective paradigm for modern psychology. There is no need, in a polytheistic psychology, to integrate, to "get it all together," or to find some ultimate blending of the many impulses and directions that erupt from the soul. A variety of gods and goddesses are to be honored, the tensions among them sustained and enjoyed.

Polytheism is one part of the psychological project Hillman describes when he takes Freud's saying, "Where id is, there let ego be," and changes it, deposing the ego's centrality. Hillman wants to encourage the ego to step aside, or at least dance without always taking the lead, and let the soul manifest its turns and pleasures. This polytheistic psychology has some Rogerian tolerance in it without the personalism, some of Gestalt concern to let images speak without letting the ego identify with the image, and a great deal of Jung's mythological sensibility without the desire to integrate and make all things conscious.

One of the stilettos that pricks the modern reader of Hillman's later book *Anima* is his claim that anima serves the important function of leading a person farther into unconsciousness. Consciousness, in the sense of reason, control, and ego, is not an essential ingredient in individuation. Hillman, in fact, never uses the words *individuation* or *unconscious*, staples in orthodox Jungian thought. In another sense, Hillman is after the consciousness to be found in dream image, fantasy, nature, and the things of culture. Reflection is not the only form consciousness can take. Something as simple as a stone exhibits a form of consciousness in its very presence, its *self-display*, to use a word that occurs frequently in Hillman's later essays.

Much of Hillman's work is a detailed elaboration of Jung's idea of the *objective psyche*. Modernism is caught up in the reductionistic notion that the psychological is coextensive with the personal, that the psyche is all ego. A more subtle modernistic formulation, favored in some Jungian writing, is that Jung's idea of *the self* embraces both ego and the unconscious, or that there is an axis between them, and the point of psychological work is to firm up that axis.

Hillman shows no interest in even this compromise of soul and ego. The soul is other, sometimes imaged in dreams and myth as a twin or double, family member or intimate, but it is still other. Essential to Hillman's psychology is a thorough acknowledgment of the integrity of the soul. He mentions that often it seems we need another actual person in life in order to encounter the soul's otherness. But there is no self to deprive the soul of its own personality.

ANIMA MUNDI: CULTURE'S SOUL

Hillman's later essays flash with the passion he brings to the soul of the world. Beginning with his theoretical essay "Anima Mundi," or "The Return of the Soul to the World" (delivered in Italian in the Palazzo Vecchio in Florence), he moves even farther from ego psychology and personalism to encounter the objective psyche in objects. His writing takes on concreteness and context that were implied in previous works. Now he studies gardens, waterworks, streets, buildings, show business, bombs, racism, ecology, work, education, and architecture. We burden ourselves, he says, when we identify personally with archetypal figures. Then we have to work feverishly on our own microcosmic lives, when we might more lightly and effectively engage in the work of the soul by becoming sensitive to the world's suffering. Our buildings are in pain, our governments are on the rocks, the arts are relegated to museums where they are explained away or reduced to technical concerns. Our personal lives may reflect these broader wounds to the world soul, and therefore a larger image of psychology itself is in order.

The field of psychology has always had a *practice*, a mode of implementing its theories. Hillman rarely writes directly about practice, yet his theory offers the basis for a radical approach to psychotherapy. For the usual one-on-one format, Hillman offers a myth for analysis that is rooted in love of the soul and in giving soul love. The great secret of archetypal psychotherapy is love for what the soul presents, even those things the therapist and patient would like to make vanish. This love comes in many forms: interest, acceptance, faithfulness, desire, attachment, friendship, and endurance.

As a whole, James Hillman's work aims toward an appreciation of the soul's beauty, its inspiring roseate hues and its bleak and terrorizing black. This accent on love and beauty spreads this psychological sensibility far beyond issues of fix, control, and cure. It takes psychology so far into the most sublime issues of philosophy, religion, and the arts that the word *psychology* applies only if it is continually redefined. The way to this Neoplatonic beauty, in ideas and in analysis, is not upward and away from the soul's earthly matrix, but through it and downward and up, in a lengthy journey not unlike those circuits of soul-work described by alchemists and Renaissance artists. It is quite proper that Hillman has been formally honored with a key to the city of Dallas and a medal from the citizens of Florence for his revival of the Renaissance psychology of culture and beauty.

Hillman's embrace of depression and pathology paradoxically leads to a psychology beyond health and normalcy, toward a cultural sensibility where soulfulness and beauty are the standards. In the end, the name taken for his work, *archetypal psychology*, implies much more than archetypes and universal images. It suggests the infinite range of psychological endeavor, rooted in everyday life and culture, but echoing the wisdom, the artfulness, and the beauty of centuries of soulful work, love, and play.

SOUL

Let me explain this a little more. Just as there are three main powers in fire—heat, light, and fleeting subtlety—so there are three similar powers in the soul's essence: the power of life, of understanding, and of desiring. . . . At different times the soul brings forth its variety of seeds more or less in profusion.

—MARSILIO FICINO
Commentary on Plato's Phaedrus

1

The Poetic Basis
of Mind

Archetypal psychology is not a psychology of archetypes. Its primary activity is not matching themes in mythology and art to similar themes in life. Rather, the idea is to see every fragment of life and every dream as myth and poetry. A city council asks James Hillman to comment on its plan to build a recreational lake. Hillman understands the immediate concerns, but he lifts the question out of its literal context and considers the need of this city for moisture of soul. It has no pool of reverie, he says. It tends to concretize whatever fantasy comes along. There is little swimming in fantasy, no fluidity of imagination, few authentic aphroditic sea pleasures. The place's soul is parched. It needs a more profound and more subtle water than a lake may provide.

All of Hillman's work—theorizing, analyzing culture, practicing therapy—presupposes what he calls a "poetic basis of mind." This is psychology rooted not in science but in aesthetics and imagination. By taking everything as poetry, Hillman frees consciousness from its thin, hard crust of literalism to reveal the depth of experience. The soul, he says, turns events into experience. But it is image that is experienced, not literalism. The city feels its lack of water and literally tries to build a lake. Only a poetic mind could penetrate that literalism and make an accurate diagnosis. This poetic vision is what Hillman means by psychology.

This work is called archetypal, *the adjective, then, because it seeks out the images in events that give rise to meaningfulness, value, and the full range of experience. It strives for depth, resonance, and texture in all that it considers. To the ancient Greek philosophers,* archai *are the basic elements out of which experience is made.* Arche-

typal psychology uses the penetrating vision of imagination to perceive those archai, *those fundamental fantasies that animate all of life.* Archetypal *means "fundamentally imaginal."*

Hillman serves the soul primarily by preserving its manifestations, and one of those is its desire to understand itself. The psyche, he says, asks for logos, and that is the basic meaning of psychology. *Metapsychology, or theory, for Hillman is not a quest for meaning beyond the soul's own imagery; rather, it is one of the ways of imagination proper to psychology. It, too, is poetry. Psychoanalytic concepts and ideas have to be heard as expressions of imagination and read as metaphors. And this approach performs a therapy on psychology itself, reminding psychology that it is not a science or a moral philosophy or a spiritual discipline. It is an imaginative activity of the soul.*

It is unpsychological, therefore, to reduce images to concepts. When we say that snakes and sticks are phallic symbols, we have slaughtered the images. When we call all female dream figures anima women, we have frozen those personalities into an abstraction. Rather than force images into fixed and confined concepts, Hillman wants us to be forced by the images. Rather than interpret a dream, Hillman prefers to let the dream interpret us. This approach gives imagination absolute priority over ego understandings and applications. The idea of a poetic basis of mind is a radical one, moving consciousness away from heroics toward a more receptive and malleable posture.

Much of the work of archetypal analysis aims at safeguarding and preserving images. The analyst watches for the tendency in a person or in society to honor its favored interpretive positions rather than the images, or to moralize against an image because it seems to go against standard values and comfortable feelings.

Given that imagination is the primary activity of the soul, psychology has to be mindful in its approach to language. Hillman treats words as beings, emissaries, not as tools or functions. He decries nominalism in all forms—making words mean what we want them to mean. Professional psychology is filled with words that long ago lost their imagistic resonance to become hollow categories in which to stuff behavior and personality.

Hillman goes so far as to say that words are persons. They speak, we listen. Words have integrity, their own histories and personalities. Imagination glimpses soul even in our words. Thus, reading Hillman is already a psychological, even therapeutic, enterprise, for it moves the mind from its fixed convictions by evoking its poetic foundations. To see through the literal to the image is to glimpse soul. Imagistic perception is psychological vision. In this sense, archetypal psychology *is a redundancy. All psychology based in aesthetics is archetypal. Psychology can tend to the soul when soul is perceived properly through image. Therefore, there may be more psychology in the fields of art and literature than in psychoanalysis.*

In an early essay on Renaissance psychology, Hillman borrowed an idea from Marsilio Ficino, the fifteenth-century Platonist who provided an inspiring philosophical base for painters and poets of his time. Ficino said, in Hillman's reading, that we need an education that runs counter to our tendencies toward naturalism and literalism. Hillman's work is largely this countereducation, *a sometimes disturbing twist of attention from what seems natural to the alternative land of image. Literalism in any field or endeavor relaxes its grip grudgingly. Therefore, Hillman holds to his countereducation in psychology with doggedness and fire, transforming medical-minded manipulations of the psyche into psychology as he defines it—archetypal, imagistic, aesthetic, and poetic.*

SOUL

Anthropologists describe a condition among "primitive" peoples called "loss of soul." In this condition a man is out of himself, unable to find either the outer connection between humans or the inner connection to himself. He is unable to take part in his society, its rituals, and traditions. They are dead to him, he to them. His connection to family, totem, nature, is gone. Until he regains his soul he is not a true human. He is "not there." It is as if he had never been initiated, been given a name, come into real being. His soul may not only be lost; it may also be possessed, bewitched, ill, transposed into an object, animal, place, or another person. Without this soul, he has lost the sense of belonging and the sense of being in communion with the powers and the gods. They no longer reach him; he cannot pray, nor sacrifice, nor dance. His personal myth and his connection to the larger myth of his people, as *raison d'être,* is lost. Yet he is not sick with disease, nor is he out of his mind. He has simply lost his soul. He may even die. We become lonely. Other relevant parallels with ourselves today need not be spelled out.

One day in Burghölzli, the famous institute in Zurich where the words *schizophrenia* and *complex* were born, I watched a woman being interviewed. She sat in a wheelchair because she was elderly and feeble. She said that she was dead for she had lost her heart. The psychiatrist asked her to place her hand over her breast to feel her heart beating: it must still be there if she could feel its beat. "That," she said, "is not my real heart." She and the psychiatrist looked at each other. There was nothing more to say. Like the primitive who has lost his soul, she had lost the loving courageous connection to life—and that is the real heart, not the ticker which can as well pulsate isolated in a glass bottle.

This is a different view of reality from the usual one. It is so radically different that it forms part of the syndrome of insanity. But one can have as much understanding for the woman in her psychotic depersonalization as for the view of reality of the man attempting to convince her that her heart was indeed still there. Despite the elaborate and moneyed systems of medical research and the advertisements of the health and recreation industries to prove that the real is the physical and that loss of heart and loss of soul are only in the mind, I believe the "primitive" and the woman in the hospital: we can and do lose our souls. I believe with Jung that each of us is "modern man in search of a soul."

Because symptoms lead to soul, the cure of symptoms may also cure away soul, get rid of just what is beginning to show, at first tortured and crying for help, comfort, and love, but which is the soul in the neurosis trying to make itself heard, trying to impress the stupid and stubborn mind—that impotent mule which insists on going its unchanging obstinate way. The right reaction to a symptom may as well be a welcoming rather than laments and demands for remedies, for the symptom is the first herald of an awakening psyche which will not tolerate any more abuse. Through the symptom the psyche demands attention. Attention means attending to, tending, a certain tender care of, as well as waiting, pausing, listening. It takes a span of time and a tension of patience. Precisely what each symptom needs is time and tender care and attention. Just this same attitude is what the soul needs in order to be felt and heard. So it is often little wonder that it takes a breakdown, an actual illness, for someone to report the most extraordinary experiences of, for instance, a new sense of time, of patience and waiting, and in the language of religious experience, of coming to the center, coming to oneself, letting go and coming home.

The alchemists had an excellent image for the transformation of suffering and symptom into a value of the soul. A goal of the alchemical process was the pearl of great price. The pearl starts off as a bit of grit, a neurotic symptom or complaint, a bothersome irritant in one's secret inside flesh, which no defensive shell can protect oneself from. This is coated over, worked at day in day out, until the grit one day is a pearl; yet it still must be fished up from the depths and pried loose. Then when the grit is redeemed, it is worn. It must be worn on the warm skin to keep its luster: the redeemed complex which once caused suffering is exposed to public view as a virtue. The esoteric treasure gained through occult work becomes an exoteric splendor. To get rid of the symptom means to get rid of the chance to gain what may one day be of greatest value, even if at first an unbearable irritant, lowly, and disguised.

(*Insearch*, 43–44, 55–56)

To understand *soul* we cannot turn to science for a description. Its meaning is best given by its context. The root metaphor of the analyst's point of view is that human behavior is understandable because it has an inside meaning. The inside meaning is suffered and experienced. It is understood by the analyst through sympathy and insight. All these terms are the everyday empirical language of the analyst and provide the context for and are expressions of the analyst's root metaphor. Other words long associated with the word *soul* amplify it further: mind, spirit, heart, life, warmth, humanness, personality, individuality, intentionality, essence, innermost, purpose, emotion, quality, virtue, morality, sin, wisdom, death, God. A soul is said to be "troubled," "old," "disembodied," "immortal," "lost," "innocent," "inspired." Eyes are said to be "soulful," for the eyes are "the mirror of the soul"; but one can be "soulless" by showing no mercy. Most "primitive" languages have elaborate concepts about animated principles which ethnologists have translated by *soul.* For these peoples, from ancient Egyptian to modern Eskimo, *soul* is a highly differentiated idea referring to a reality of great impact. The soul has been imaged as the inner man, and as the inner sister or spouse, the place or voice of God within, as a cosmic force in which all humans, even all things living, participate, as having been given by God and thus divine, as conscience, as a multiplicity and as a unity in diversity, as a harmony, as a fluid, as fire, as dynamic energy, and so on. One can "search one's soul" and one's soul can be "on trial." There are parables describing possession of the soul by and sale of the soul to the devil, of temptations of the soul, of the damnation and redemption of the soul, of development of the soul through spiritual disciplines, of journeys of the soul. Attempts have been made to localize the soul in specific body organs and regions, to trace its origin to sperm or egg, to divide it into animal, vegetable, and mineral components, while the search for the soul leads always into the "depths."

The terms *psyche* and *soul* can be used interchangeably, although there is a tendency to escape the ambiguity of the word *soul* by recourse to the more biological, more modern *psyche. Psyche* is used more as a natural concomitant to physical life, perhaps reducible to it. *Soul,* on the other hand, has metaphysical and romantic overtones. It shares frontiers with religion.   (*Suicide,* 44–45, 47)

By *soul* I mean, first of all, a perspective rather than a substance, a viewpoint toward things rather than a thing itself. This perspective is reflective; it mediates events and makes differences between ourselves and everything that happens. Between us and events, between the doer and the deed, there is a reflective moment—and soul-making means differentiating this middle ground.

It is as if consciousness rests upon a self-sustaining and imagining substrate—an inner place or deeper person or ongoing presence—that is simply there even when all our subjectivity, ego, and consciousness go into eclipse. Soul appears as a factor independent of the events in which we are immersed. Though I cannot identify soul with anything else, I also can never grasp it by itself apart from other things, perhaps because it is like a reflection in a flowing mirror, or like the moon which mediates only borrowed light. But just this peculiar and paradoxical intervening variable gives one the sense of having or being a soul. However intangible and indefinable it is, soul carries highest importance in hierarchies of human values, frequently being identified with the principle of life and even of divinity.

In another attempt upon the idea of *soul* I suggested that the word refers to that unknown component which makes meaning possible, turns events into experiences, is communicated in love, and has a religious concern. These four qualifications I had already put forth some years ago. I had begun to use the term freely, usually interchangeably with *psyche* (from Greek) and *anima* (from Latin). Now I am adding three necessary modifications. First, *soul* refers to the *deepening* of events into experiences; second, the significance *soul* makes possible, whether in love or in religious concern, derives from its special *relation with death*. And third, by *soul* I mean the imaginative possibility in our natures, the experiencing through reflective speculation, dream, image, and *fantasy*—that mode which recognizes all realities as primarily symbolic or metaphorical.

(*Re-Visioning*, x)

ARCHETYPAL FANTASY

This first two-horned topic invites a second and equally difficult one. What is fantasy? Here I follow C. G. Jung very closely. He considered the fantasy images that run through our daydreams and night dreams, and which are present unconsciously in all our consciousness, to be the primary data of the psyche. Everything we know and feel and every statement we make are all fantasy based, that is, they derive from psychic images. These are not merely the flotsam of memory, the reproduction of perceptions, rearranged leftovers from the input of our lives.

Rather, following Jung I use the word *fantasy-image* in the poetic sense, considering images to be the basic givens of psychic life, self-originating, inventive, spontaneous, complete, and organized in archetypal patterns. Fantasy-images are both the raw materials and finished products of psyche, and they are the privileged mode of access to knowledge of soul. Nothing is more primary. Every notion in our minds, each perception of the world and sensation in ourselves must go through a psychic organization in order to "happen" at all. Every single feeling or observation occurs as a psychic event by first forming a fantasy-image.

Here I am working toward a psychology of soul that is based in a psychology of image. Here I am suggesting both a *poetic basis of mind* and a psychology that starts neither in the physiology of the brain, the structure of language, the organization of society, nor the analysis of behavior, but in the processes of imagination.

By calling upon Jung to begin with, I am partly acknowledging the fundamental debt that archetypal psychology owes him. He is the immediate ancestor in a long line that stretches back through Freud, Dilthey, Coleridge, Schelling, Vico, Ficino, Plotinus, and Plato to Heraclitus—and with even more branches which have yet to be traced. Heraclitus lies near the roots of this ancestral tree of thought, since he was the earliest to take psyche as his archetypal first principle, to imagine soul in terms of flux and to speak of its depth without measure.

Depth psychology, the modern field whose interest is in the unconscious levels of the psyche—that is, the deeper meanings of the soul—is itself no modern term. *Depth* reverberates with a significance, echoing one of the first philosophers of antiquity. All depth psychology has already been summed up by this fragment of Heraclitus: "You could not discover the limits of the soul *(psyche)*, even if you traveled every road to do so; such is the depth *(bathun)* of its meaning *(logos)*." Ever since Heraclitus brought soul and depth together in one formulation, the dimension of soul is depth (not breadth or height) and the dimension of our soul travel is downward.

❧

One more word we need to introduce is *archetype*. The curious difficulty of explaining just what archetypes are suggests something specific to them. That is, they tend to be metaphors rather than things. We find ourselves less able to say what an archetype is literally and more inclined to describe them in images. We can't seem to touch one or point to one, and rather speak of what they are like. Archetypes throw us into an imaginative style of discourse. In fact, it is precisely as metaphors that Jung—who reintroduced the ancient idea of archetype into modern psychology—writes of them, insisting upon their indefinability. To take an archetypal perspective in psychology leads us, therefore, to envision the basic nature and structure of the soul in an imaginative way and to approach the basic questions of psychology first of all by means of the imagination.

Let us then imagine archetypes as the *deepest patterns of psychic functioning*, the roots of the soul governing the perspectives we have of ourselves and the world. They are the axiomatic, self-evident images to which psychic life and our theories about it ever return. They are similar to other axiomatic first principles, the models or paradigms, that we find in other fields. For "matter," "God," "energy," "life," "health," "society," "art" are also fundamental metaphors, archetypes perhaps themselves, which hold whole worlds together and yet can never be pointed to, accounted for, or even adequately circumscribed.

All ways of speaking of archetypes are translations from one metaphor to another. Even sober operational definitions in the language of science or logic are no less metaphorical than an image which presents the archetypes as root ideas, psychic organs, figures of myth, typical styles of existence, or dominant fantasies that govern consciousness. There are many other metaphors for describing them: immaterial potentials of structure, like invisible crystals in solution or form in plants that suddenly show forth under certain conditions; patterns of instinctual behavior like those in animals that direct actions along unswerving paths; the *genres* and *topoi* in literature; the recurring typicalities in history; the basic syndromes in psychiatry; the paradigmatic thought models in science; the worldwide figures, rituals, and relationships in anthropology.

But one thing is absolutely essential to the notion of archetypes: their emotional possessive effect, their bedazzlement of consciousness so that it becomes blind to its own stance. By setting up a universe which tends to hold everything we do, see, and say in the sway of its cosmos, an archetype is best comparable with a god. And gods, religions sometimes say, are less accessible to the senses and to the intellect than they are to the imaginative vision and emotion of the soul.

The archetypal perspective offers the advantage of organizing into clusters or constellations a host of events from different areas of life. The archetype of the hero, for example, appears first in *behavior*, the drive to activity, outward exploration, response to challenge, seizing and grasping and extending. It appears second in the *images* of Hercules, Achilles, Samson (or their cinema counterparts) doing their specific tasks; and third, in a style of *consciousness*, in feelings of independence, strength, and achievement, in ideas of decisive action, coping, planning, virtue, conquest (over animality), and in psychopathologies of battle, overpowering masculinity, and single-mindedness.   (*Re-Visioning*, xi, xii–xiv)

IMAGINAL METHOD

The use of allegory as a defense continues today in the interpretations of dreams and fantasies. When images no longer surprise us, when we can expect what they mean and know what they intend, it is because we have our "symbologies" of established meanings. Dreams have been yoked to the systems which interpret them; they belong to schools—there are "Freudian dreams," "Jungian dreams," etc. If long things are penises for Freudians, dark things are shadows for Jungians. Images are turned into predefined concepts such as passivity, power, sexuality, anxiety, femininity, much like the conventions of allegorical poetry. Like such poetry, and using similar allegorical techniques, psychology too can become a defense against the psychic power of personified images.

If the mother in our dream, or the beloved, or the wise old counselor, says and does what one would expect, or if the analyst interprets these figures conventionally, they have been deprived of their authority as mythic images and persons and reduced to mere allegorical conventions and moralistic stereotypes. They have become the personified conceits of an allegory, a simple means of persuasion that forces the dream or fantasy into doctrinal compliance. The image allegorized is now the image in service of a teaching.

In contrast, archetypal psychology holds that the true iconoclast is the image itself which explodes its allegorical meanings, releasing startling new insights. Thus the most distressing images in dreams and fantasies, those we shy from for their disgusting distortion and perversion, are precisely the ones that break the allegorical frame of what we think we know about this person or that, this trait of ourselves or that. The "worst" images are thus the best, for they are the ones that restore a figure to its pristine power as a numinous person at work in the soul.   (*Re-Visioning*, 8)

There is an invisible connection within any image that is its soul. If, as Jung says, "image is psyche," then why not go on to say, "images are souls," and our job with them is to meet them on that soul level. I have spoken of this elsewhere as befriending, and elsewhere again I have spoken of images as animals. Now I am carrying these feelings further to show operationally how we can meet the soul in the image and understand it. We can actively imagine it through word play which is also a way of talking with the image and letting it talk. We watch its behavior—how the image behaves within itself. And we watch its ecology—how it interconnects, by analogies, in the fields of my life. This is indeed different from interpretation. No friend or animal wants to be interpreted, even though it may cry for understanding.

We might equally call the unfathomable depth in the image, love, or at least say we cannot get to the soul of the image without love for the image.

❧

Our method can be done by anyone in analysis or out. It requires no special knowledge—even if knowledge of symbols can help culturally to enrichen the image, and knowledge of idioms and vocabulary can help hear further into the image. By letting the image itself speak, we are suggesting that words and their arrangements (syntax) are soul mines. But mining doesn't require modern technical tools. (If it did, no one would ever have understood a dream or an image until modern psychology came along!) What does help mining is an eye attuned to the dark. (We shall have to take up later the question of *training*, how to catch the eye to read the image, the ear to hear it.) . . . .

After this we can now essay a statement about what it is that makes an image *archetypal*. We have found our axiomatic criteria—dramatic structure, symbolic universality, strong emotion—not required in our actual operations with an image. We have found instead that an archetypal quality emerges through (a) precise portrayal of the image; (b) sticking to the image while hearing it metaphorically; (c) discovering the necessity within the image; (d) experiencing the unfathomable analogical richness of the image.

Since any image can respond to these criteria, any image can be considered archetypal. The word *archetypal* as a description of images becomes redundant. It has no descriptive function. What then does it point at?

Rather than pointing *at* something, *archetypal* points *to* something, and this is *value*. By attaching *archetypal* to an image, we ennoble or empower the image with the widest, richest, and deepest possible significance. *Archetypal*, as we use it, is a word of importance (in Whitehead's sense), a word that values.

❧

Should we carry this conclusion over to other places where we use *archetypal*, to our psychology itself, then by *archetypal psychology* we mean a psychology of value. And our appellative move is aimed to restore psychology to its widest, richest, and deepest volume so that it would resonate with soul in its descriptions as unfathomable, multiple, prior, generative, and necessary. As all images can gain this archetypal sense, so all psychology can be archetypal when it is released from its surface and seen through to its hidden volumes. *Archetypal* here refers to a move one makes rather than a thing that is. Otherwise, archetypal psychology becomes only a psychology of archetypes.

In most contexts where we come across the word *archetypal*, especially in relation with image ("*that* is an archetypal image"), archetypal could readily be replaced by one or another of the backgrounds on which it relies: mythical, religious, institutional, instinctual, philosophical, or literary.

But there is a difference of feeling between saying "the circle is a scientific or philosophical idea" and saying, "the circle is an archetypal idea." *Archetypal* adds the further implication of basic root structure, generally human, a necessary universal with consequents. The circle is not just any scientific idea; it is basic, necessary, universal. *Archetypal* gives this kind of value.

Now if the value implication is taken literally, we begin to believe that these basic roots, these universals *are*. We have moved from a valuation adjective to a thing and invented substantialities called archetypes that can "back up" our sense of archetypal value. Then we are forced to gather literal evidence from cultures the world over and make empirical claims about what is defined to be unspeakable and irrepresentable.

We do not need to take archetypal in this literal sense. Then the implications of basic, deep, universal, necessary, all those implications carried by the word *archetypal*, add richer value to any particular image.

This re-visioning of archetypal implies that the more accurate term for our psychology in its *operational* definition is *re-visioning*. In what we do we are more re-visionists than archetypalists; or, we evoke archetypes (gods and myths) in order to re-vision psychology. The value for re-visioning psychology of a psychology of the archetypes is that it provides a metaphorical tool of widest, richest, and deepest volume. It conforms with the soul value we wish to give to and find in our work. ("Inquiry into Image," 82–85)

LANGUAGE

In the modern language games of Wittgenstein, words are the very fundamentals of conscious existence, yet they are also severed from things and from truth. They exist in a world of their own. In modern structural linguistics, words have no inherent sense, for they can be reduced, every single one of them, to basic quasi-mathematical units. The fantasy of a basic number of irreducible elements out of which all speech can be constituted is a dissecting technique of the analytic mind which applies logical atomism to *logos* itself—a suicide of the word.

Of course there is a credibility gap, since we no longer trust words of any sort as true carriers of meaning. Of course, in psychiatry, words have become schizogenetic, themselves a cause and source of mental disease. Of course we live in a world of slogan, jargon, and press releases, approximating the "newspeak" of Orwell's *1984*.

As one art and academic field after another falls into the paralyzing coils of obsession with language and communication, speech succumbs to a new semantic anxiety. Even psychotherapy, which began as a *talking cure*—the rediscovery of the oral tradition of telling one's story—is abandoning language for touch, cry, and gesture. We dare not be eloquent. To be passionate, psychotherapy now says we must be physical or primitive. Such psychotherapy promotes a new barbarism. Our semantic anxiety has made us forget that words, too, burn and become flesh as we speak.

A new angelology of words is needed so that we may once again have faith in them. Without the inherence of the angel in the word—and *angel* means originally "emissary," "message-bearer"—how can we utter anything but personal opinions, things made up in our subjective minds? How can anything of worth and soul be conveyed from one psyche to another, as in a conversation, a letter, or a book, if archetypal significances are not carried in the depths of our words?

We need to recall the angel aspect of the word, recognizing words as independent carriers of soul between people. We need to recall that we do not just make words up or learn them in school, or ever have them fully under control. Words, like angels, are powers which have invisible power over us. They are personal presences which have whole mythologies: genders, genealogies (etymologies concerning origins and creations), histories, and vogues; and their own guarding, blaspheming, creating, and annihilating effects. *For words are persons.* This aspect of the word transcends their nominalistic definitions and contexts and evokes in our souls a universal resonance.

❧

Freud's *talking cure* is also the cure of our talk, an attempt at that most difficult of cultural tasks, the rectification of language: the right word. The overwhelming difficulty of communicating soul in talk becomes crushingly real when two persons sit in two chairs, face to face and knee to knee, as in an analysis with Jung. Then we realize what a miracle it is to find the right words, words that carry soul accurately, where thought, image, and feeling interweave. Then we realize that soul can be made on the spot simply through speech. Such talk is the most complex psychic endeavor imaginable—which says something about why Jung's psychology was a *cultural* advance over Freud's style of talking cure, free autistic associations on the couch.

All modern therapies which claim that action is more curative than words (Moreno) and which seek techniques other than talk (rather than in addition to it) are repressing the most human of all faculties—the telling of the tales of our souls. These therapies may be curative of the child in us who has not learned to speak or the animal who cannot, or a spirit daimon that is beyond words because it is beyond soul. But only continued attempts at accurate soul-speech can cure our speech of its chatter and restore it to its first function, the communication of soul.

Soul of bulk and substance can be evoked by words and expressed in words; for myth and poetry, so altogether verbal and "fleshless," nonetheless resonate with the deepest intimacies of organic existence. A mark of imaginal man is the speech of his soul, and the range of this speech, its self-generative spontaneity, its precise subtlety and ambiguous suggestion, its capacity, as Hegel said, "to receive and reproduce every modification of our ideational faculty," can be supplanted neither by the technology of communication media, by contemplative spiritual silence, nor by physical gestures and signs. The more we hold back from the risk of speaking because of the semantic anxiety that keeps the soul in secret incommunicado, private and personal, the greater grows the credibility gap between what we are and what we say, splitting psyche and logos. The more we become tied by linguistic self-consciousness, the more we abdicate the ruling principle of psychological existence. . . . Man is half-angel because he can speak. The more we distrust speech in therapy or the capacity of speech to be therapeutic, the closer we are to an absorption into the fantasy of the archetypal subhuman, and the sooner the archetypal barbarian strides into the communication ruins of a culture that refused eloquence as a mirror of its soul.

(Re-Visioning, 8–9, 217–218)

While other nineteenth-century investigators were polluting the archaic, natural, and mythic in the outer world, psychology was doing much the same to the archaic, natural, and mythic within. Therapeutic depth psychology shares this blame, since it shares nineteenth-century attitudes. It gave names with a pathological bias to the animals of the imagination. We invented psychopathology and thereby labeled the *memoria* a madhouse. We invented the diagnoses with which we declared ourselves insane. After subtly poisoning our own imaginal potency with this language, we complain of a cultural wasteland and loss of soul. The poison spreads; words continually fall "mentally ill" and are usurped by psychopathology, so that we can hardly use them without their new and polluted connotations: *immature, dissociation, rigid, withdrawn, passive, transference, fixation, sublimation, projection* (the last three notably different in alchemy), *resistance, deviate, stress, dependence, inhibition, compulsion, illusion, split, tranquilized, driven, compensation, inferiority, derange, suppression, depression, repression, confusion*—these words have been psychologized and pathologized in the past 150 years.

So Psyche requests the psychologist to remember his calling. Psychological remembrance is given by the kind of speech that carries remembrance within it. This language is both of culture and uncultured, is both of art and artless. It is a mythic, metaphoric language, a speech of ambiguities that is evocative and detailed, yet not definitive, not productive of dictionaries, textbooks, or even abstract descriptions. Rather, it is a speech that leads to participation, in the Platonic sense, in and with the thing spoken of, a speech of stories and insights which evoke, in the other who listens, new stories and new insights, the way one poem and one tune ignite another verse and another song. It is conversation, letters, tales, in which we reveal our dreams and fantasies—and our psychopathology. It evokes, calls forth, and creates psyche as it speaks. It speaks of mood: of "sadness" and "despair" before "depression"; of "rage" before "aggression"; of "fear," "panic," and "anguish" before "anxiety attacks." This speech is "not fashioned in schools," and it will be "simple and rude," as Tertullian said. It will have "corporeal similitudes," that is, body images, speaking from and reaching to the imaginal body in order to provoke the soul's movements. It must be speech that works as an "imaginative agent," stirring fantasy. Such speech has impact because it carries body in it; it is speech alive, the word itself alive, not a description about a psychic state by a psychologist, not carefully defined, but freely imagined. . . .

Such speech meets every human at the ultimate levels, beyond education, age, or region, just as the themes of our dreams, panics, and passions are common to all humanity. If the language is of the street and workshop, then psychology has already taken another step out of the consulting room. The soul's confusions and pains need words which mirror these conditions through imagination. Adequate descriptions of the soul's states will depend less upon right definition than upon accurate transmission of style.

(*Myth of Analysis*, 205–206, 208)

CONSCIOUSNESS

If "becoming conscious" has its roots in reflection and if this instinct refers to the anima archetype, then consciousness itself may more appropriately be conceived as based upon anima than upon ego.

The ego as base of consciousness has always been an anachronistic part of analytical psychology. It is a historical truth that our Western tradition has identified ego with consciousness, an identification that found formulation especially in nineteenth-century psychology and psychiatry. But this part of Jung's thought does not sit well with either his notion of psychic reality or his therapeutic goals of psychic consciousness. What brings cure is an archetypal consciousness, and this notion of consciousness is definitely not based upon ego. . . .

The "relativization of the ego," that work and that goal of the fantasy of individuation, is made possible, however, from the beginning if we shift our conception of the base of consciousness from ego to anima archetype, from I to soul. Then one realizes from the very beginning (a priori and by definition) that the ego and all its developmental fantasies were never, even at the start, the fundament of consciousness, because consciousness refers to a process more to do with images than will, with reflection rather than control, with reflective insight into, rather than manipulation of, *objective reality*. We would no longer be equating consciousness with one phase of it, the developmental period of youth and its questing heroic mythology. Then, too, while educating consciousness even in youth, the aim of nourishing anima would be no less significant than that of strengthening ego.

Instead of regarding anima from the viewpoint of ego where she becomes a poisonous mood, an inspiring weakness, or a contrasexual compensation, we might regard ego from soul's perspective where ego becomes an instrument for day-to-day coping, nothing more grandiose than a trusty janitor of the planetary houses, a servant of soul-making. This view at least gives ego a therapeutic role rather than forcing it into the antitherapeutic position, a stubborn old king to be relativized. Then, too, we might relativize the myth of the hero, or take it for what it has become today for our psyche—the myth of inflation—and not the secret key to the development of human consciousness. The hero myth tells the tale of conquest and destruction, the tale of psychology's "strong ego," its fire and sword, as well as the career of its civilization, but it tells little of the culture of its consciousness. Strange that we could still, in a psychology as subtle as Jung's, believe that this king-hero, and his ego, is the equivalent of consciousness. Images of this psychological equivalence were projected from television screens straight and live from the heroic-ego's great contemporary epic in Vietnam. Is this consciousness?

Basing consciousness upon soul accords with the Neoplatonic tradition—which we still find in Blake—where what today is called ego-consciousness would be the consciousness of the Platonic cave, a consciousness buried in the least-aware perspectives. These habits and continuities and daily organizations of personality certainly cannot encompass the definition of consciousness, a mystery that still baffles every area of research. To put it together with ego limits consciousness to the perspectives of the cave which today we would call the literalistic, personalistic, practicalistic, naturalistic, and humanistic fallacies. From the traditional psychology (of Neoplatonism), ego-consciousness does not deserve the name of consciousness at all.

Consciousness arising from anima would therefore look to myth, as it manifests in the mythologems of dreams and fantasies and the pattern of lives; whereas ego-consciousness takes its orientations from the literalisms of its perspectives, i.e., that fantasy it defines as "reality."

Because fantasy-images provide the basis of consciousness, we turn to them for basic understanding. *Becoming conscious* would now mean becoming aware of fantasies and the recognition of them *everywhere* and not merely in a "fantasy world" separate from "reality." Especially, we would want to recognize them as they play through that "mirror in which the unconscious becomes aware of its own face" (*CW* 14, §129), the ego, its thought structures and practical notions of reality. Fantasy-images now become the instrumental mode of perceiving and insighting. By means of them we realize better what Jung so often insisted upon: the psyche is the subject of our perceptions, the perceiver through fantasy, rather than the object of our perceptions. Rather than analyzing fantasies, we analyze by means of them; and translating reality into fantasy-images would better define becoming conscious than would the former notion given by ego of translating fantasy into realities. . . .

In particular, the fantasies arising from and giving insight into attachments would refer to anima consciousness. Because anima appears in our affinities, as the *fascinosum* of our attractions and obsessions, where we feel most personal, here this consciousness best mythologizes. It is a consciousness *bound to life,* both at the level of the vital, vegetative soul as it used to be called (the psychosomatic symptom as it is now called) and at the level of involvements of every kind, from petty passions, gossip, to the dilemmas of philosophy. Although consciousness based on anima is inseparable from life, nature, the feminine, as well as from fate and death, it does not follow that this consciousness is naturalistic, or fatalistic, otherworldly and morose, or particularly "feminine." It means merely in these realms it turns; these are the metaphors to which it is attached.

Attachment now becomes a more significant term in anima consciousness than do those more guilt-making, and thus ego-referent, terms like *commitment, relatedness,* and *responsibility.* In fact, the relativization of the ego means placing in abeyance such metaphors as: choice and light, problem solving and reality testing, strengthening, developing, controlling, progressing. In their place, as more adequate descriptions of consciousness and its activities, we would use metaphors long familiar to the alchemy of analytical practice: fantasy, image, reflection, insight, and, also, mirroring, holding, cooking, digesting, echoing, gossiping, deepening.

(*Anima,* 87-89, 93-97)

W hen myths say gods have blue hair or blue bodies, they have. The gods live in a blue place of metaphor, and they are described less with naturalistic language than with poetic "distortion." Mythical talk must be full of hyperbole; the gods live in the highs and deeps. To depict them rightly we need the expressionist's palette, not the impressionist's. Precisely this shift into mythical perception occurs with the *unio mentalis:* we now *imagine* the nature of reality, and dark blue becomes the right color to express Dionysus's hair, because it is the natural, reasonable hue for the hair of this god in this hymn, a most realistic depiction.

Although the *caelum* here, as *unio mentalis* and quintessence, is a late stage, it is sometimes (Paracelsus, Figulus) said to be the prerequisite for all alchemical operations whatsoever. The mind from the beginning must be based in the blue firmament, like the lazuli stone and sapphire throne of mysticism, the azure heaven of Boehme, *philos sophia*. The blue firmament is an image of cosmological reason; it is a mythical place that gives metaphorical support to metaphysical thinking. It is the presentation of metaphysics in image form. These upper vaults of stone confirm the solidity of invisible thought in a mythical manner and they show the mythical foundations of thought; they allow, even command, a philosophy that reaches to just such cosmological heights and depths, the full extension and glory of imagination as philosophy, philosophy as imagination, in the *terra alba* of the imaginal as described by Corbin.

If the *caelum* must be present to begin with, then to do alchemy one must be confirmed in imaginal durabilities, transcending mere psychological perspectives and metaphorical implications. The metaphorical twist that the adjective blue gives in the immense variety of its uses in vernacular speech, removing ordinary things from their ordinary sense, is only the beginning of the epistrophic return of all things to their imaginal ground. The mind itself must be drenched in blue, cosmological.

Alchemy begins before we enter the mine, the forge, or laboratory. It begins in the blue vault, the seas, in the mind's thinking in images, imagining ideationally, speculatively, silveredly, in words that are both images and ideas, in words that turn things into flashing ideas and ideas into little things that crawl, the blue power of the word itself, which locates this consciousness in the throat of the *visuddha cakra* whose dominant color is a smoky purple-blue.

The *caelum*, then, is a condition of mind. Envision it as a night sky filled with the airy bodies of the gods, those astrological constellations which are at once beasts and geometry and which participate in all things of the world as their imaginal ground. The *caelum* does not of course take place in your head, in your mind, but your mind moves in the *caelum*, touches the constellations, the thick and hairy skull opens to let in more light, their light, making possible a new idea of order, a cosmological imagination whose thought accounts for the cosmos in the forms of images.   ("Blue," 44–45)

2

Many Gods,
Many Persons

In a dream commonly reported, the dreamer is driving along a highway when the car suddenly swerves onto the shoulder or onto a dirt road cutting off at an angle or into a field. Apparently it isn't always easy to keep to the straight and narrow, to maintain one's vision on a single path. Yet there is the nagging feeling that it's only right to "get your act together," to have a goal in mind, and to fight off temptations toward dispersion. To stray from single-mindedness is, in the imagery of the dream, deviant behavior—de-via, "off the road."

James Hillman characteristically finds necessity in deviancy. Instead of making a norm of singleness of soul, he portrays the psyche as inherently multiple. He does not use a mild word such as polycentric or multifaceted for this multiplicity. Rather, he takes a word from religion and mythology, polytheism, implying an essential and profound division in the soul.

In his essay "Psychology: Monotheistic or Polytheistic?" Hillman places polytheism alongside Carl Jung's ideas of anima and animus. Although the point is rarely made, Jung suggests a deep division in the psyche. Anima and animus are two very different sources of meaning and fantasy, much deeper than ego, that are difficult to unite in "marriage" or "syzygy." Hillman takes this division, made along the lines of gender, and opens it further mythologically into images of the gods and goddesses. For him, polytheistic mythology offers an excellent metaphoric background for imagining the psyche in its multiplicity.

A polytheistic psyche is not the same as a fragmented soul. Some, when they hear of Hillman's emphasis on polytheism, complain that his psychology is one more version of a more general cultural fragmentation, of a piece with pathological splintering in modern art, life, and politics. But Hillman diagnoses cultural fragmentation as the return of repressed polytheism. When we chase multiplicity from our own self-definition, we are condemned to live out fragmentation in society. In Hillman's view, we need a psychology that gives place to multiplicity, not demanding integration and other forms of unity, and at the same time offering a language adequate to a psyche that has many faces. Hillman's psychological polytheism does not portray a life of chaos but one of many elements rising and falling in prominence, conflicting and dovetailing, in a rich counterpoint of themes and episodes.

Psychological polytheism is not psychotic dissociation or moral relativity; quite the opposite. Repression of multiplicity returns in the form of disintegration. The heroic ego, trying so hard to get it all together, sets up a condition of psychic fragmentation. We are so used to valuing integration and unity that any suggestion of multiplicity sends us off into extremes. Polytheism, however, means "many," not "any." It is not that anything goes, but that the soul has many sources of meaning, direction, and value.

The psyche is not only multiple, it is a communion of many persons, each with specific needs, fears, longings, styles, and language. The many persons echo the many gods who define the worlds that underlie what appears to be a unified human being. The persons of dream represent the many personalities who have a role in the psyche's everyday dramas. A polytheistic psychology looks carefully at the relations between dream figures, giving them a hearing, allowing each his due, even those dream persons the ego finds objectionable and threatening.

The images of polytheistic mythology are themselves therapeutic because they give place to the soul's variety and conflict. We can imagine tensions when we have an orientation in the first place that acknowledges many different directions in the psyche. A bias toward monotheism shudders to find many tendencies in tension and aims toward a unified resolution. A polytheistic position holds tension so that all parties concerned find a way to coexist.

Psychological polytheism, therefore, is not only a matter of quantities—many gods and many impulses, but also quality. It implies a life that can embrace conflicting directions, one that doesn't resort to hierarchies and overarching principles to impose order. The psychological environment of a polytheistic viewpoint is accepting and receptive to voices that differ and sometimes breed conflict. The anxiety that derives from heroic efforts toward integration eases in a condition of polytheism. At the same time, the guiding principle of polytheism is to give each divine figure the attention he or she requires.

A relaxed ego that honors the many offers considerable rewards. We find vitality in tension, learn from paradox, gather wisdom by straddling ambivalence, and gain confidence in trusting the confusion that naturally arises from multiplicity. The sign of a soulful life is its rich texture and its complexity. The soul's complexes, therefore, are not to be simply ironed out, because they are the stuff of human complexity.

Before we try to resolve a conflict, Hillman insists we look at our belief in conflict. In any conflict, there usually lies a secret heroism that enjoys struggle or a secret martyr who wants to be torn apart. In a polytheistic view of the psyche, conflicts no longer seem so decisive. From the start, the motive in polytheism is to honor all sides. The idea is not to conquer or be conquered. There is no one hierarchical, unified head.

In the context of polytheism it is virtuous not to be integrated and centered, but to be flexible, embracing, tolerant, patient, and complicated. The varieties of experience do not have to be harmonized. Balance, integration, and wholeness, important values in a monotheistic psychology, have no place in polytheism, which demands a stretching of the heart and imagination. The polytheistic soul is richly textured and texted. It has many qualities of character and is the theater where many stories are enacted, many dreams mirrored.

POLYTHEISM

Which fantasy governs our view of soul-making and the process of individuation—the many or the one?

The very sound of the question shows already to what extent we are ruled by a bias toward the one. Unity, integration, and individuation seem an advance over multiplicity and diversity. As the self seems a further integration than anima/animus, so seems monotheism superior to polytheism.

Jung used a polycentric description for the objective psyche. The light of nature was multiple. Following the traditional descriptions of the *anima mundi*. Jung wrote of the *lumen naturae* as a multiplicity of partial consciousness, like stars or sparks or luminous fishes' eyes. A polytheistic psychology corresponds with this description and provides its imagistic formulation in the major traditional language of our civilization, i.e., classical mythology. By providing a divine background of personages and powers for each complex, polytheistic psychology would find place for each spark. It would aim less at gathering them into a unity and more at integrating each fragment according to its own principle, giving each god its due over that portion of consciousness, that symptom, complex, fantasy, which calls for an archetypal background. It would accept the multiplicity of voices, the Babel of the anima and animus, without insisting upon unifying them into one figure, and accept too the dissolution process into diversity as equal in value to the coagulation process into unity. The pagan gods and goddesses would be restored to their psychological domain.

We would consider Artemis, Persephone, Athena, Aphrodite, for instance, as more adequate *psychological* backgrounds to the complexity of human nature than the unified image of Maria, and the diversity expressed by Apollo, Hermes, Dionysus and Hercules, for instance, to correspond better with psychological actualities than any single idea of self, or single figure of Eros, or of Jesus and Yahweh. Not that Maria, Eros, Jesus, and Yahweh are false—far, far from it; only that they, like Zeus too, tend to present themselves in descriptions which dominate through unification, thus losing the values shaped by each of the other gods and goddesses.

Focus upon the many and the different (rather than upon the one and the same) also provides a variety of ways of looking at one psychic condition. There are many avenues for discovering the virtues in a psychic phenomena. Depression, say, may be led into meaning on the model of Christ and his suffering and resurrection; it may through Saturn gain the depth of melancholy and inspiration, or through Apollo serve to release the blackbird of prophetic insight.

From the perspective of Demeter depression may yield awareness of the mother-daughter mystery, or, through Dionysus, we may find depression a refuge from the excessive demands of the ruling will.

This emphasis upon many dominants would then favor the differentiation of the anima/animus. Quite possibly—and now this is my claim and contention—closer interest in a variety of divine hypostases and their processes displayed in myth will prove more psychological, even if less religious (in the monotheistic sense of religion). This interest will more likely produce more insights into emotions, images and relationships, even if it will be less encouraging for a theology of evolutional wholeness. It will more likely reflect accurately the illusions and entanglements of the soul, even if it satisfies less the popular vision of individuation from chaos to order, from multiplicity to unity, and where the health of wholeness has come to mean the one dominating the many.

Polytheistic psychology obliges consciousness to circulate among a field of powers. Each god has his due as each complex deserves its respect in its own right. In this circularity of *topoi* there seem no preferred positions, no sure statements about positive and negative, and therefore no need to rule out some configurations and *topoi* as "pathological"; pathology itself will require a polytheistic re-visioning. When the idea of progress through hierarchical stages is suspended, there will be more tolerance for the nongrowth, nonupward, and nonordered components of the psyche. There is more room for variance when there is more place given to variety. We may then discover that many of the judgments which have previously been called psychological were rather theological. They were statements about dreams and fantasies and behavior, and people too, coming from a monotheistic ideal of wholeness (the self), that devalues the primal multiplicity of souls. . . .

Babel and the proliferation of cults in the Hellenistic period always seem a degeneration. . . . One might, however, consider the proliferation of cults as a *therapeia* ("worship, service, and care") of the complexes in their many forms. Then one could understand the psychic fragmentation supposedly typical of our times as the return of the repressed, bringing a return of psychological polytheism. Fragmentation would then indicate many possibilities for individuation and might even be the result of individuation: each individual struggling with his daimones. If there is only one model of individuation can there be true individuality? The complexes that will not be integrated force recognition of their autonomous power. Their archetypal cores will not serve the single goal of monotheistic wholeness. Babel may be a religious decline from one point of view and it may be a psychological improvement, since through the many tongues a fuller discordant psychic reality is being reflected. So the current delight in superstitions, astrology, witchery, and oracles has a psychological significance even if they be considered inferior religion. Through these images and practices anima/animus aspects of the psyche begin to find traditional reflection and containment in an impersonal background. Without the gods, who offer differentiated models for the peculiar psychic phenomena of anima and animus, we see them as projections. Then we try to take them back with introverted measures. But "The individual ego is much too small, its brain much too feeble, to incorporate all the projections withdrawn from the world. Ego and brain burst asunder in the effort; the psychiatrist calls it schizophrenia" (*CW* 11, §145). Without a consciously polytheistic psychology are we not more susceptible to an unconscious fragmentation called schizophrenia?

Monotheistic psychology counters what it must see as disintegration and breakdown with archetypal images of order (mandalas). Unity compensates plurality. Polytheistic psychology would meet this so-called disintegration in its own language, by means of archetypal likeness: *similis similibus curantur.* Each particular phenomenon in an experience of breakdown would be viewed less in terms of the construct *breakdown.* Instead it would be led back *(epistrophé)* to its archetypal source—and the idea of breakdown itself would be articulated more precisely in terms of the hero, the puer, Hermes, Dionysus, Demeter, and their differing styles. There would be less need for compensation through opposites.

The restoration of the gods and goddesses as psychic dominants reflects truly both the varied beauty and messy confusion, and tragic limitation, of the anima/animus, their fascinating multiplicity, their conflicts, their lack of ethical cohesion, their tendency to draw us deep through life and into death. Polytheistic psychology can give sacred differentiation to our psychic turmoil and can welcome its outlandish individuality in terms of classical patterns.

As I have spelled out in several later writings, *psychological* polytheism is concerned less with worship than with attitudes, with the way we see things and place them. Gods, for psychology, are neither believed in nor addressed directly. They are rather adjectival than substantive; the polytheistic experience finds existence qualified with archetypal presence and recognizes faces of the gods in these qualifications. Only when these qualities are literalized, set apart as substances, that is, become theologized, do we have to imagine them through the category of belief.

✢

I preferred Lopez's formulation: "The many contains the unity of the one without losing the possibilities of the many." This restates the Neoplatonist idea of *skopos:* the thematic unity of intention, the aim or target which gives an internal necessity and fittingness to each part of a work of art. Here the one is not something apart and opposed to the many, leaving them as inchoate fragmented bits, but it appears as the unity of each thing, that it is as it is, with a name and a face.

As a psychic reality, the one appears only as this or that image: a voice, a number, a whirlwind, a universal idea, etc. And, it appears as the unity of each particular event, discoverable phenomenally only within eachness. The arguments that the one is ground of the many, their continuity, or the whole which embraces them all are again biases of monotheistic consciousness attempting to usurp a more ultimate, more basic and superior place in a metapsychological system, where system itself belongs to senex rhetoric. We must watch out for words like *ground,* and *whole,* and *all,* and remember that unity too can be imagined polytheistically. To polytheistic consciousness, the one does not appear as such but is contained as one among many and within each of the many, as Lopez says.

✢

Polytheism is not necessarily half of a philosophical pair, requiring monotheism for its other side. In itself polytheism is a style of consciousness—and this style should not even be called *polytheistic,* for strictly, historically, when polytheism reigns there is no such word. Where the daimones are alive *polytheism, pantheism, animism,* and even *religion* do not appear. The Greeks had *daimones* but not these terms, so we ought to hold from using monotheistic rhetoric when entering that imaginative field and style we have been forced to call *polytheistic.*

Then we might better discover this other psychological eye by imagistic, mythic, and poetic means, releasing intuitive insights from sensate particular events. The psyche, and the world's psyche too, would show its patterns in tales and images and the physiognomic qualities of things. The whole show would be different, and indeed psychic life is *show,* both the comedy and agony of drama, and *schau,* each appearance an imagistic essence, a showing forth; revelations, theophanies.

When William James described *A Pluralistic Universe,* he set this sentence in italics: *"Reality MAY exist in distributive form, in the shape not of an all but of a set of eaches, just as it seems to be."* Then he added: "There is this in favor of eaches, that they are at any rate real enough to have made themselves at least appear to everyone, whereas the absolute [wholeness, unity, the one] has as yet appeared immediately to only a few mystics, and indeed to them very ambiguously."

Eachness: that is the place I share with James—and with Jung, for what else is individuation but a particularization of the soul.

("Monotheistic or Polytheistic?" 110, 114–116, 116–117, 125–126, 129, 131, 133)

I think too that the underworld teaches us to abandon our hopes for achieving unification of personality by means of the dream. The underworld spirits are plural. So much is this the case that the *di manes* (underworld spirits), who were the Roman equivalent of the Greek *theoi chthōnioi,* have no native singular form. Even individual dead persons were spoken of plurally, as *di manes.* "The ancient Egyptian was thought to live after death in a multiplicity of forms, each of these forms was the full man himself." The underworld is an innumerable community of figures. The endless variety of figures reflects the endlessness of the soul, and dreams restore to consciousness this sense of multiplicity. The polytheistic perspective is grounded in the chthonic depths of the soul. A psychotherapy that reflects these depths can therefore make no attempt at achieving undivided individuality or encouraging a personal identity as a unified wholeness. Instead, psychotherapeutic emphasis will be upon the disintegrative effects of the dream, which also confronts us with our moral disintegrity, our psychopathic lack of a central hold on ourselves. Dreams show us to be plural and that each of the forms that figure there are "the full man himself," full potentials of behavior. Only by falling apart into the multiple figures do we extend consciousness to embrace and contain its psychopathic potentials.

(Dream and the Underworld, 41)

*P*olytheistic psychology refers to the inherent dissociability of the psyche and the location of consciousness in multiple figures and centers. A psychological polytheism provides archetypal containers for differentiating our fragmentation and, what is of utmost significance, offers another perspective to pathology. The interconnection between the "splinter psyches" of our multiple persons and the many gods and goddesses of polytheism is brought out in this passage from Jung:

If tendencies towards dissociation were not inherent in the human psyche, fragmentary psychic systems would never have been split off; in other words, neither spirits nor gods would have ever come into existence. That is also the reason why our time has become so utterly godless and profane: we lack all knowledge of the unconscious psyche and pursue the cult of consciousness to the exclusion of all else. *Our true religion is a monotheism of consciousness, a possession by it,* coupled with a fanatical denial of the existence of fragmentary autonomous systems.

(CW 13, §51, emphasis added)

When the monotheism of consciousness is no longer able to deny the existence of fragmentary autonomous systems and no longer able to deal with our actual psychic state, then there arises the fantasy of returning to Greek polytheism. For the "return to Greece" offers a way of coping when our centers cannot hold and things fall apart. The polytheistic alternative does not set up conflicting opposites between beast and Bethlehem, between chaos and unity; it permits the coexistence of all the psychic fragments and gives them patterns in the imagination of Greek mythology. A "return to Greece" was experienced in ancient Rome itself, and in the Italian Renaissance, and in the Romantic psyche during the times of revolution. In recent years it has been an intrinsic part of the lives of such artists and thinkers as Stravinsky, Picasso, Heidegger, Joyce, and Freud. The "return to Greece" is a psychological response to the challenge of breakdown; it offers a model of disintegrated integration.   *(Re-Visioning,* 26–27)

PERSONS

The persons I engage with in dreams are neither representations *(simulacra)* of their living selves nor parts of myself. They are shadow images that fill archetypal roles; they are personas, masks, in the hollow of which is a *numen.* . . .

The former teacher, or my professor, in a dream is not only some intellectual potential of my psychic wholeness. More deeply, this figure is the archetypal mentor, who, for now, in this dream, wears the robes of this schoolteacher or that professor. The childhood love in my dreams is not only a special feeling tone that I may rediscover and unite with now as I age. More deeply this youth from then, living in remembrance, is the archetypal *kore* or *puer* who comes in the shape of this or that personal memory. In dreams, we are visited by the daimones, nymphs, heroes, and gods shaped like our friends of last evening. . . .

In their names are their souls—an individual's name and his Ba were interchangeable, as if we only get our true names from the underworld in relation with death. To see through a dream-person into his or her psychic reality requires an attentive ear to names.

Even when they have no names or are named only functionally or situationally, these names can be imagined as epithets. So we get the unknown woman, the cashier, the mechanic, the owner.

We get figures doing things: the running boy, the driving woman, the worrying brother. Then, should we put capital letters on these figures, we approximate the epithets of the gods: The Man in the Shirt, The Sunburnt Girl, The Huge Black Cop.

(*Dream and the Underworld*, 60–63)

Personifying not only aids discrimination; it also offers another avenue of loving, of imagining things in a personal form so that we can find access to them with our hearts. Words with capital letters are charged with affect, they jump out of their sentences and become images. The tradition of depersonifying recognized full well that personified words tend to become cherished and sacred, affecting the reason of the heart. Hence nominalists disparage the personified style of expression, calling it rhetoric with emotive meaning only. But this very recognition, that personifying emotionalizes, shifts the discussion from nominalism to imagination, from head to heart.

The image of the heart—*l'immagine del cuor*—was an important idea in the work of Michelangelo who was strongly influenced by the Platonist tradition. Imagining with the heart refers to a mode of perception that penetrates through names and physical appearances to a personified interior image, from the heart to the heart. When Michelangelo portrayed Lorenzo and Giuliano Medici in the Sacristy of San Lorenzo, the features which he depicted were unnatural, not as they appeared in life but rather transfigured to conform with the true image of their persons in the heart. While the scientific Renaissance (Bacon and Galileo) insisted on the primacy of sense perception, Michelangelo's *immagine del cuor* implied that *perception is secondary to imagination.* By imagining through and beyond what the eye sees, the imagination envisions primordial images. And these present themselves in personified forms.

Nearer our own times another Mediterranean, the Spaniard Miguel de Unamuno (1864–1936), returned to the relationship of heart and personified images and explained the necessary interdependence between love and personifying. . . . He sums up, saying: "Our feeling of the world, upon which is based our understanding of it, is necessarily anthropomorphic and mythopeic." Loving is a way of knowing, and for loving to know, it must personify. Personifying is thus a way of knowing, especially knowing what is invisible, hidden in the heart.

In this perspective personifying is not a lesser, primitive mode of apprehending but a finer one. It presents in psychological theory the attempt to integrate heart into method and to return abstract thoughts and dead matter to their human shapes.

⚜

Multiplication of persons occurs in two kinds of clinical conditions. First, it may happen when the importance of any single individual becomes so overwhelming to a patient that he must split the individual's image, multiplying it into more manageable parts. The patient then has two doctors, or more, with the same name (or several names for the same doctor), two or more beloveds or dead spouses, or even two or more selves. In this way personifying is protective; it prevents an unbearable concentration of numinous power in any single figure.

Second, multiplication of persons may be used as a therapeutic tool in order to bring home the realization that "the ego complex is not the only complex in the psyche." By actively imagining the psyche into multiple persons, we prevent the ego from identifying with each and every figure in a dream and fantasy, each and every impulse and voice. For the ego is not the whole psyche, only one member of a commune. Therapy works through the paradox of admitting that all figures and feelings of the psyche are wholly *mine*, while at the same time recognizing that these figures and feelings are free of my control and identity, not *mine* at all.

Personifying helps place subjective experiences "out there," thereby we can devise protections against them and relations with them. Through multiplicity we become internally more separated; we become aware of distinct parts. Even should unity of personality be an aim, "only separated things can unite," as we learn from the old alchemical psychologists. Separation comes first. It is a way of gaining distance. This *separatio* (in the language of alchemy) offers internal detachment, as if there were now more interior space for movement and for placing events, where before there was a conglomerate adhesion of parts or a monolithic identification with each and all, a sense of being stuck in one's problem.

Essential to this internal separation is naming the personalities; as if only by naming the animals in Eden could Adam become who he was. Through naming, they became *they*, and Adam could now recognize and be separate from each of their characters. His leonine, wolfish, and apelike aspects were no longer him, or his, but "out there" sharing the same garden. By objectifying in this personified manner, we can be spared other objective methods which psychology employs for similar purposes. Naming with images and metaphors has an advantage over naming with concepts, for personified namings never become mere dead tools. Images and metaphors present themselves always as living psychic subjects with which I am obliged to be in relation. They keep me aware of the power of the words I work with, whereas concepts tend to delude me into nominalism.

Whether *personifying* occurs in a patient as a protection or in a therapist as a means of making separations, its purpose is the same: *to save the diversity and autonomy of the psyche from domination by any single power*, whether this domination be by a figure of archetypal awe in one's surroundings or by one's own egomania. Personifying is the soul's answer to egocentricity.

Besides its clinical appearance, personifying happens with each of us, every night, in dreams. The dream is the best model of the actual psyche, because it shows various styles of consciousness copresent in one scene. These styles are embodied in persons who are embroiled with each other. So psychologists say: dreams show you your conflicts. But conflicts presuppose wishes, viewpoints, whole styles of personality different from the ego-complex. These we see in the dream's drama, which is also a critique of the ego-complex from the viewpoints of the other members of the troupe. The secondary personalities in waking life usually find their way to criticize the ego's rule only through symptomatic interferences (psychopathologies), but in dreams they turn the tables and show the ego its limitations. . . .

By employing the dream as model of psychic actuality, and by conceiving a theory of personality based upon the dream, we are imagining the psyche's basic structure to be *an inscape of personified images.* The full consequences of this structure imply that the psyche presents its own imaginal dimensions, operates freely without words, and is constituted of multiple personalities. We can describe the psyche as a polycentric realm of nonverbal, nonspatial images.

Myth offers the same kind of world. It too is polycentric, with innumerable personifications in imaginal space.

(Re-Visioning, 14–15, 31–33)

The figures whom Jung encountered were Elijah, Salome, and a black serpent. Soon Elijah transformed into Philemon. . . . The cosmos brought by Elijah, Salome, the black serpent, and Philemon—this "Egypto-Hellenistic atmosphere with a Gnostic coloration"—was the very one that could sustain the act which Jung was performing. I can hardly stress this enough: the figures whom Jung first met and who convinced him of the reality of their psychic being by extending to him personal relations with the powers of the psyche, these figures derive from the Hellenistic world and its belief in daimones. (*Daimon* is the original Greek spelling for these figures who later became *demons* because of the Christian view and *daemons* in positive contradistinction to that view.)

Jung's descent to the "land of the dead" presented him with his spiritual ancestors, who, through Jung, ushered in a new daimonology and angelology.

Know Thyself in Jung's manner means to become familiar with, to open oneself to and listen to, that is, to know and discern, daimones. Entering one's interior story takes a courage similar to starting a novel. We have to engage with persons whose autonomy may radically alter, even dominate our thoughts and feelings, neither ordering these persons about nor yielding to them full sway. Fictional and factual, they and we, are drawn together like threads into a *mythos*, a plot, until death do us part. It is a rare courage that submits to this middle region of psychic reality where the supposed surety of fact and illusion of fiction exchange their clothes.

(Healing Fiction, 54–55)

3

Imaginal Practice:
Greeting the Angel

Readers complain that James Hillman offers little in the way of technique and method. He speaks strongly against guided imagery, Gestalt techniques, the interpretation and application of images for life, drug-induced reverie, and studies in symbolism. While it is true one looks in vain in Hillman for a manual explaining how to work with images, he does provide some precise guidelines for elaborating images and for preserving their integrity.

Of primary importance in archetypal practice is one's attitude toward an image. Hillman says over and over that he wants to preserve the phenomena. "Stick to the image" has become a rule of thumb. This means not translating images into meanings, as though images were allegories or symbols. As he says, if there is a latent dimension to an image, it is its inexhaustibility, its bottomlessness. Even subtle moves with an image can turn it into a concept or link it into an abstract group of family symbols.

Hillman also advises that an image comes with a moral claim. It haunts or obsesses until we respond to it in some fashion. It may suggest an internal necessity or a limitation, or it may require direct action. Images are daimones offering indications of fate. In a climate of modernism, imagination is often taken lightly. Relying on images for an ethical sensibility would seem to promote relativity. Anything goes. But Hillman recognizes a profound, subtle, complex morality in taking images seriously. Knowing our fantasy life is to know ourselves profoundly. From that particular kind of self-knowledge that is beyond ego comes a strong sense of destiny. In this sense, imagination provides a solid moral grounding.

A different yet important kind of grounding also arises from psychological ideas. *Modern psychology suffers from a debilitating anti-intellectualism. Instead of ideas, it relies on research designs, quantitative studies, simple and literalistic catalogs of illness, and a wide range of techniques. Or, it goes in the opposite direction where feelings are the final moral arbitrator. One of Hillman's radical contributions to psychology is to ground psychology once again in ideas that have depth and texture, and to propose ideas with intellectual passion.*

In many writings, Hillman presents "rules" for working with images that are similar to the "rules" artists follow in their work. These rules protect the individuality of the image and yet let it speak more loudly than it would without this work. One rule, for instance, is to consider all the details and the context of an image. If you dreamed of a snake last night, that snake is not identical to the one that appeared to Adam and Eve, although it may be related. Hillman recommends that we take an olfactory approach to images, knowing them with the intimacy of smell.

Because we take imagination lightly, we are often tempted to ground an image outside itself. A dream takes its meaning and weight from a past memory or a current problem. A painting is of special value because it represents a classic myth. A work of literature is prized because it teaches an important moral lesson. In all these instances, the image suffers from neglect. Its own presence, pregnant and full of implication, can't get through all the attempts to ground it.

An image, Hillman says, appears as representative of the entire pandemonium of images. Christian iconography often shows the air teeming with angels, but only Gabriel announces the message of ultimate importance to the Virgin. A particular image, Hillman notes, is a necessary angel waiting for a response. How we greet this angel will depend on our sensitivity to its reality and presence.

IDEAS

We shall be assuming the passionate importance of psychological ideas. . . . The soul requires its own ideas, in fact, soul-making takes place as much through ideation as in personal relationships or meditation. *One aim of this book is the resuscitation of ideas* at a time in psychology when they have fallen into decline and are being replaced by experimental designs, social programs, therapeutic techniques.

There seems to be nothing more astounding in the field of psychology than its scarcity of interesting ideas. Whole schools are built upon one book, and one book upon one idea, and that often a simplification or a borrowing. The ideational process in psychology is far behind its methodology, instruments, and applications—and far, far behind the psyche's indigenous richness. In this century since Freud and Jung and the wealth of ideas they introduced—from libido, projection, and repression to individuation, anima/animus, and archetype, to pick but a handful—how few have been the ideas generative of psychological reflection! Technical concepts proliferate in the jargon of a profession, but these are short-lived fruit flies feeding on the sound fruit.

Ideas decline for many reasons. They too grow old and hollow, become private and precious; or they may detach from life, no longer able to save its phenomena. Or they may become monomanic, one particular idea crediting itself with more value than all others, and in opposition to them. Today action is thought of within this polarity, which at its extreme would make action blind and ideas impotent. An old cliché, the bodiless head of academic psychology, is converting into a new cliché, the headless body of therapeutic psychology—a current demonstration of action against ideation.

I would remove discussion of ideas from the realm of thought to the realm of psyche. It is their appearance in the psyche, their significance as psychic events, their psychological effect and reality as experiences relevant for soul, that demand our attention as psychologists.

For us ideas are ways of regarding things *(modi res considerandi)*, perspectives. Ideas give us eyes, let us see. The word *idea* itself points to its intimacy with the visual metaphor of knowing, for it is related both to the Latin *videre* ("to see") and the German *wissen* ("to know"). Ideas are ways of seeing and knowing, or knowing by means of insighting. Ideas allow us to envision, and by means of vision we can know. Psychological ideas are ways of seeing and knowing soul, so that a change in psychological ideas means a change in regard to soul and regard for soul.

Our word *idea* comes from the Greek *eidos,* which meant originally in early Greek thought, and as Plato used it, both that which one sees—an appearance or shape in a concrete sense—and that by means of which one sees. We see them, and by means of them. Ideas are both the shape of events, their constellation in this or that archetypal pattern, and the modes that make possible our ability to see through events into their pattern. By means of an idea we can see the idea cloaked in the passing parade. The implicit connection between having ideas to see *with* and seeing ideas themselves suggests that the more ideas we have, the more we see, and the deeper the ideas we have, the deeper we see. It also suggests that ideas engender other ideas, breeding new perspectives for viewing ourselves and world.

Moreover, without them we cannot "see" even what we sense with the eyes in our heads, for our perceptions are shaped according to particular ideas. Once we considered the world flat and now we consider it round; once we observed the sun rotate around the earth, and now we observe the earth turn around the sun; our eyes and their perceptions did not change with the Renaissance. But our ideas have changed, and with them what we "see." And our ideas change as changes take place in the soul, for as Plato said, soul and idea refer to each other, in that an idea is the "eye of the soul," opening us through its insight and vision.

Therefore the soul reveals itself in its ideas, which are not "just ideas" or "just up in the head," and may not be "pooh-poohed" away, since they are the very modes through which we are envisioning and enacting our lives. We embody them as we speak and move. We are always in the embrace of an idea. Therapy has as important a job to do with ideas as it has with symptoms and feelings, and the investigation of a person's ideas are as revealing of his archetypal structure as are his dreams and his desires. No one concerned with soul dare say, "I am not interested in ideas" or "Ideas are not practical."

Ideas remain impractical when we have not grasped or been grasped by them. When we do not get an idea, we ask "how" to put it in practice, thereby trying to turn insights of the soul into actions of the ego. But when an insight or idea has sunk in, practice invisibly changes. The idea has opened the eye of the soul. By seeing differently, we do differently. Then *how* is implicitly taken care of. *How?* disappears as the idea sinks in—as one reflects upon *it* rather than on how to do something with it. This movement of grasping ideas is vertical or inward rather than horizontal or outward into the realm of doing something. The only legitimate *How?* in regard to these psychological insights is: "How can I grasp an idea?"

Since psychological ideas, or insights as I have sometimes called them, reflect soul, the question of comprehending them turns on one's relation with soul and how the soul learns. The answer to this has always been "by experience," which is tantamount to turning the question back upon itself, since one of the main activities of soul as we defined them at the beginning of this book is precisely that of changing "events into experiences." Here we are specifying how events become experiences, saying that the act of seeing through events connects them to the soul and creates experiences. Simply to participate in events, or to suffer them strongly, or to accumulate a variety of them, does not differentiate or deepen one's psychic capacity into what is often called a wise or an old soul. Events are not essential to the soul's experiencing. It does not need many dreams or many loves or city lights. We have records of great souls that have thrived in a monk's cell, a prison, or a suburb. But there must be a vision of what is happening, deep ideas to create experience. Otherwise we have had the events without experiencing them, and the experience of what happened comes only later when we gain an idea of it—when it can be envisioned by an archetypal idea.

The soul learns less in psychology than in psychologizing—a difference we shall soon be explaining in detail. It learns by searching for itself in whatever ideas come to it; it gains ideas by looking for them, by subjectivizing all questions, including the *How?* To give any direct answer to *How?* betrays the activity of soul-making, which proceeds by psychologizing through all literal answers. As it gains ideas by looking for them, the soul loses ideas by putting them into practice in answer to *How?*

There is in fact a direct relation between the poverty of ideas in academic and therapeutic psychology and their insistence upon the practical. To work out answers to psychological questions not only immediately impoverishes the ideational process, but also means falling into the pragmatic fallacy—the assumption that ideas are valued by their usefulness. This fallacy denies our basic premise: that ideas are inseparable from practical actions, and that theory itself is practice; there is nothing more practical than forming ideas and becoming aware of them in their psychological effects. Every theory we hold practices upon us in one way or another, so that ideas are always in practice and do not need to be put there.

Finally, psychological learning or psychologizing seems to represent the soul's desire for light, like the moth for the flame. The psyche wants to find itself by seeing through; even more, it loves to be enlightened by *seeing through itself*, as if the very act of seeing through clarified and made the soul transparent—as if psychologizing with ideas were itself an archetypal therapy, enlightening, illuminating. The soul seems to suffer when its inward eye is occluded, a victim of overwhelming events. This suggests that all ways of enlightening soul—mystical and meditative, Socratic and dialectic, Oriental and disciplined, psychotherapeutic, and even the Cartesian longing for clear and distinct ideas—arise from the psyche's need for vision. (*Re-Visioning*, 115–116, 121–123)

RESPONDING TO IMAGES

Imaginational morality is essentially *not* in my judgment as to whether the daimones I behold are good or bad, *nor* does it lie in the application of imagination (how I put what I discover from images into life's actions). Rather this morality lies in recognizing the images religiously, as powers with claims. . . .

Jung attributes the moral moment to the responding ego, whereas I would psychologize the question further, asking why does the moral question arise at all in his mind after the encounter with images? Possibly the moral concern is the result of the encounter itself and so enters Jung's narrative at this juncture. As these imaginal figures bring a sense of internal fate, so they bring an awareness of internal necessity and its limitations. We feel responsible to them and for them. A mutual caring envelopes the relationship, or, as this situation was put in antiquity, the daimones are also guardian spirits. Our images are our keepers, as we are theirs.

From the outside, the appearance of the daimones seems to offer ethical relativity: a paradise of seductions and escapades. But this fantasy of ethical relativity betrays a consciousness that is not yet inside the imaginal world, that does not Know Thyself from within its images. In other words, the question of ethical relativity which raises its head whenever one speaks of a "pandemonium of images" and a plurality of gods is answered by the dedication which the images demand. It is they—not we—who demand meticulous crafting into jeweled idols; they, who call for ritualized devotions, who insist they be consulted before we act. Images are the compelling source of morality and religion as well as the conscientiousness of art. And, as we do not make them up, so we do not make up our response to them, but are "taught" this response by them as moral instances. It is when we lose the images that we become moralistic, as if the morality contained within the images becomes a dissociated, free-floating guilt, a conscience without face.

When an image is realized—fully imagined as a living being other than myself—then it becomes a *psychopompos*, a guide with a soul having its own inherent limitation and necessity. It is this image and no other, so that the conceptual questions of moral pluralism and relativism fade in front of the actual engagement with the image. The supposed creative pandemonium of the teeming imagination is limited to its phenomenal appearance in a particular image, that specific one which has come to me pregnant with significance and intention, a necessary angel as it appears here and now and which teaches the hand to represent it, the ear to hear, and the heart how to respond. There is thus revealed through this engagement a *morality of the image*. Psychological morality which derives from the imaginal is no longer a "new ethics" of shadow integration by means of that same old Kantian ego and its heroic wrestlings with abstract dualisms. The ego is no longer the place where morality resides, a philosophical position that had wrested morality from the imagination thereby demonizing it. Instead, it is the daimon who is our preceptor, our *spiritus rector*.

When we study Jung carefully as to *why* one undertakes active imagination, we find these basic reminders. They can be presented as a *via negativa* of cautions, similar to the sober restraint that imbues Freud's analytical mode with a religious piety.

1. Active imagination is not a spiritual discipline, not a way of Ignatius of Loyola or of Eastern yoga, for there are no prescribed or proscribed fantasies. One works with the images that arise, not special ones chosen by a master or a code.

2. Active imagination is not an artistic endeavor, not a creative production of paintings and poems. One may aesthetically give form to the images—indeed one should try as best one can aesthetically—though this is for the sake of the figures, in dedication to them and to realize their beauty, and not for the sake of art. The aesthetic work of active imagination is therefore not to be confused with art for exhibition or publication.

3. Active imagination aims not at silence but at speech, not at stillness but at story or theater or conversation. It emphasizes the importance of the word, not the cancellation of the word, and thus the word becomes a way of *relating,* an instrument of feeling.

4. Thus it is not a mystical activity, performed for the sake of illumination, for reaching select states of consciousness (samadhi, satori, unity with all things). That would be imposing a spiritual intention upon a psychological activity; that would be a domination of, even a repression of, soul by spirit.

5. Nor, however, does this last mean that active imagination is a psychological activity in only the personal sense—for the sake of curing symptoms, calming or abreacting terrors and greeds, bettering families, improving and developing personality. Such would be to demean the daimones into personal servants whose concern must then be with problem solving those delusions we call realities because we have not seen through to their fantasies, their guiding images that project them along.

6. Yet, active imagination is not a psychological activity in the transpersonal sense of *theurgy* (ritual magic), the attempt to work with images by and for the human will. From both sides of archetypal psychology's tradition—Plotinus and Freud—we have been warned against opening floodgates to the "black tide of mud of

occultism." Active imagination becomes popularist superstitious theurgy when we activate the images artificially (drugs), perform it routinely as a ritualism, foster special effects (synchronicities), further divinatory abilities (turning to inner voices to interpret dreams), use it to augment self-confidence in decisions (power). Each and all of these uses are no longer modes of self-knowledge but of self-aggrandizement, now covered by the innocent label *psychic growth*. Faust still pervades, perverts, our Know Thyself, turning it into a drive beyond the limits which that maxim originally implied: "Know that you are but human, not divine." Active imagination as theurgic divination would work on the gods rather than recognizing their workings in us. We reach too far, missing the daimones that are present every day, and each night too. As Plotinus said: "It is for them to come to me, not for me to go to them."

So, Jung's method of interior imagining is for none of these reasons—spiritual discipline, artistic creativity, transcendence of the worldly, mystical vision or union, personal betterment, or magical effect. Then what for? What is the aim?

Primarily, it aims at healing the psyche by re-establishing it in the metaxy from which it had fallen into the disease of literalism. Finding the way back to the metaxy calls up a mythical mode of imagining such as the Platonic Socrates employed as a healer of souls. This return to the middle realm of fiction, of myth carries one into conversational familiarity with the cosmos one *inhabits*. *Healing* thus means "Return" and *psychic consciousness* means "Conversation," and a *healed consciousness* lives fictionally, just as healing figures like Jung and Freud become under our very eyes fictional personages, their factual biographies dissolving and coagulating into myths, becoming fictions so they can go on healing.

Therefore, active imagination, so close to art in procedure, is distinct from it in aim. This is not only because active imagination foregoes an end result in a physical product, but more because its intention is Know Thyself, self-understanding, which is as well its limit—the paradoxical limit of endlessness that corresponds with the Heraclitean endlessness of psyche itself. Self-understanding is necessarily uroboric, an interminable turning in a gyre amid its scenes, its visions and voices.

From the viewpoint of narrative, the visions and voices are an unfolding story without end. Active imagination is interminable because the story goes into death and death is endless—who knows where it has its stop? From the viewpoint of narrative, self-understanding is that healing fiction which individuates a life into death. From the imagistic viewpoint, however, self-understanding is interminable because it is not in time to begin with. Know Thyself is revelatory, nonlinear, discontinuous; it is like a painting, a lyric poem; biography thoroughly gone into the imaginative act. We may fiction connections between the revelatory moments, but these connections are hidden like the spaces between the sparks or the dark seas around the luminous fishes' eyes, images Jung employs to account for images. Each image is its own beginning, its own end, healed by and in itself. So, Know Thyself terminates whenever it leaves linear time and becomes an act of imagination. A partial insight, this song now, this one image; to see partly is the whole of it. *(Healing Fiction, 60–62, 78–80)*

Our method has been partly described by Henry Corbin when writing of *ta' wil*, which he says means: *"reconduire, ramener une chose à son origine et principe, à son archetype."* As he says further: "In *ta' wil* one must carry sensible forms back to imaginative forms and then rise to still higher meanings; to proceed in the opposite direction (to carry imaginative forms back to the sensible forms in which they originate) is to destroy the virtualities of the imagination." For us, it is the conservation and exploration and vivification of the imagination and the insights derived therefrom, rather than the analysis of the unconscious, that is the main work of therapy.

("Pothos," 50)

To see the archetypal in an image is thus not a hermeneutic move. It is an imagistic move. We amplify an image by means of myth in order not to find its archetypal meaning but in order to feed it with further images that increase its volume and depth and release its fecundity. Hermeneutic amplifications in search of meaning take us elsewhere, across cultures, looking for resemblances which neglect the specifics of the actual image. Our move, which keeps archetypal significance limited within the actually presented image, also keeps meanings always precisely embodied. No longer would there be images without meaning and meaning without images. The neurotic condition that Jung so often referred to as "loss of meaning" would now be understood as "loss of image," and the condition would be met therapeutically less by recourse to philosophy, religion, and wisdom, and more by turning directly to one's actual images in which archetypal significance resides.

Unless we maintain this distinction between inherent significance and interpretative meaning, between insighting an image and hermeneutics, we shall not be able to stay with the image and let it give us what it bears. We shall have the meaning and miss the experience, miss the uniqueness of what is there by our use of methods for uncovering what is not there. We shall forget that wholeness is not only a construction to be built or a goal to achieve, but, as Gestalt says, a whole is presented in the very physiognomy of each event.   (*Typologies*, 37–38)

SENSING IMAGES

The dream begins: "In some kind of a cave, a dark cavern. The whole place slopes backward and downward from where I'm standing. . . ." This seems a simple presentation of optical vision. I can see myself standing, and behind me, as on a stage set or in a photograph, the ground and walls sloping back and down. Then, as I stay there *looking* at the image, I begin *hearing* "backward" and "downward" in a second sense. (Perhaps this resounding of the image is an effect of this image itself, its echoing cavernous resonance.) The scene is no longer a simple descriptive reproduction; now it has a second sense of implications. Metaphorical insight emerges through hearing while seeing.

Insight occurred largely because I slowed my reading of the image from narrational sequence (what happened next? and then, and then?) to poetic imagistic reading. In narrational reading, the sense emerges at the end, whereas in imagistic reading there is sense throughout. Most poetry (not the heroic epic, of course) is printed on the page in a form that forces the eye to slow itself to the cadence of the images.

Now, the second level of *backward and downward* is given with the first, and not added to it as an interpretation. The classical Gestalt psychology of Köhler and Koffka would consider the menacing pull of the dark cavern to be as important and primary as the speleological description. For them, description is always physiognomy. We do not project the second sense onto the first, since the quality of depth is immediately presented *to the senses* by the scene itself, that it slopes back and down, that it is a cave, that it is dark.

Freud might have gone yet further, saying that the primary level of the dream scene is the latent meaning of *sloping backward and downward* (regression toward the mother) which the dream manifests in a speleological metaphor. I think a trained psychological mind works the way in which I am here imagining Freud. Such a person would not have to look at the scene first as a photograph; he would start right off hearing the image with metaphorical insight. He would see the sense in it even while sense-perceiving it—or even before. A second sense would be immediately intuited and felt as present whatever the situation. I wonder whether Freud's idea of latent meaning needs to be taken so literally. Perhaps, *latency* (in childhood, in dream content, in psychosis) merely intends to remind us not to stay in a manifest position. It is a sign that says: "keep digging."

The sense of smell alone may be a better analogy for image-sensing than both seeing and hearing together, because smell is both more concrete, and less. Heraclitus, for instance, considered smell to be *the* mode of psychic perception (a proposition treated more fully in my *The Dream and the Underworld*). When Heraclitus further implies that the nostrils are the most discriminating of the sense organs, and that the gods distinguish by means of aroma, he is referring to invisible perception or the perception of invisibles. Like perceives like: the invisible, intangible, inaudible psyche perceives invisible, inaudible, intangible essences. Sensate intuition or intuitive sensation.

Even the word *essence* has a double sense: both a highly volatilized substance like a perfume and a primary principle, seed-idea, form. Smell involves us in what is most sensate and most subtle; primitive and primordial in one and the same sense. I do believe that the divine mode of the gods or the underworld mode of souls is not so far apart from what you call *our animal sensing*.

Protestor: "You mean to say that we smell images!"

I mean to say that smelling is the best sense analogy for imagining for these reasons: First, we commonly hold smell to be more gutsy than sight and sound. So the sense of smell gives a sense of body depth to whatever is smelled. By smelling an image, I am implying the image has body.

Second, smell is commonly held to be the most parasitical sense, that is, it has hardly any language of its own—something we already discovered about imagination. Smells, like images, are *reflections, effluvia:* the odor of a rose, the scent of burnt toast, the stench of a refinery. Odor, scent, and stench have no smell of their own, no content without a particular body. Smells cannot stand alone. They must be linked to an image: rose odor, toast scent, refinery stench. On the analogy with smell, therefore, the sense of an image inherently *sticks to the image* and cannot leave the image without losing its sense.

It follows, third, that a smell refers to a particular image in which the smell inheres. It conjures a unique event and favors discrimination among unique events. If we want to understand an image for itself, we must smell it out. We need a good nose for differences, *diakrisis* of the spirits, that imaginative precision which is the main aim of the imaginal method.

Fourth, smelling images guards us against optical illusions about seeing images. If an image is not *what* you see but the *way* you see, then smell reminds us that we don't have to see an image to sense it. In fact, smell reminds us that we can't see them, keeps them deliteralized, like the old definition of archetype: nonpresentable form. So, by *smelling* images, we keep the archetypal as an actual sensation in the image, without having to exaggerate this sensation by calling it numinous or tremendous.

Protestor: "All these sensation details. It's like Wundt's laboratory revisioned. Are you sure you're not a sensation type—or is this the compulsion of your inferior function?"

We are all sensation types as soon as we are seized by an image. Can anyone image without sensing? The moment you leave sensing out of imagining, it is imagining that becomes an inferior function: sheer fantasy, mere imaginings, only a dream. Let me go on.

Fifth, smells are all there at once, like images. There is no beginning, middle and end, like stories. We are less likely to read images narratively.

Sixth, unlike the words of our other senses (*touch, see,* etc.), *smell* has a *bad* connotation. Something negative, offensive, is carried along with the sense, so that smell reminds us of our native aversion to images. We don't altogether like them. Iconoclasm is inherent to the image itself. The cult and worship of images requires flowers and incense, as if to sweeten (as Adolf Guggenbühl says) what is also inherently obnoxious. There is an intolerable aspect to *every* image, as image. Its habitation in the undersense of things is their underworld and "death." An image as a simulacrum is but a shadow of life and the death of concretistic faith. Imagining implies the death of the natural, organic view of life and this repels our common sense. Hence, the underworld stinks; dung and corpses; brimstone. Images are demonic, of the very devil; keep a distance. Have a keen nose.

Seventh, the cognition of smell is like a recognition. Smells bring the remembrance of Platonic recollection together with an instinctual reaction. Lured by musk, swayed by damp honeysuckle, we respond to the aphroditic evocation and recognize love arising without previous learning. Reflex and reflection together. The smelled image is both immediate and remembered, both animal and memorial.

Eighth, smells cannot be summoned. Though they may evoke remembrance of things past, we cannot willfully recollect them as we can a room or a tune. We are subject to them, assailed by them, translated into their world: with one whiff of mixed lavendar, cedar, and camphor, I become a little boy excitedly hiding in a chest—imagination utterly beyond control of will. The egoless spontaneity of smell is similar to that of imagining.

Ninth, this spontaneity beyond control of will, however, is not beyond limit. It does not imply imagination as flight into pure possibility, as if one could imagine anything. No, smell is always of something, so imagining is always held within the bounds of a specific image—this image, right here, under your nose. This is what I mean by "the body of the image": its particular limits which are its shape and its way of working. If, as Jung says, psychic reality is simply that which works in the psyche, then what does this working, and always in a specifically patterned way, is the body of the image. Images don't work for us when we cannot sense their body. And it is our nose that reminds us that images have bodies, are animals.

Protestor: "If I take you seriously, it would mean that images are actually perceived by an animal nose at an instinctual level, and that they must have, in some sense or other, an animal body. Aren't you merely elaborating what Jung always insisted upon: images and instincts are inseparable?"

Let's leave it right there: images as instincts, perceived instinctually; the image, a subtle animal; the imagination, a great beast, a subtle body, with ourselves inseparably lodged in its belly: imagination, an animal mundi and an anima mundi, both diaphanous and passionate, unerring in its patterns and in all ways necessary, the necessary angel that makes brute necessity angelic; imagination, a moving heaven of theriomorphic gods in bestial constellations, stirring without external stimulation within our animal sense as it images its life in our world.   ("Image-Sense," 137, 140–142)

IMAGINATION, THE GROUND OF CERTAINTY

Unless the multiplicities of white are kept as its shadows—as blues, as creams, as the wan and pale feelings of gray—the whitening becomes sheer blankness. Here is a reflective consciousness that perceives without reaction, a kind of frank stare, chilled and numbed, lunar, curiously deadened within its own anima state that should have brought it life.

So, to keep whiteness from blinding itself with simplicities (instead of multiplicities), a reduction needs to be performed on the albedo, but in its own style which means turning up the heat in an anima fashion. New lunatic intensities, demanding active imaginations and fermentations that lead to ever-finer discriminations (white against white), adding weight to light and rubbing the silver to more clarified reflections. This means friction, more accurate tuning of responses, and keeping to the lunatic fringe—noticing the oddity of behavior and feeling when images are first reality. We whiten the earth by earthing our whiteness. So, put the heat on anima attractions, soulful philosophizings, delicate aestheticisms, petty perceptions, global moods, lovey-dovey coziness, and the nymphic gossamer illusions that promise lions. Don't literalize the relief of the albedo into relaxation: pull the plug on Mary's bath. Silver is hard and it likes heat and truth; its telos is yellow and red, bright and loud. Get at essentials; stick to the image; greet the angel. This white earth of the imaginal is also a territory of essences, principles, *archai* (as in Corbin). The aim of reduction is not to stay stuck to the nigredo nose in the dirt but, as Berry writes, to come to "the essential, the quintessence of one's nature." To achieve this intensity of soul, whether in an hour of analysis, in a close relationship, in language, study or art, takes as much sweat as shoveling through the stable with Hercules. These essences stand out the further we can move into each image, each fantasy, each event, working at distinctions within them rather than comparisons between them. For in the albedo the very method of psychoanalysis changes from an Aristotelian observation of similarities (and its ultimate reduction downward to common denominators) to the study of singularity, each phenomenon a thing in itself, allowing and forcing the necessary angel to appear as the body in the image making its behavioral demands on the soul.

A double dove, both male and female, appears in one of Jung's own dreams, and from that dream and Robert Grinnell's analysis of it, we can take a final cue as to the doves' significance, or how the silvered psyche works in our consciousness. I shan't recapitulate the dream. It is in Jung's biography. But the result of the dove's appearance, its transformation into a little girl—and do not such girls "belong" to Diana?—its speech to him and its vanishing into *blue* air, adds something more to the gift of speech and the gift of interpretation from above downward. The result of the dove was, as Grinnell brings out, the gift of faith in images, a psychological faith, which permits belief and enjoins conviction, a fervid animal faith in the depths, a dove in the belly that gives one the sense that the psyche is the first reality and that we are always soul.

What is reflection then when there is no subject reflected, neither emotion nor external object? No fact at all? The very idea of reflection transmutes from witness of a phenomenon, a mirroring of something else, to a resonance of the phenomenon itself, a metaphor without a referent, or better said, an image.

Mental events as images do not require and cannot acquire further validation by reference to external events. The soul's life is not upheld as correct by virtue of exteriority. But neither are mental events validated by virtue of my *having* a dream, *thinking* an idea or *feeling* an experience. We are beyond soul as a conglomerate of subjective functions, with imagination merely one function among others, a bureau in the department of mind. (Imagination imagines itself in this bureaucratic fashion only when it must give report of itself in the language of historical psychology that denied imagination any valid place to begin with.) Psychic events do not require my reports in the language of functions and experiences in order to be. They do not require my reports at all. Soul need no longer be captured by subjectivity, a mind owning its events and distinct from them. Neither wax tablet, cage of birds, ghost in the machine, iceberg or saddleback—functional models all, attempting to account for, give support to, a subjective base for psychic events. Let it go. We can dispel subjectivity and yet still have soul. No subject needed, neither conscious nor unconscious, neither empirical nor transcendental, neither personal ego nor impersonal self. Personal pronouns can lose their hold: whose is that cat, this music, the idea which *I* am writing now? The event is there, shining. Have we thought it, or has it appeared, epiphanic amid that birthing turmoil which we call work. And who are *we* to say? Let events belong to themselves, or to the others. "All things are full of gods." said Euripides; it is *their* personal belongings that furnish our world. The event is there—though not in a mirror, for if the mirror vanish the event will still be there. Or better: the event is the mirror self-sustaining its own reflection. Have faith in the everlasting indestructible ground of images. They do not need us. . . .

Strange to find imagination as the ground of certainty, that nothing is more certain than fantasy—it is as it is. It can be subjected to the noetic procedures of cognition but these cannot negate it. It still stands, and more firmly than the doubts with which it is assailed by noetic inquiry. When the mind rests on imaginal firmament, then thinking and imagining no longer divide against each other as they must when the mind is conceived in the categories of *nous*. Now *nous* can as well be *psyche;* the noetic, the psychological. Knowledge comes from and feeds the soul, the *epistrophé* of *data* to its first meaning "gifts." Knowledge is received by the soul as understanding, in exchange for which the soul gives to knowledge value and faith. Knowledge can again believe in itself as a virtue. Here is knowledge not opposed to soul, different from feeling or life, academic, scholarly, sheerly intellectual or merely explanatory *(erklärendes)*, but knowledge as a necessity demanded by the silvered mind by means of which the soul can understand itself. In this white country where the barriers between soul and intellect do not try to keep each other out, psyche is itself a kind of knowing, a keen accounting, a wit of what is there; and *nous* is psychological, engaged in intelligent interlocutions among its images. The entire dialectic of philosophy becomes whitened to talk among imaginal figures. We take part in a symposium going on forever: mental life, an extraordinary banquet. Through this inquiring conversation and this display of the image by means of its rhetoric, psyche becomes knowledgeable, noetically aware of itself, though not as defined by *nous* (which limits psychological knowledge to the cognition of experience, introspection of the interiority of time, structures of transcendental subjectivity and the operations of its logic). Instead of these philosophical constrictions on psychological knowledge, psyche becomes aware by means of an imaginal method: the ostentation of images, a parade of fantasies as imagination bodies forth its subtleties. *Nous* observer of *psyche*, seeing in her mirror how his mind actually proceeds. *Nous* at last psychological: all its cognitive instrumentarium become lunatic, the logic of images; psyche with logos. Here in the white earth psychology begins.

("Silver (II)," 48–52)

ANGELIC INTERPRETATION

Man is created as an image, in an image, and by means of his images. Therefore he appears first of all to the imagination so that the perception of personality is first of all an imaginative act (to which sensation, emotion, and ideation contribute but do not determine). Modern psychological methods of examining images and imagination in terms of sensations or feelings start the wrong way around. Since imagination forms us into our images, to perceive a person's essence we must look into his imagination and see what fantasy is creating his reality. But to look into imagination we need to look with imagination, imaginatively, searching for images with images. You are given to my imagination by your image, the image of you in your heart as Michelangelo, as Neoplatonism, as Henry Corbin would say, and this image is composed not only of wrinkles, muscles, and colors accreted through your life, though they make their contribution to its complexity. To see you as you are is an imagination, as Lavater says, of structure, the divine image in which your essence is shaped.

❧

We may look at man theriomorphically, by which I do not mean merely genetically or in an evolutional sense. I mean rather that the gods themselves show their shapes the world over as animals, so that the animal is also an *imago dei*, a face of our eternal nature. By perceiving the animal in man we may perceive rudiments of divinity, essential archetypal modes of consciousness—leonine, hawklike, mousy, piggish—essential natures in the psyche that suppose paleolithic indelibility, and are our guardians.

The perspective I am suggesting here considers that the first psychological difference between humans and animals resides in how we regard each other. Humans regard animals differently than animals regard animals (and humans), so a first step in restoring Eden would be to regain the animal eye.

Here we are taking up Jung's idea—presented first at Eranos—that image and instinct are inseparable components of a single spectrum. As there are images in instincts, so we might say there are instincts in images. Images are bodies. Animal images in art, religion, and dreams are not merely depictions *of* animals. Animal images are also showing us images *as* animals, living beings that prowl and growl and must be nourished; the imagination, a great animal, a dragon under whose heaven we breathe its fire.

Darwin considered the animal *expression* in physiognomy to be primary. Gestalt responded by considering the animal *perception* of physiognomy to be primary. If the world presents itself in expressive shapes like animals, then there must be an eye that can see shapes, as animals. To read lines on the face of the world we need an animal eye. This eye not only sees man as animal but by means of the animal, seeing each other with an animal eye. To this eye, image and type appear together. There is no abstraction of one from the other, no *ology*. As T. E. Hulme, the imagist, put it: "We must judge the world from the status of animals, leaving out 'Truth,' etc." Wallace Stevens states in his poems that the animal is the first idea, the myth before the myth, whose perception is of physiognomic *Gestalt*, as a "lion roars at the enraging desert." This bird before the sun of our ordinary round and mind, this "dove in the belly" perceives, and creates with its response, the innate intelligibility of the world. This animal comes in our dreams, this animal—or is the dove an angel?— perceives *sub specie aeternitatis*, the brute eye that reads character in the flesh, and, like Lavater, instantly feels like and dislike. The animal eye perceives and reacts to the animal image in the other.

(*Typologies*, 44, 54–56)

Dreams show bugs have something to teach. They demonstrate the intentions of the natural mind, the undeviating faith of desire, and the urge to survive.

They bring the community consciousness of a swarm and hive, a *Gemeinschaftsgefuehl*, a cosmic sympathy, deeper than a social contract. They conjoin and enjoy the contrary elements of earth and air, show amazing capacities to conform and transform, and are resolute in their persistence to draw a dreamer out of the shelters of human habitation, the sheltering limits of human habits. At the end we feel they want us, these winged creatures with their astonishing eyes. They come to us in dreams which is what angels are supposed to do. Startling, terrifying, sudden: is this the only way angels can now enter our world which has no openings for their welcome?

At least we may consider this angelic interpretation, the bug as strange angel, almost small enough to fit its definition of beauty dancing on a pinhead (the very instrument we use to fix bugs in classificatory death). To survive as they survive, we must utterly transform the shapes of our thought, as they risk all in their transformations. Our minds cannot go far enough out on a limb. This angelic view calls us to look again, respecting who they are, what they are, why they are in the dream, and further, how meet them, even care for them—these miraculous shapes and behaviors, each intricate appearance, a superb archaic ability, faultless, pious, comical, grave, intense, seeking us out while we sleep.

("Going Bugs," 70)

4

Therapy: Fictions
and Epiphanies

The word therapy is loaded with medical connotations, so James
Hillman takes it back to be bathed in etymological fantasies in order
to have a pristine sense of its nature. For the Greeks, the word meant
"service, attendance, and nursing." This notion of therapy lies deep
in Hillman's approach to symptoms, dreams, and images. He attends
to them and serves them, even when they challenge or contradict the
taste and intentions of society or the person who presents them.

To this somewhat familiar etymology Hillman adds another
more curious one. The word, he says, is connected to the word
throne and relates therapy to chair. He might have alluded to ancient
images of Asklepiós, Greek god of healing, sitting in his chair, his
dog at his feet. And, he might have mentioned Sigmund Freud's
famous couch. Even today, the chair is intimately involved in our
image of therapy. The chair suggests reflection, conversation, stillness, interiority, support, and ordinariness. The therapist, Hillman
says, is like a chair eliciting numinous projections. These are some
of the fantasies that arise in therapy. The patient has a chair, too—his
own support, his own identification with Asklepiós, his own source
of fantasy. It is a condition of mutual dependency.

Hillman makes a statement that stands out like an axiom: "The
disease which the experience of death cures is the rage to live." In
Re-Visioning Psychology Hillman says that the soul has a special
relation to death. Here we find death entering therapy. The "rage
to live" is the one-sided affection for life that one often sees in
tandem with symptoms. The patient wants to restore life to its
former ease and tempo. But therapy, when it beckons soul, brings

a dose of death. It reveals eternal aspects of what appears to be only ongoing life. It invites the deep, underworld perspective that is full of revelation but also disappointing the ego that is attached to life.

Hillman states another axiom, "Until the soul gets what it wants, it must fall ill again." The therapist attends to the soul, to dreams and symptoms, for instance, in order to find out what the soul wants. One looks for the myth of the symptom. Therapy searches out fantasy and desire. Hillman assumes that even in symptomatic behavior there are signs of the soul's telos, the directions it wants to take. A symptom is an opportunity as well as a suffering. The therapist has to find its poetry and its dramatic form.

Hillman moves on to yet another puzzling statement: "To be psychological means to see myself in the masks of this particular fiction that is my fate to enact." Here we are not looking for the true self, some core hidden beneath the fictions and enactments of life. Rather, we are seeking the personas, the characters we are in the various dramas of the soul. The god in this case is Dionysus, divine patron of theater and the dramatic aspect of life. The "poetic basis of mind" now becomes the "dramatic forms of life." The archetypal therapist operates at the level of fiction. We are always in a dramatic episode, even when we are analyzing the dramas of life. Notice that Hillman is not merely making a passing observation about psychodrama. He makes the point that to see oneself wearing the Dionysian masks is to be psychological. Carl Jung said that psyche is image. Hillman says that to be psychological is to be thoroughly imaginal.

Reference to drama and mask also gets the ego out of the center of the picture. Hillman often uses metaphors from alchemy or images of animals to show that will, action, and decision are lodged in the soul by nature. It is unnecessary to call on psychology's standard fiction of a central command post called ego-consciousness.

Hillman presents this idea in another way. In therapy one notices a movement from case history to soul history, from literal anxieties and heroics to myth and enduring memory. In place of an anxious drive to live properly and love sufficiently, fate and the qualities and turns of one's soul come to the forefront.

Some have seen in Hillman's attitude the effects of the archetypal positive mother, because he does not look at dreams and behavior for what is wrong or missing. He does not feel that the psyche is "out to get you" or "do you in." He calls this attitude psychological faith or following the anima. By affirming what is, he suggests *that the psyche rests so firmly in age-old archetypal realities of gods, myths, culture, and nature that the movements in the human soul have intentions that can be trusted.*

From the viewpoint of Promethean therapy, where the goal is to outwit the gods on behalf of human intentions, archetypal therapy appears quite mysterious. What do you do if you aren't interested in cure, if you respect symptoms? The answer is that therapist and patient are quite active in their respective chairs riding the moods and fantasies of the anima, reaching for their assigned masks, incubating in the dreams, and entering the mythic drifts of life's episodes.

CARE OF THE SOUL

The Greek word *therapeia* refers also to care. The root is *dher*, which means "carry, support, hold," and is related to *dharma*, the Sanskrit meaning "habit" and "custom" as "carrier." The therapist is one who carries and takes care as does a servant (Greek = *theraps*, *therapon*). He is also one to lean upon, hold on to, and be supported by, because *dher* is also at the root of *thronos* = throne, seat, chair. Here we strike an etymological root of the analytical relationship. The chair of the therapist is indeed a mighty throne constellating dependency and numinous projections. But the analysand also has his chair, and the analyst is both servant and supporter of the analysand. Both are emotionally involved and the dependence is mutual. However, this dependence is not personal, upon each other. Rather it is a dependence upon the objective psyche which both serve together in the therapeutic process. By carrying, by paying careful attention to and devotedly caring for the psyche, the analyst translates into life the meaning of the word *psychotherapy*. The psychotherapist is literally the *attendant of the soul*.   (Suicide, 115–116)

The psyche is *not* unconscious. *We* are, we patients, we analysts. The psyche is constantly making intelligible statements. It's making dreams and symptoms, it's making fantasies and moods. It's extraordinarily intentional, purposive. But the system of therapy has projected "the unconscious" into the patient's psyche, which, then because of opposites, means that the analyst must be conscious. Both patient and analyst tend to believe this system. But the point is that consciousness floats; a psychic fluidum, as Mesmer might have called it, wrapping around and all through the analytical session. It doesn't belong to either party. Sometimes the patient has an insight, and another moment the analyst is conscious by simply being reticent, and another moment the consciousness is really in the image.

For instance, a black snake comes in a dream, a great big black snake, and you can spend a whole hour with this black snake talking about the devouring mother, talking about the anxiety, talking about the repressed sexuality, talking about the natural mind, all those interpretive moves that people make, and what is left, what is vitally important, is what that snake is doing, this crawling huge black snake that's walking into your life . . . and the moment you've defined the snake, interpreted it, you've lost the snake, you've stopped it, and then the person leaves the hour with a concept about my repressed sexuality or my cold black passions or my mother or whatever it is, and you've lost the snake. The task of analysis is to keep the snake there, the black snake, and there are various ways for keeping the black snake . . . see, the black snake's no longer necessary the moment it's been interpreted, and you don't need your dreams any more because they've been interpreted.

But I think you need them all the time, you need that very image you had during the night. For example, a policeman, chasing you down the street . . . you need that image, because that image keeps you in an imaginative possibility . . . if you say, "Oh, my guilt complex is loose again and is chasing me down the street," it's a different feeling, because you've taken up the unknown policeman into your ego system of what you know, your guilt. You've absorbed the unknown into the known (made the unconscious conscious) and nothing, absolutely nothing has happened, nothing. You're really safe from that policeman, and you can go to sleep again. Your interpretation protects your sleep. I want to let the psyche threaten the hell out of you by keeping that policeman there chasing you down the street, even now as we talk. The policeman is more important than what we say about him: I mean *the image is always more inclusive, more complex* (it's a complex, isn't it?) *than the concept.* Let's make that a rule. That's why "stick to the image" is another rule in archetypal psychology. So who is the policeman? Is he guilt, or is he the sense of the law, is he the sense of order, is he the sense of the city, the *polis?* Has he something to do with an inherent structure of consciousness that wants something from you, or reminds you of something, calls you to him? Otherwise he wouldn't be chasing you. You need to keep the policeman there so that you can learn what he is up to and what keeps you running, and running in the street, into the street.

The images are where the psyche is. People say, "I don't know what the soul is," or "I've lost my soul" or whatever. To me the place to look when you feel that way is immediately to the images that show where you are with your soul in your dreams. "I don't know where the hell I am, I am all confused, I've just lost my job . . . everything is happening." Where do you look when you feel that way? . . . The place to look is not only to your feelings, not to your interpretations, not ask help from a third person necessarily, but ask yourself what were you in the image? Where's your imagination? That immediately *locates* you somewhere, into your own psyche. Whereas the introspection doesn't help at all, chasing one's shadow, questioning why did I do this, why do I do that and why did they do this. An instant turmoil: the Hindus call it *vritta,* turning the mind on itself like an anthill. But when you have an image of an anthill you know where you are: you're in the middle of an anthill, they're going in fifty different directions at once, *but the ants are* doing *something.* It seems desperate to me only because I say it shouldn't be an anthill. But an anthill has an internal structure, it is an organization. So the gift of an image is that it affords a place to watch your soul, precisely what it is doing.

Of course, if instead of the language of concept—the anthill is your confusion (and then you think, "Oh, I always get confused; when somebody leaves me, I get confused; when I get rejected, I don't know where I am; I just walk in a thousand different directions"—and you begin with subjectivism, that subjective importance about yourself). Instead of that kind of language, you can talk to the confusion in the language of the image, which is an anthill. The ants are swarming: some are going up, some are coming down, some are carrying eggs somewhere, some are taking care of I don't know what, carrying a dead one. . . . There's a great deal going on, let's see what the ants are doing. And I am not thinking about confusion anymore, I'm *watching the phenomenon,* and seeing phenomenologically what is happening. I am no longer caught in my own subjectivity. I'm fascinated with what's going on, and this attentiveness is quieting. I can see it scientifically—watch as a naturalist does. The phenomenologist of the psyche is also a naturalist of the psyche, watching the way it produces what it produces. I might see the ants suddenly all eating each other up. It's no use saying that is a destructive scene that's happening: I have to wonder about purposefulness, too. Let's watch: maybe the psyche is taking care of the problem by itself. We don't know in advance; we have to stick with the image, stay in the imagination. "Oh, oh, they just started crawling on my feet, eating my feet. I can't stand it. They are crawling up my legs. I'm going crazy." Now the image is vividly coming to life. Still, stay with it, what is your reaction? I can brush them off, I can run around in circles. I can get a dish of honey to attract them elsewhere. I can sing them an ant song. You see, I can do something in relationship to the actual thing that is happening. But what I don't do, won't do is interpret the ants. You saw that move—"They're crawling up my legs. I'm going crazy"—that shift from image to interpretation—and *that* makes you crazy.

The hermeneutic move made the craziness. Who says you are going crazy? What you actually feel is the ants crawling up your legs. Then there are other questions to be put into this scene. I mean you have to locate yourself in it, extend the terrain a bit, not a lot, not too much, but a bit. Have you stepped on the ants, have you tried to cross their path, have you put your foot unknowingly into an anthill? Step away! It's a certain animal movement. An animal sense of living. This is the active relation to the image that we want to get going through therapy.   (*Inter Views,* 53–56)

CASE STORIES

As an analysis proceeds, it moves inward from the case history toward the soul history, that is, it explores complexes more for their archetypal meanings and less for their traumatic history. Soul history is recaptured by separating it from obfuscations in case history. The immediate family, for instance, become the real people they are, undistorted by inner meanings which they had been forced to carry. The rediscovery of soul history shows itself in the reawakening of emotion, fantasy, and dream, in a sense of mythological destiny penetrated by the transpersonal, and by spontaneous acausal time. It reflects the "cure" from a chronic identification of the soul with outer events, places, and people. As this separation occurs, one is no longer a case but a person. Soul history emerges as one sheds case history, or, in other words, as one dies to the world as an arena of projection. Soul history is a living obituary, recording life from the point of view of death, giving the uniqueness of a person *sub specie aeternitatis*. As one builds one's death, so one writes one's own obituary in one's soul history.

❧

For the Eskimos, when one falls ill, one takes on a new name, a new diseased personality. To get over a disease, one must quite literally "get over" it by transcending it, that is, by dying. The only hope for cure lies in the death of the ill personality. Health requires death.

Perhaps this is what Socrates meant with his last obscure words about owing a sacrificial cock to Asklepiós. Once the cocky pride of life that crows hopefully at each day's dawning is sacrificed, the instinct for tomorrow is yielded. Death then is the cure and the salvation and not just a last, worst stage of a disease. The cock crow at dawn also heralds resurrection of the light. But the victory over disease and the new day begins only when the ambition for it has been abandoned upon the altar. The disease which the experience of death cures is the rage to live. . . .

An analyst often finds himself purposely passing by the symptoms appearing in his practice. Rather than investigate these symptoms, he turns to the person's life which has fostered the pathology. His premise is that the disease has its meaning in the life of the patient and he tries to understand this meaning. He cannot hold out the usual hope for cure or even relief of symptoms. His analytical experience says that *the hope which the patient presents is part of the pathology itself.* The patient's hope arises as an essential part of the constellation of his suffering. It is frequently governed by impossible demands to be free of suffering itself. The same condition that constellated the symptoms is just the condition which these symptoms are interrupting and killing—or curing. Therefore, an analyst does not hope for a return to that condition out of which the symptoms and the hope for relief arose.

Because hope has this core of illusion it favors repression. By hoping for the *status quo ante*, we repress the present state of weakness and suffering and all it can bring. Postures of strength are responsible for many major complaints today—ulcers, vascular and coronary conditions, high blood pressure, stress syndrome, alcoholism, highway and sport accidents, mental breakdown. The will to fall ill, like the suicide impulse, leads patient and physician face to face with morbidity, which stubbornly returns in spite of all hope to the contrary. One might ask if medical hope itself is not partly responsible for recurrent illness; since it never fully allows for weakness and suffering the death experience is not able to produce its meaning. Experiences are cheated of their thorough effect by speedy recovery. *Until the soul has got what it wants, it must fall ill again.* And another iatrogenic vicious circle of recurrent illness begins.

(Suicide, 79, 156–158)

A colleague once told me about a new patient walking out on her when she challenged the thematic mode of the patient's story. The patient presented himself as a rather sick case, having been more or less steadily in therapy for fifteen of his thirty-six years; things had not much changed (alcohol, homosexuality, depressions, money worries), and he had tried many kinds of therapy. My colleague said: "For me, you are a new case, and I don't accept that you are as sick as you believe you are. Let's begin today." By refusing his web of constructions, she also cut him off from his supporting fiction. He did not return. His story still made sense to him: an incurable, but still a dues-paying member of the therapeutic traffic. He wanted analysis and the analyst to fit into his story.

A second case, this one from my practice: psychotic episodes, hospitalizations with medical abuses, seductions, and violations of rights, shock treatments and "helpful drugs." I took this story like a past another woman might tell of: falling in love in high school and marrying the boy next door, having a loving husband, children, and a spaniel, a story of making it. In other words both are consistent accounts exposing a thematic motif which organizes events into experience. Both of these women, this one from her percale sheets and the other from her canvas straitjacket—to put the fantasy figuratively—might come in to therapy, desperate, saying precisely the same thing: "It doesn't make any sense; I've wasted the best years of my life, I don't know where I am, or who I am." The senselessness derives from a breakdown in the thematic motif: it no longer holds events together and gives them sense, it no longer provides the mode of experiencing. The patient is in search of a new story, or of reconnecting with her old one.

I believed her story to be her sustaining fiction, but that she had not read it for its hermetic possibilities, its covert meanings. She had taken her story literally in the clinical language in which it had been told her, a tale of sickness, abuse, wastage of the best years. The story needed to be doctored, not her: it needed reimagining. So I put her years of wastage into another fiction: she knew the psyche because she had been immersed in its depths. Hospital had been her finishing school, her initiation rites, her religious confirmation, her rape, and her apprenticeship with psychological realities. Her pedigree to survival and diploma was her soul's endurance through, and masochistic enjoyment of, these psychological horrors. She was indeed a victim, not of her history but of the story in which she had put her history.

You will have noticed that my colleague contested a story of sickness and I confirmed one, but that both of us clashed with the presenting fiction, thereby beginning the battle of stories which is an essential aspect of face-to-face therapy and of clinical case conferences. We saw this already in Freud with Dora. He took her story and gave it a new plot, a Freudian plot: and part of this plot is that it is good for you; it's the best plot because it cures, which is the best denouement of the therapeutic genre.

The talk going on in depth analysis is not merely the analysis of one person's story by the other, and whatever else is going on in a therapy session—ritual, suggestion, eros, power, projection—it is also a contest between singers, reenacting one of the oldest kinds of cultural enjoyments that we humans know. This is partly why therapy pretends to being creative, and I use that word advisedly to mean originating of significative imaginative patterns, *poiesis*. Successful therapy is thus a collaboration between fictions, a re-visioning of the story into a more intelligent, more imaginative plot, which also means the sense of mythos in all the parts of the story.

Unfortunately we therapists are not aware enough that we are singers. We miss a lot of what we could be doing. Our ways of narration are limited to four kinds: epic, comic, detective, social realism. We take what comes—no matter how passionate and erotic, how tragic and noble, how freakish and arbitrary—and turn it all into one of our four modes. First, there are the cases showing the ego's development, especially out of childhood, through obstacles and defeats: heroic epic. Second, the tales of tangles, the confused identities and uncertain genders, the impossible bumbling inadequacies of the foolish victim, but which come out with a happy end of adjustment: comic. Third, unmasking hidden plots through clues and crises, indefatigably tracking down what went wrong by a taciturn but twinkle-eyed, pipe-puffing detective, not too unlike Holmes or Poirot. Fourth, the detailed descriptions of small circumstances, true to life, the family as a misfortune, environmental conditions as another, all presented with lugubrious sociological terminology and the heavy-handed panned shots of tendentious importance: social realism.

Psychology would do better to turn directly to literature rather than to use it unaware. Literature has been friendly to us, openly incorporating a good deal from psychoanalysis. Those in literature see the psychology in fiction. It's our turn to see the fiction in psychology.

For instance, we might look at the picaresque mode. Its central figure does not develop (or deteriorate), but goes through episodic, discontinuous movements. His narrative ends abruptly without achievement for there is no goal so the denouement can neither be the resolution of comedy nor the fatal flaw of tragedy. Rather than using such large programmed scales, success and failure are measured by the flavor of daily experiences. (There is precise attention paid to eating, dressing, money, sex.) There are tales within tales that do not further a plot, showing that psychic history goes on in many places at once—meanwhile, back on the farm, in another part of the forest—and in many figures at once. Other personages of the story are as interesting as the main character, just as the other figures within our dreams and fantasies often bear more upon our fates than does the ego. There are no lasting relationships, and much emphasis upon personas, the garbs and masks of life at all levels, especially the shadow world of pimps, thieves, bastards, charlatans, and pompous dignitaries. These figures, in us each, are the realm of picaresque reflection, of seeing through every established stance, yet without moral implication. And though the picaresque character suffers defeat, depression, and betrayal, he does not progress by means of suffering into light.

From the tragic perspective such a way of framing a case history is a waste; soul demands something more metaphysically important. From the comic viewpoint there would have to be a resolution, some sort of accepting awareness and adaptation to the society which to the picaresque person is always hostile. From the heroic standpoint, the picaresque mode is a psychopathic parody of the individuation epic—but then individuation might be a paranoid organization of the picaresque. The same tale told as social realism would turn into a political tract, as indeed anarchism and the picaresque thrive best in Spanish soil.

But I have made my exhibition: case histories have different fictional styles and may be written in a variety of fictional genres. And therapy may be most helpful when a person is able to place his life within this variety, like the polytheistic pantheon, without having to choose one against the others. For even while one part of me knows the soul goes to death in tragedy, another is living a picaresque fantasy, and a third engaged in the heroic comedy of improvement. (*Healing Fiction*, 16–19)

DRAMATIC TENSIONS

If psychotherapy is to understand the dreaming soul from within, it had best turn to "theatrical logic." The nature of mind as it presents itself most immediately has a specific form: Dionysian form. Dionysus may be the force that through the green fuse drives the flower, but this force is not dumb. It has an internal organization. In psychology this language speaks not genetically, not biochemically in the information of DNA codes, but directly in Dionysus's own art form, theatrical poetics. This means the dream is not a coded message at all, but a display, a *Schau,* in which the dreamer himself plays a part or is in the audience, and thus always involved. No wonder that Aristotle placed psychotherapy *(catharsis)* in the context of theater. Our lives are the enactment of our dreams; our case histories are from the very beginning, archetypally, dramas; we are masks *(personae)* through which the gods sound *(personare).* Like dreams, inner fantasy too has the compelling logic of theater.

Dionysian consciousness understands the conflicts in our stories through dramatic tensions and not through conceptual opposites; we are composed of agonies not polarities. Dionysian consciousness is the mode of making sense of our lives and worlds through awareness of mimesis, recognizing that our entire case history is an enactment, "either for tragedy, comedy, history, pastoral, pastoral-comical, historical-pastoral, tragical-historical, tragical-comical-pastoral," and that to be "psychological" means to see myself in the masks of this particular fiction that is my fate to enact.

Finally, to view ourselves from within a drama refers to the religious origins, not only of drama, but of the mythical enactments that we perform and name with the mask of "behavior."

. . . A young, divorced teacher, a German woman who lived with her daughter, embodied a vigorous animus development in

Jung's sense, or a masculine protest in Adler's. Her own daughter did not carry her soul values because her daughter was too much like a younger edition of herself, an adaptive, go-ahead little girl. Instead there appeared another little girl in her fantasy, an as-if daughter, dark with big eyes such as one sees on famine posters and save-the-children appeals. Sometimes this little girl was also a little boy, between seven and eleven: the psychic hermaphrodite. The woman speaks to her fantasy child: "What do you want then?"

> *Child:* To be let be, and never have to do anything. You are always pushing me around.
> *Woman:* I want you to grow up.

(Do you notice that we have already switched to what the woman wants. The child is on the defensive.)

> *Child:* What's better about that?
> *Woman:* Then you won't be such a sick drag.
> *Child:* If I have to grow up for your sake, I won't.
> *Woman:* Stubborn!

(The woman writes: I was furious and breathing very hard.)

The child starts to cry. Then it says, "Teach me. I don't know how. I want to learn." (With this the woman suddenly finds herself sobbing, for she is after all a teacher. She said she was crying "not as a child but as herself." She realized that this child of her soul was why she was a teacher—by vocation as well as profession.) The next evening she returned to the dialogue:

> *Woman:* First you said you want to be let be and then you say teach me. I don't understand you.
> *Child:* You don't understand me.
> *Woman:* If I let you be, I'm not teaching and if I'm teaching I'm not letting you be. I don't know what to do with you.
> *Child:* You don't know what to do with me.
> *Woman:* You make me feel stupid. I never feel more inferior than when I'm with you.
> *Child:* Good, now you can teach me.
> *Woman:* I still don't understand.
> *Child:* When you understand you can't teach me because then you don't respect my ignorance. For you, understanding me

has equaled pushing me around. Please teach me things you know, things you read. Teach me psychology, about psyche. I want to learn to think, to understand, and not how to behave.

Let me point out here the close interplay between thinking and feeling. They are not antitheses. Here, feeling for the child is teaching it to think. I can also point out the Adlerian content to this dialogue: only when she becomes inferior to her inferiority does the therapy of that inferiority, the child, begin. But my main intent with this piece of soul fiction or active imagination is to show the relevance of psychology for psychotherapy, that the soul wants to learn psychology, wants thoughtful formulations of itself, and that this is a mode of its healing. This woman listened. She began to read psychology differently, not learning it for information to apply it to education, or to become an analyst, but in connection with her experience, especially in connection with her inferiority, her weak and dumb child.   (*Healing Fiction*, 37–38, 40, 117–119)

PSYCHOLOGICAL FAITH

Imagination and its development is perhaps a religious problem, because imagination becomes real only through belief. As theology tells us, belief is an act of faith, or it is faith itself as a primary investment of energy in something which makes that something "real." Inner life is pale and ephemeral (just as is the outer world in depressed states) when the ego does not turn to it, believe in it, and endow it with reality. This investment, this commitment to inner life, increases its importance and gives it substance. The interest one pays soon pays interest. The frightening forces become gentler and more manageable, the inner woman more human and reliable. She no longer only seduces and demands; she begins to reveal the world into which she draws one and even gives an account of herself, her function and purpose. As this "she" becomes more human, the moods one is subject to become less difficult and personal and are replaced by a steadier emotional undertone, a feeling-tone, a chord. No longer in conflict with her, more energy is now disposable to consciousness, which shows that the energy spent in this discipline comes back in a new form. However, as in a physical system, no more can come out than is put in. Only devotedly faithful attention can turn fantasy into imagination.

This faithful attention to the imaginal world, this love which transforms mere images into presences, gives them living being, or rather reveals the living being which they do naturally contain, is nothing other than *remythologizing*. Psychic contents become *powers, spirits, gods*. One senses their presence as did all earlier peoples who still had soul. These presences and powers are our modern counterparts of former pantheons of living beings, of animated soul parts, protective household gods, and ominous daimones. These beings were *mythical* in that they were part of a *tale* or psychic drama. The same archetypal dramas are played in us and by us, and through us for our behalf, once the imaginal aspect of our lives and of life itself is given attention. Attention is the cardinal psychological virtue. On it depends perhaps the other cardinal virtues, for there can hardly be faith nor hope nor love for anything unless it first receives attention.

There is a further consequent of the credit one pays to the images of the soul. A new feeling of self-forgiveness and self-acceptance begins to spread and circulate. It is as if the heart and the left side were extending their dominion. Shadow aspects of the personality continue to play their burdensome roles but now within a larger tale, the myth of oneself, just what one is which begins to feel as if that is how one is meant to be. My myth becomes my truth; my life symbolic and allegorical. Self-forgiveness, self-acceptance, self-love; more, one finds oneself sinful but not guilty, grateful for the sins one has and not another's, loving one's lot even to the point of desire to have and to be always in this vivid inner connection with one's own individual portion. Such strong experiences of religious emotion seem to be the gift again of the anima. This time she has a special quality that might best be called Christian and which only begins to reveal itself—this *anima naturaliter christiana*—after long attentive care has been given to much of the psyche that might not be Christian.

The third step is gratuitous. It refers to the free and creative appearance of imagination, as if the inner world now come to life begins to act spontaneously, by itself, undirected and even unattended by ego-consciousness. The inner world not only begins more and more to take care of itself, producing crises and resolving them within its own transformations, but it also takes care of you, your ego-worries and ego-claims. This is the feminine Shakti of India at a higher state; it is also the nine Muses responsible for culture and creativity. One feels lived by imagination.   (*Insearch*, 118–120)

The work of soul-making is concerned essentially with the evocation of psychological faith, the faith arising from the psyche which shows as faith in the reality of the soul. Since psyche is primarily image and image always psyche, this faith manifests itself in the belief in images: it is *idolatrous*, heretical to the imageless monotheisms of metaphysics and theology. Psychological faith begins in the *love of images*, and it flows mainly through the shapes of persons in reveries, fantasies, reflections, and imaginations. Their increasing vivification gives one an increasing conviction of having, and then of being, an interior reality of deep significance transcending one's personal life.

Psychological faith is reflected in an ego that gives credit to images and turns to them in its darkness. Its trust is in the imagination as the only uncontrovertible reality, directly presented, immediately felt. Trust in the imaginal and trust in soul go hand in hand, as depth psychologists have recognized. The reverse is also true: when imagination is not evoked, there is a deep-seated lack of confidence to imagine fantasies in regard to one's problems and to be free of the ego's literalizations, its sense of being trapped in *reality*. Lack of psychological faith is compensated by exaggerated personalizing, a fantastic need for people (and a need for fantastic people), of which transference on the analyst is only one manifestation.

Soul-making, as work on anima through images, offers a way of resolving the dependencies of transference. For it is not the therapist or any actual person whatever who is the keeper of my soul beyond all betrayals, but the archetypal persons of the gods to whom the anima acts as bridge. The shaping of her amorphous moods, sulfuric passions, bitter resentments, and bubbles of distraction into

distinct personalities is the main work of therapeutic analysis or
soul-making. Therefore it works in imagination, with imagination,
and for imagination. It discovers and forms a personality by disclosing and shaping the multiple soul personalities out of the primary
massa confusa of arguing voices and pushing demands.

(Re-Visioning, 50–51)

Isn't *devotio* to anima the calling of psychology? So, another deep-
seated reason for this book is to provide grounding for the vision of
soul in psychology, so that psychology doesn't abandon itself to the
archetypal perspectives of the child and developmentalism or the
mother and material causalism. The vision of soul given by anima
is more than just one more perspective. The call of soul convinces;
it is a seduction into psychological faith, a faith in images and the
thought of the heart, into an animation of the world. Anima attaches
and involves. She makes us fall into love. We cannot remain the
detached observer looking through a lens. In fact, she probably
doesn't partake in optical metaphors at all. Instead, she is continually
weaving, stewing, and enchanting consciousness into passionate attachments away from the vantage point of a perspective.

(Anima, ix–x)

THE GUIDING ANIMA

It is yet to be established that we find a truer and more authentic
relationship with soul by dispensing with its living carrier in concrete existence. To break off a complex-ridden relationship charged
with anima projections would be to literalize her into the person
carrying the projections. Every prescription or proscription concerning what to do or how to behave literalizes. This is as true for

actions in the "inner" world as for the "outer." Internalizing can become just as literal as acting out.

Whenever internalization through sacrifice means putting the knife to concrete life because it is concrete—e.g., renouncing "marriage with the anima," or sexuality, or tangible fascinations for the sake of the self's individuation process—then there has been no internalization whatsoever, merely a more radical literalization. Instead of internalization through sacrifice, there is literalization through suppression. Then, sacrifice itself has been literalized as denying, cutting, or killing concrete life, and internalization has been placed literally "inside" one's head or skin.

Likewise externality is not "out there" in the concrete, extraverted world. It refers to the evident, obvious, prima facie, or superficial aspect of all events ("inner" or "outer"). We fall into externality all the time, even when internalizing in active imagination, taking the figures at face value, listening to their counsel literally, or simply by having to do active imagination at all in order to find depth, interiority, fantasy, and anima. Then the world of psychic images and the anima figure within this world hold magic sway. One is in thrall to Mistress Soul. No matter how introvertedly performed, this is externality, acting in, literalism, absolutizing, or whatever else one likes to call it.

So let us not imagine anima bridging and mediating inward only as a sibylline benefactrice, teaching us about all the things we did not know, the girl guide whose hand we hold. This is a one-way trip, and there is another direction to her movement. She would also "unleash forces" of the collective unconscious, for across her bridge roll fantasies, projections, emotions that make a person's consciousness unconscious and collective. She makes us like everyone else, mouthing the same clichés, chasing the same ephemera, clinging to the same needs. As mediatrix to the eternally unknowable she is the bridge *both* over the river into the trees *and* into the sludge and quicksand, making the known ever more unknown. The deeper we descend into her ontology, the more opaque consciousness becomes. Then to follow her we must declare like the alchemists that understanding moves from the known to the unknown in an epistemology based upon the dictum *ignotum per ignotius.* Anima explanations point to the unconscious and make us more unconscious. She mystifies, produces sphinxlike riddles, prefers the cryptic and occult where she can remain hidden: she insists upon uncertainty. By leading whatever is known from off its solid footing, she carries every question into deeper waters, which is also a way of soul-making.

⚜

Anima consciousness clings to unconsciousness, as the nymphs adhere to their dense wooden trees and the echoes cannot leave their caves. It is an attached consciousness that sits like a small bird with a small voice upon the back of materia prima, roiling in the sludge of our stupidities, and so our possibility of greatest anima consciousness is where we are most unconsciously involved. Consequently, I have emphasized gossip, petty resentments, clinging needs, kitschy tastes, backbiting, old scores, and pouts. Not because these refer to inferior feelings of the anima or inferior femininity. Not at all. These conditions of intense attachment are thick with prima materia, offering the best ground for anima insights.

Anima consciousness not only relativizes ego consciousness but also relativizes the very idea of consciousness itself. It then is no longer clear when we are psychologically conscious and when unconscious. Even this fundamental discrimination, so important to the ego-complex, becomes ambiguous. Ego therefore tends to regard anima consciousness as elusive, capricious, vacillating. But these words describe a consciousness that is mediated to the unknown, conscious of its unconsciousness and, so, truly reflecting psychic reality.

⚜

Projections occur between parts of the psyche, not only outside into the world. They occur between internal persons and not only onto external people. The alchemical idea of projection referred to *interior* events. Ruland's alchemical dictionary describes projection as a "violent interpenetration" of substances; there is a "sudden egression" which is projected over a matter by another matter therewith transforming it. Projection too can be psychologized; we can take back projection itself, interiorizing it as an activity going on blindly between anima and animus within.

Each anima figure projects a particular sort of animus figure and vice versa. A Hebe wants a Hercules and Hercules does it for Hebe—and not just on the college campus between cheerleader and linebacker but "in here." My hebephrenic soul, young and silly and tied by social conventions, the bride and her shower, produces an ego that comes home like a hero showing off and bearing trophies. Or, within the smiling, innocent girl is ruthless ambition in a lion-skin, forever wrestling old age and able to harrow hell itself.

Another, more intellectual example: during anima imagining of whatever sort—spiteful, lascivious, or productive—an animus spirit rises up and begins to criticize. Precisely here is the origin of the critical spirit as that part of fantasy which detaches itself, abstracts, makes comparisons, and looks down. This animus serves soul by separating mind from mood to gain distance. However, as an animus bound in tandem with anima, this critical spirit still retains traces of moodiness, now "objectified" into opinion. So it is not altogether freed of subjectivism. (Little wonder that critics seem anima-ridden and opinionated, both.) The objective spirit, that goal of our Western intellectual endeavor, is an attempt of the soul to free itself by means of the animus from the valley of its attachments. And the figure in dreams who judges is the one who both frees us from anima imprisonments and sentences us with his opinions.

(*Anima*, 123–125, 133–135, 141, 175–177)

I singled out Ulysses as the one hero—if we must call him that— who had differentiated relations with many female figures and goddesses, relations which furthered his journey, making survival possible. It is hard to point at any one of these figures—wife, mother, queen, nurse, mistress, enchantress, or goddess Athena—as most telling. ("He recognized all these women," concludes Book 22.) There is, however, a subtle sea change in Ulysses after the encounter with Nausicaa, who bears traditional traits of what Jung calls *anima*. After bathing in her stream Ulysses is renewed.

I would suggest that his multiple relations with anima, implied by the scar and the suffering that lie in his name, is the secret of his epithet, *polytropos*, "of many turns," or "turned in many ways" by which he is described in the very first line of the epic. Ulysses is not locked into opposites. He does not suffer from one-sidedness. In him there need be no conflict between senex and puer. His is an *anima* consciousness, which also helps account for his successful descent to the underworld. . . .

With all this in mind we may turn again to the scene of the nurse washing Ulysses's legs and feet, understanding now this moment of recognition-through-disguise as revelation of essence. The scar by which he is known is the mark of soul in the flesh. It is the seal of anima, the somaticized psyche. His flesh has become wound, just as our flesh "hurts all over" when we enter wounded consciousness. Now, we can see that this generalization of a symptom into the pathologized condition of complaining pain is an attempt at giving full body to the wound by letting the body be fully sensitized by the wound. Odysseus, the pained one, is the personification of pathologized consciousness—like Christ in his way, and Dionysus in his. The wounded body has become the embodied wound; and, as embodied, as built into his existence in the leg that carries him and walks with him, his woundedness is also his hidden understanding and grounding support.   ("Ulysses' Scar," 119–121)

WORLD

The way through the world
Is more difficult to find than the way beyond it.
—WALLACE STEVENS, "Reply to Papini"

5

Anima Mundi

According to the ancient Greek philosopher Thales, "the whole world is full of gods." The idea that the world itself in all its particulars has soul was reborn in the Renaissance and now it is taken up in archetypal psychology. In the writings of James Hillman, Robert Sardello, Ginette Paris, Wolfgang Giegerich, and other archetypalists, this is not just a philosophical and mystical notion. If psychology is by definition work with the soul, and if nature and culture have soul, then psychology must concern itself with this larger sphere.

Hillman argues strongly against reducing soul to personal subjectivity, naming personalism as one of the burdens of the modern era. Psychology assumes that only humans are persons, and therefore we are given the impossible responsibility of carrying the full weight of soul. We tend to interpret everything in terms of personal relationships. Even therapy is often defined as the interaction of two persons, and the goal in therapy is the personal development or growth of the private individual.

The soul is not of itself personal. Of course, the psyche presents itself in images of persons and in personal feelings, but it is more than personal. Carl Jung used the phrase objective psyche, suggesting that when we look into the soul, we are looking at something with its own terrain, its own history and purposes, and its own principles of movement and stasis. The interested, noninterfering tone Hillman usually takes when dealing with manifestations of the soul derives in large measure from this conviction that the soul has its own reasons.

To the archetypal psychologist the world, too, is a patient in need of therapeutic attention. When our fantasy of the world deprives it of personality and soul, we tend to treat this "inanimate" world badly. We place all our psychological attention on interior

95

events and intimate relationships, withdrawing that attention from the world. But if the world has subjectivity, we have to have a relationship with it. Therefore, as Hillman says, we can be in the world through the heart rather than the head. We can feel our congenital ties to the things of nature and of culture, discovering our actual attachments and thereby developing new intimacies with what has been previously dismissed as dead throwaway matter.

Hillman refuses to see personality in the world of things as projection of our own fantasies. While it is true that we perceive the world's soul through a refined and strong imagination, that doesn't mean that the world is alive only through our fantasy of it. Nature, architecture, politics, economics, and even city transportation are filled with fantasy that lies beyond our projections. Archetypal psychology tries to unveil that imagery. The point is not to dissect the world's soul for the mere pleasure of analysis and understanding, but to remember the world's body so that we can become more aware of how it affects us and relate to it as person to person. We might also find in that relationship, as we would with a human patient, areas of suffering in need of special attention. Here, Hillman's point is that therapy on our own souls is ultimately ineffective without equal attention to the world soul.

Hillman's essay on nature is especially interesting in this regard. If we take nature literally and romanticize its beauty and harmony, then we stand a chance of losing touch with the "natural beauty" of culture, of the things we make. For his notion of soul, Hillman relies on alchemists who describe soul as an opus, "a work." He also keeps in mind the quotation from John Keats that describes the world as the "vale of soul-making." Hillman uses this as a motto for archetypal psychology. Culture can be defined as the work of soul-making.

To his theory of anima mundi Hillman adds many essays on the soul of ordinary things, from city streets to the ceiling in a room, thereby restoring a sensibility for the affections and sensitivities of things. If the world has soul, then each thing in its own way will manifest consciousness and affect. If it is difficult to imagine this soul, then perhaps that difficulty only demonstrates how much subjectivity we humans have usurped. Yet it is abundantly clear how much soul we can find on an ocean beach, in a cabinetmaker's shop, or on a neighborhood street. Returning soul to the world not only attends to the world, it offers more opportunity to engage in the work of soul ourselves.

NATURE ALIVE

Acry went through late antiquity: "Great Pan is dead!" Plutarch reported it in his "On the Failure of the Oracles," yet the saying has itself become oracular, meaning many things to many people in many ages. One thing was announced: nature had become deprived of its creative voice. It was no longer an independent living force of generativity. What had had soul, lost it: or lost was the psychic connection with nature. With Pan dead, so too was Echo; we could no longer capture consciousness through reflecting within our instincts. They had lost their light and fell easily to asceticism, following sheepishly without instinctual rebellion their new shepherd, Christ, with his new means of management. Nature no longer spoke to us—or we could no longer hear. The person of Pan the mediator, like an ether who invisibly enveloped all natural things with personal meaning, with brightness, had vanished. Stones became only stones—trees, trees; things, places, and animals no longer were this god or that, but became "symbols" or were said to "belong" to one god or another. When Pan is alive then nature is too, and it is filled with gods, so that the owl's hoot *is* Athena and the mollusk on the shore *is* Aphrodite. These bits of nature are not merely attributes or belongings. They are the gods in their biological forms. And where better to find the gods than in the things, places and animals that they inhabit, and how better to participate in them than through their concrete natural presentations. Whatever was eaten, smelled, walked upon or watched, all were sensuous presences of archetypal significance. When Pan is dead, then nature can be controlled by the will of the new God, man, modeled in the image of Prometheus or Hercules, creating from it and polluting in it without a troubled conscience. (Hercules, who cleaned up Pan's natural world first, clubbing instinct with his willpower, does not stop to clear away the dismembered carcasses left to putrefy after his civilizing, creative tasks. He strides on to the next task, and ultimate madness.) As the human loses personal connection with personified nature and personified instinct, the image of Pan and the image of the devil merge. Pan never died, say many commentators on Plutarch, he was repressed. Therefore, as suggested above, Pan still lives, and not merely in the literary imagination. He lives in the repressed which returns, in the psychopathologies of instinct which assert themselves, as Roscher indicates, primarily in the nightmare and its associated erotic, demonic and panic qualities.

Panic, especially at night when the citadel darkens and the heroic ego sleeps, is a direct *participation mystique* in nature, a fundamental, even ontological experience of the world as alive and in dread. Objects become subjects; they move with life while one is oneself paralyzed with fear. When existence is experienced through instinctual levels of fear, aggression, hunger or sexuality, images take on compelling life of their own. The imaginal is never more vivid than when we are connected with it instinctually. The world alive is of course animism; that this living world is divine and imaged by different gods with attributes and characteristics is polytheistic pantheism. That fear, dread, horror are natural is wisdom. In Whitehead's term *nature alive* means Pan, and panic flings open a door into this reality.

There is no access to the mind of nature without connection to the natural mind of the nymph. But when nymph has become witch and nature a dead objective field, then we have a natural science without a natural mind. Science devises other methods for divining nature's mind, and the nymph factor becomes an irregular variable to be excluded. Psychologists then speak of the anima problem of the scientist. But the nymph continues to operate in our psyches. When we make magic of nature, believe in natural health cures and become nebulously sentimental about pollution and conservation, attach ourselves to special trees, nooks and scenes, listen for meanings in the wind and turn to oracles for comfort—then the nymph is doing her thing.   ("Pan," 24–25, 33, 54)

In place of the familiar notion of psychic reality based on a system of private experiencing subjects and dead public objects, I want to advance a view prevalent in many cultures (called primitive and animistic by Western cultural anthropologists), which also returned for a short while in ours at its glory through Florence and Marsilio Ficino. I am referring to the world soul of Platonism, which means nothing less than the world ensouled. . . .

Let us imagine the *anima mundi* as that particular soul spark, that seminal image, which offers itself through each thing in its visible form. Then *anima mundi* indicates the animated possibilities presented by each event as it is, its sensuous presentation as a face bespeaking its interior image—in short, its availability to imagination, its presence as a *psychic* reality. Not only animals and plants ensouled as in the Romantic vision, but soul is given with each thing, God-given things of nature and man-made things of the street.

The world comes with shapes, colors, atmospheres, textures—a display of self-presenting forms. All things show faces, the world not only a coded signature to be read for meaning, but a physiognomy to be faced. As expressive forms, things speak; they show the shape they are in. They announce themselves, bear witness to their presence: "Look, here we are." They regard us beyond how we may regard them, our perspectives, what we intend with them, and how we dispose of them. This imaginative claim on attention bespeaks a world ensouled. More—our imaginative recognition, the childlike act of imagining the world, animates the world and returns it to soul.

Then we realize that what psychology has had to call *projection* is simply *animation,* as this thing or that spontaneously comes alive, arrests our attention, draws us to it. This sudden illumination of the thing does not, however, depend on its formal, aesthetic proportion which makes it "beautiful"; it depends rather upon the movements of the *anima mundi* animating her images and affecting our imagination. The soul of the thing corresponds or coalesces with ours. This insight that psychic reality *appears* in the expressive form or physiognomic quality of images allows psychology to escape from its entrapment in "experience." Ficino releases psychology from the self-enclosures of Augustine, Descartes, and Kant, and their successors, often Freud and sometimes Jung. For centuries we have identified interiority with reflexive experience. Of course, things are dead, said the old psychology, because they do not *experience* (feelings, memories, intentions). They may be animated by our projections, but to imagine their projecting upon us and each other their ideas and demands, to regard them as storing memories or presenting their feeling characters in their sensate qualities—this is magical thinking. Because things do not experience, they have no subjectivity, no interiority, no depth. Depth psychology could go only to the intra- and inter- in search of the interiority of soul.

Not only does this view kill things by viewing them as dead; it imprisons us in that tight little cell of ego. When psychic reality is equated with experience, then ego becomes necessary to psychological logic. We have to invent an interior witness, an experiencer at the center of subjectivity—and we cannot imagine otherwise.

With things returned again to soul, their psychic reality given with the *anima mundi*, then their interiority and depth—and depth psychology too—depend not on their experiencing themselves or on their self-motivation but upon self-witness of another sort. An object bears witness to itself in the image it offers, and its depth lies in the complexities of this image. Its intentionality is substantive, given with its psychic reality, claiming but not requiring our witness. Each particular event, including individual humans with our invisible thoughts, feelings, and intentions, reveals a soul in its imaginative display. Our human subjectivity too appears in our display. Subjectivity here is freed from literalization in reflexive experience and its fictive subject, the ego. Instead, each object is a subject, and its self-reflection is its self-display, its radiance. Interiority, subjectivity, psychic depth—all out there, and so, too, psychopathology.

Hence, to call a business *paranoid* means to examine the way it presents itself in defensive postures, in systematizations and arcane codes, its delusional relations between its product and the speaking about its product, often necessitating gross distortions of the meanings of such words as *good, honest, true, healthy*, etc. To call a building *catatonic* or *anorexic* means to examine the way it presents itself, its behavioral display in its skinny, tall, rigid, bare-boned structure, trimmed of fat, its glassy front and desexualized coldness and suppressed explosive rage, its hollow atrium interior sectioned by vertical shafts. To call consumption *manic* refers to instantaneity of satisfaction, rapid disposal, intolerance for interruption (flow-through consumption), the euphoria of buying without paying (credit cards), and the flight of ideas made visible and concrete in magazine and television advertising. To call agriculture *addictive* refers to its obsession with ever-higher yields, necessitating ever-more chemical energizers (pesticides, herbicides) at the expense of other life forms and to the exhaustion of agriculture's earthen body. . . .

We have tried hitherto in depth psychology to regain the psyche of the world by subjectivist interpretations. The stalled car and blocked driveway became my energy problems; the gaping red construction site became the new *operatio* going on in my Adamic body. We could give subjectivity to the world of objects only by taking them into our interior subject, as if they were expressing our complaint. But that stalled car, whether in my dream or in my driveway, is still a thing unable to fulfill its intention; it remains there, stuck, disordered, claiming attention for itself. The great wound in the red earth, whether in my dream or in my neighborhood, is still a site of wrenching upheaval, appealing for an aesthetic as much as a hermeneutic response. To interpret the world's things as if they were our dreams deprives the world of its dream, its complaint. Although this move may have been a step toward recognizing the interiority of things, it finally fails because of the identification of interiority with only human subjective experience.

Attention to the qualities of things resurrects the old idea of *notitia* as a primary activity of the soul. *Notitia* refers to that capacity to form true notions of things from attentive noticing. It is the noticing on which knowledge depends. In depth psychology, *notitia* has been limited by our subjective view of psychic reality so that attention is refined mainly in regard to subjective states. This shows in our usual language of descriptions. When for instance I am asked, "How was the bus ride?" I respond, "Miserable, terrible, desperate." But these words describe me, my feelings, my experience, not the bus ride which was bumpy, crowded, steamy, cramped, noxious, with long waits. Even if I noticed the bus and the trip, my language transferred this attention to notions about myself. The *I* has swallowed the bus, and my knowledge of the external world has become a subjective report of my feelings.

An aesthetic response does require these feelings but it cannot remain in them; it needs to move back to the image. And the way back to the bus ride necessitates words which notice its qualities.

("Anima Mundi," 77–80, 85)

If God-given and man-made are an unnecessary, even false, opposition, then the city made by human hands is also natural in its own right. Surely, it is as *natural* to human beings to make burial grounds, marketplaces, political and social communities, and to erect structures for worship, education, protection, and celebration as it is for them to gather nuts and berries, trap animals, or hoe the soil. Cities belong to human nature; nature does not begin outside the city walls. Therefore, the city does not have to copy the green world in order to be beautiful, a habit which puts a premium on suburbia, each citizen with his private tree, turf, and Toro. Urban beauty would not draw its standards from approximation to wild nature, requiring potted trees and vine interiors, noisy artificial waterwalls that impede the natural flow of running conversation, and plastics that fake the look of leather and stone. Again, pop art in sculptural forms has revealed the simple, genuine givenness of plastic masses that do not imitate anything prior to themselves.

Second, if we can take back the experience of God-givenness from its location only in nature, then we might be able to find this experience elsewhere. The great cathedrals of Europe, for instance, were God-given and man-made both—and these were built at a time when the large outdoors was usually felt to be haunted by evil. The soul's need for beauty was met mainly by urban events such as pageants, music, contests, and feasts centered around the huge cathedrals and their stalls. What we now turn to nature for—inspiration in the face of might and majesty, wonder over intricacy, rhythms, and detail—could as well appear in our constructions. Skyscrapers, power stations, airports, market halls, and hotels can be reimagined as structures for the soul to find beauty, rather than conceived merely as secular and cost-efficient service functions.

Third, the imitation of nature changes. We would imitate the process of nature rather than what the process has made, the way of nature rather than the things of nature, *naturans* rather than *naturata* as the philosophers say. It would be less a matter of building a false river through a mall than of building a mall so it reminds of a draw, reflecting the actual way nature works this specific Texan geography. It would be less a matter of planting trees in a row along a sidewalk than of making the sidewalk itself meander organically as if it were itself growing along with irregular ramifications. We would remember nature in the way we construct so that nature echoes in the constructed object.

The majestic, descending torrent of the Fort Worth Water Garden hasn't a single leaf, a single loose pebble: it is utterly *unnatural*—stone, cement, hidden piping plunked down into the usual downtown wasteland. Yet that construction completely overwhelms with the experience we expect from natural beauty—its wild adventure, its encompassing grandeur. The Henry Moore sculpture in the city hall plaza of Dallas is more *natural* than the trees around it, even though they are organic. The Moore piece remembers nature's contours, skin, and volumes. The trees, however, are engineered according to a designer's plans, enlarged plantings from an architectural-scale model. (Perhaps that is why they haven't been able to grow since having been stuck down there five years ago.) The Moore sculpture does not imitate a great beast, a mother and brood, a group of hills—yet those echoes resonate within it. Children touch it, play around it. They ignore the unnatural trees.

The imitation of nature could then employ technical means as it has done for centuries in the arts. The garden, after all, is not nature but art; in fact, it is nature imitating art. The restitution of a natural environment would not require the literal transplantation of whole biospheres "parked" into set-aside preserves but would rather suggest miniature biospheres all through the city: hybrid dwarf shrubs, songbirds in cages, window boxes and vegetable plots, fishponds, insect vivaria, terraria. Botany and biology would be honorably represented on the staff of city hall instead of serving only academia and servicing the drug industry. I am suggesting here the imitation of nature as a miniaturization of nature such as the Japanese practice. I am suggesting a reduction in the scale of awe from a romantic and sublime immersion in vastness to joy in pondering the particular.

Fourth, we would no longer let the National Park Service, the Sierra Club, or God take care of our need for beauty by protecting or fostering wilderness. We could come to a more psychological notion of wilderness following the definition inherent in the rules governing wilderness areas: enter and enjoy but make no mark. Disturb nothing, pollute nothing, leave no trace—if possible, not even a footprint.

This definition psychologically implies that wherever we tread with that attitude we are creating the experience of wilderness. When we move with senses acute, listening, watching, breathing in tune with the world about us, recognizing its priority and ourselves as guests, witnessing its "God-givenness," then we have made a wilderness area or moment. The restoration of the pristine starts in a fresh attitude toward what is, whatever and wherever it is. . . .

Last, and this is most important to the psychologist practicing in America. There could be a profound shift in therapy of soul. Soul could be reclaimed from soulful places out there filled with God-given beauty, as if soul were given to us automatically, by osmosis, when we stand beneath a redwood or hear the waves on the shore. Once we recognize, however, that the need for beauty must be met, but that scenic, physical nature is not the only place it can be met, we would take the soul back into our own hands, realizing that what happens with it is less given and more made—made through our work with it in the actual world by making that actual world reflect the soul's need for beauty.   ("Natural Beauty," 52–55)

CITY AND SOUL

Without images, we tend to lose our way. This happens, for example, on freeways. Rectangular signs, uniform in size and all painted green (or all painted brown at the airport) with numbers and letters, are not images, but magnified verbal concepts. We don't know where we are except by means of an abstract process of reading and thinking, remembering and translating. All eyeballs and head. Lost is the bodily sense of orientation. We might even consume less gasoline—all those wrong turns—if our way through the city were landmarked by images like those of the old crossroads, the hangman's tree, the sign of the red ox, the fountain.

The soul wants its images, and when it doesn't find them, it makes substitutes; billboards and graffiti, for instance. Even in East Germany and China where ads are not allowed, slogans still are written large on walls and placards posted. Spontaneously, the human hand makes its mark, insisting on personalized messages, as human nature everywhere immediately chalks its initials on monuments.

These marks made in public places, called the *defacing of monuments,* actually put a face on an impersonal wall or oversized statue. The human hand seems to want to touch and leave its touch, even if by only obscene smears and ugly scrawls. So, let us make sure that the hand has its place in the city, not only by means of shops for artisans and displaying crafts, but also by animating and bringing culture to the walls and stones and spaces left bleakly untouched by the human hand. Surely, a city's masterpieces of engineering form and architectural inspiration would not be despoiled by the presence of images that reflect the "soul" through the hand.

The last of these different ideas of soul that are reflected in a city is the notion of human relations. That is probably what comes first to your mind when you think of soul—the relations between human beings, at eye level in particular. When we think of the cities, our contact with them (with New York, for instance) is craning the neck upward. The rube tourist goes to New York sightseeing its wonders, and ends his vacation with a stiff neck. Yet, the eye-level relation between human beings is a fundamental part of soul in cities. The faces of things—their surfaces, their facings—how we read what meets us at eye level. How we see into each other, look at each others' faces, read each other—that is how soul contact takes place. So a city would need places for these eye-level human contacts. Places for meeting. A meeting is not only public meeting, it is meeting in public; people meeting each other. Pausing where it's possible to have a moment of eye-level touching. If the city doesn't have places for pausing, how is it possible to meet? Strolling, eating, talking, gossiping. Terribly important in city life are those places where gossip can take place. People stand by the water cooler and tell about what's happening and that gossip is the very life of the city. We speak differently from behind a desk than we do in the coffee alcove. Who saw whom where, what, what's new, what's happening—here is some of the psychological life of the city. That grapevine of gossip.

We also need body places. Places where bodies see each other, meet each other, are in touch with each other, like the people who leave their offices in Paris and swim in the Seine River or have a lunch break in Zurich and swim in the lake, or skate. This emphasizes the relationship of body to the daily life of the city, bringing one's physical body into the town. In other words, I am emphasizing the place of intimacy within a city, for intimacy is crucial to the soul. When we think of soul and soul connections, we think of intimacy and this has nothing to do with how big the city is or how tall the buildings are. There is always the possibility for corners, for pauses, for being together in broken-up interiors where intimacy is possible.

Let's use, as an image of this aspect of soul in city, one of the main streets of Dallas: Lovers Lane. If you imagine a city as a place for lovers, then you may understand the idea I'm trying to express. I don't believe love interferes with business or efficiency or tax base or retail sales or any of the rest—at all. I think a city is built on human relations, of people coming together, and it would increase, if anything, the very things that are desirable in a city. So, it is not a matter of splitting again into two things, that is, work and pleasure, city and soul, public daytime and private nighttime, because that cuts soul off from city. There have always been places built within the city where there is a break with the seeming purpose of the city. It is only recently, of course, that we think the purpose of cities is economical or political. The purpose of the city from the beginning was something instinctual in human beings to build them: To want to be together, to imagine, talk, make, and exchange. One needs those, so-called marketplaces, places where the break can take place. . . .

A city that neglects the soul's welfare makes the soul search for its welfare in a degrading and concrete way, in the shadow of those same gleaming towers. Welfare, mainly an inner-city phenomenon, is not only an economic and social problem, it is predominantly a psychological problem. The soul that is uncared for—whether in personal or in community life—turns into an angry child. It assaults the city which has depersonalized it with a depersonalized rage, a violence against the very objects—storefronts, park monuments, public buildings—which stand for uniform soullessness. What city dwellers in their rage have in recent years chosen to attack, and chosen to defend (trees, old houses, and neighborhoods), is significant.

Once the barbarians who attacked civilization came from outside the walls. Today they spring from our own laps, raised in our own homes. The barbarian is that part of us to whom the city does not speak, that soul in us who has not found a home in its environs. The frustration of this soul in face of the uniformity and impersonality of great walls and towers, destroys like a barbarian what it cannot comprehend, structures which represent the achievement of mind, the power of will, and the magnificence of spirit, but do not reflect the needs of soul. For our psychic health and the well-being of our city, let us continue to find ways to make place for soul.

("City and Soul," 3–6)

The eighteenth century took care of this need of the soul for indirection in a canny manner. Into the walking areas there were constructed what the common people called "ha ha's": surprising sunken fences, hidden hedges, boundary ditches which, when come upon suddenly, called forth a "ha ha," stopping the progress of the walk, forcing the foot to turn and the mind to reflect.

How strange this is to us today: Imagine, while walking from your parked car toward your visual objective, being blocked by an open culvert trench or a chain barrier that you had not previously perceived. Your "ha ha" would be fury—a public complaint, a lawsuit. When we walk today, it is mainly a walking with the eye. We want no mazes, no amazements. We have sacrificed the foot to the eye. Older cities often grew up around the traces of the feet: paths, corners and enclosures, crossings. These cities followed the inherent patterns of the feet rather than the planned designs of the eye.

Clearly, the automobile seems a further development of eye consciousness rather than foot consciousness. Despite an old word for the car, *locomobile,* its locomotion is a visual experience. Hence, walking on a highway because the car broke down is a horrifying, depersonalizing experience. Out there is revealed to the foot as burrs, weeds, holes, trash, and roaring leviathans at one's back. Of course new cities have sidewalk problems since the foot is ignored. The streets soon become criminal regions: roll up the window, lock the door, don't linger. Street crime begins psychologically in a walkless world; it begins on the drawing board of that planner who sees cities as collections of highrise buildings and convenience malls, with streets as mere efficient modes of access.

Development planners have radically affected our notions of cities, leading us to forget that cities spring up from below; they rise from their streets. Cities are streets, avenues of commerce and exchange, the low-country world of physical thronging, a congregation pounding the pavements in curiosity, surprise, and encounter, human life not above the melee but right in it. Cities depend on walking for their vitality. . . .

What can we do? May a psychologist question proposals for malls without foot imagination, and may he raise doubts about underground tunnels for pedestrians, or recommend interesting downtown sidewalks rather than glassed-in walkways? May he propose things that are noticeable to the eye and yet draw the foot into exploration—like complexities, nooks, watercourses, levels, shifts of perspectives? It is surely not the psychologist who lays out the span between parking lot and building, for if he did it might be more a mode of encountering faces, with posters and paintings, places for pausing, rather than an eerie cement gray space to hurry through in fear, where place is remembered neither by eye nor foot but conceptually—a code-lettered stub clutched in the hand. Yes, I suppose the psychologist would build "ha ha's" in the paths of progress, wanting every design for a street project to be imagined not only in terms of getting there, but also in terms of being there.   ("Walking," 4–6)

I want now to claim that the ceiling is the most neglected segment of our contemporary interior—interior in both architectural and psychological senses of the word. Whether oppressively close and ugly . . . or removed altogether in vaulting A-frames or atria to the roof, the ceiling is the unconsidered, the unconscious, presenting interiority without design, with no sense of inherent order.

What statements are these ceilings making? What are they saying about our *psychic* interiors? If looking up is that gesture of aspiration and orientation toward the higher order of the cosmos, an imagination opening toward the stars, our ceilings reflect an utterly secular vision—short-sighted, utilitarian, unaesthetic. Our heads reach up and open into a meaningless and chaotic white space. The world above has merely a maintenance function, God the repairman called on when things break down.

Curiously, however, the *perspective* from above still remains. Look at our usual blueprints, our usual models. They are drawn from above as floor plans; the view is down from the ceiling. The place from which the gods have fled is now where the planner sits. We must remember here that renewal of spirit occurs within an enclosed space, under some sort of ceiling. Ancient kings, as far back as the pharaohs, placed themselves under a canopy, a tent, a dome—walls were incidental—and thereby the interior man, the soul, received renewed vitality. The ceiling did indeed refer to heaven, to *ciel*, as our popular and mistaken etymology of ceiling continues to insist.

For *ceiling* doesn't come from *ciel*, French for "heaven, sky." Covering the room, enclosing it, that feeling of interior designed space—that there is design to the interior, and this design renews the human spirit—is the true root of the word. It derives from *celure*, via Middle English (*celynge, silynge, syling,* and *selure* [*celure*]) for "tapestry, canopy, hangings," finally coming to *ceil*, meaning "to line with woodwork."

Ceilings became white only during the Enlightenment, the eighteenth century, with the refinement of the plasterer's art. Previously all the detail was exposed: joists, beams, the reverse of the floor above. Then the detail was enhanced by carving the beams, painting, gilding, stucco, plaster, so that looking up fed the imagination. The eye traversed an intriguing pattern of rhythmical and inherent relationships—where function (joists, floorboards) and beauty were inseparable. Ceilings emphasized design—and I do not mean only the magnificent ones painted to represent the heavens and the gods.

Inside the Latin root of the word itself (*celum, caelatura, caelo*) is the idea of design as burnishing, chiseling, engraving. The upper aspect of our interior space is an intricately fashioned and figured design. The ceiling is a place of images to which imagination turns its gaze to renew vitality. The true ceiling, then, as derived from the word is not a flat white rectangular space studded with incidental equipment, but a magnificent artifice of imagery. The ceiling up there corresponds with the richness of human imagination. It is this our heads can open into and find protection under.

Which brings us to the quality of light and ceiling fixtures. You all feel the difference when the overhead light is turned off and standing lamps, table lamps, go on. You know the kind of interior that emerges—like a Vuillard or a Bonnard room, an effect used in the movies to change the atmosphere toward intimacy and interiority. Single uniform brightness gives way to shadings of color, reflection, and the sense of nearness to the light within the reach of the hand—as to a candle or a fireplace.

Overhead lighting belongs originally to large state halls, banquet rooms, exhibitions, factories, and markets, where very high ceilings and expansive floor plans demanded flooding of light from above. A splendor both marvelous and functional, indoors, yet lit as the sun-filled world. The light fixtures themselves became objects of awe. They have of course given way, in most cases, to what the maintenance crew can get at and clean up, as low-cost as possible.

Now we apply the same overhead lighting in the smallest cubicles with the lowest ceilings. We sit bathed in a merciless, shadowless enlightenment, democratically falling on all alike, straight down—a spotlight like that used to break criminals into confession, a brilliant clarity like for an anatomical dissection. The light does not group the furniture, encircle it. Instead, each thing is distinct, isolated from each other thing. Interiority is gone: the flickering feeling of the cave, lighting that makes this piece of room here different from that over there. The room receives the massive doses of illumination of summer outdoors: uniform, bright, cloudless. And timeless: it is always noon indoors. We cannot tell because of these ceiling lights what time of day it is, what the weather, what the season of the year.

Moreover, you do not want to raise your eyes, to look into fluorescent fixtures, at the bright bulb in the track can. You keep your head down—a depressive posture, outlook limited to the horizontal or the downward state. In such light what does the soul do with its shadows, where find interiority? Does the soul not shrink into even deeper personal interiors, into more darkness, so that we feel cut off, alienated, prey to the darkest of the dark: guilts, private sins, fears, and horror fantasies. I am suggesting some of our most oppressive psychological ills come out of the ceiling.

To conclude this psychoanalysis of the ceiling, a word on moldings. At the retreat of the Dallas Institute on Architecture and Poetry, Robert Sardello gave a remarkable, thought-provoking paper in which he examined the place of the right angle in the design of modern cities. He pointed out that the right angle is an abstract expression for the ancient archetypal directions of heaven and earth, sky god and earth mother, the vertical and horizontal dimensions reduced to a simple pair of intersecting lines, much like the tool used by carpenters, the *square*, the Greek word for which is *norma* (from which we have norms, normal, normalcy). The simple right angle normalizes our entire world from the grid plan of city plats to the graph paper on which we calculate and display the living curves of economic activity.

Modern Bauhaus design exposes this conjunction of father sky and mother earth. The joint is laid bare. Moldings resolve the shock, the violence of their direct rectangular conjunction. Moldings provide a skirt, a curtain covering the exposed pornography, the crotch shot of ceiling joining wall in bare fluorescent light. Moldings are not merely a Victorian cover-up, a delicate discretion—they are an erotic moment in a room, a detail that softens the vertical, letting it come down gently through a series of ripples, heaven into earth, earth into heaven, the secular and the divine, not cut apart and placed at right conflicting purposes, a leap, a gap (as we often see a black line at the ceiling's edge where the two directions have receded from each other, the Sheetrock not quite meeting, the taping and mud inadequate).

The problem of how to conclude a ceiling, its edge or end, was particularly a concern of Islamic builders, who had to set circular domes on square rooms. Squaring of the circle and circling of the square, the meeting of two worlds, gave rise to extraordinarily ornate corners rich with embellished moldings. Rich fantasies develop at the juncture where the ceiling descends into the living space of everyday. . . .

My purpose with these physical details is to make a psychological point. I want to preserve and restore the simple gesture of looking upward. If our society suffers from failures of imagination, of leadership, of cohesive far-sighted perspectives, then we must attend to the places and moments where these interior faculties of the human mind begin. Remember the psalm: "I shall lift up mine eyes—from whence cometh my help." That primordial gesture toward the upper dimension, that glance above ourselves, yet not lofty, spacey, and dizzy, may be where the first bits of interior change take place. This change of soul can take place inside our ordinary rooms.

("Ceiling," 79–82, 84)

The Salt of Soul, the Sulfur of Spirit

Because James Hillman is an advocate of soul, he often takes a position that is sharply critical of spirituality, especially the kind of spirituality that seeks to escape or transcend the pleasures and demands of ordinary earthly life. His way of distinguishing soul from spirit is unfamiliar to many. In ordinary usage, spirit and soul are almost interchangeable. But the distinction is central for Hillman. He sees the attitudes and activities of spirit, especially spirituality that is split off from soul, as a threat to values of soul.

The modern world assumes a two-tiered reality: body and mind, or matter and spirit. Hillman reinstates the Neoplatonic view that soul is the "in-between" factor keeping mind in touch with body and matter with spirit. Fantasy and image make spirituality and material endeavors soulful.

Soul, Hillman says with his metaphor of peaks and vales, resides in the valleys of experience. Soul is always tethered to life in the world. It can't be separated from the body, from family, from the immediate context, from mortality. Spiritual efforts, important in their own right, tend to transcend these limitations of the valley. Motivated by spiritual concerns, men and women leave their families to join dedicated communities. They focus their attention on afterlife, cosmic issues, idealistic values and hopes, and universal truths. They try to perfect the body with yogas and diets and demanding exercise routines. Spirit is to be found not only in church, but also in the gym, on the corporate ladder, and in higher education.

It is this lofty, high-reaching, transcendent brand of spirituality that gains a monopoly and bruises the soul. When spirit is imagined as above human life, as fundamentally masculine, as abstracting and distancing, and as pure and uncontaminated, the soul is particularly denigrated. For soul is always in the thick of things: in the repressed, in the shadow, in the messes of life, in illness, and in the pain and confusion of love. Spirituality often seeks to transcend these lowly conditions of the soul. But to transcend them is to lose touch with the soul, and a split-off spirituality, with no influence from the soul, readily falls into extremes of literalism and destructive fanaticism.

It could be objected that on his own ground Hillman is rather spiritual himself. His extensive theories form a metapsychology, a philosophy of soul. He loves to challenge philosophy and religion. He seems to avoid soulful elements in his writing. You find few case histories, little autobiography, rare anecdotes. However, the spirit is grounded to soul in other ways. Hillman takes history as myth; he usually gives the autobiography and geography of an idea and, most telling of all, he treats his own work as fiction, as a mythology of soul made of fragments from history, religion, philosophy, and literature. As a scholar he is a bricoleur, a handyman, an artist, as has been said, of the psyche.

Soul also enters Hillman's writing as shadow. He allows contradictions and ambiguities to rise to the surface. He speaks with the soul's passion, sometimes abandoning balance and fairness on behalf of repressed and undervalued elements. He gives almost perverse, loving attention to abused expressions of the psyche: panic, masturbation, paranoia, superficiality, and gossip.

If Hillman criticizes spirituality that soars up and away from the muddy contexts of the soul, he is favorable toward the fiery sulfuric spirit that burns with passion. But even this hot spirit "coagulates," becomes quickly fixed in literalism. Nevertheless, it accounts for the passionate lure of things and people. It is the "flammable face of the world."

In contrast, the soul finds its enduring fixity in its salt, in the blood, sweat, and tears of ordinary life. Life with soul is filled with felt experience. Events have bite and flavor and are taken in with full subjective participation. Hillman's approach to archetype is itself more soul-oriented in its attention to particulars than other spiritual methods that emphasize the global and eternal aspects.

Hillman does not advocate a compensatory move away from spirit into soul. What he does call for is a critical view of spirit that does not hinder imagination from participating in truth, dogma, and general laws. Tradition teaches that spirit nourishes soul. Hillman's *psychology attempts to bring abundant imagination to religion, philosophy, theology, spiritual practice, the intellectual life, language, and the spirited ways of everyday life so that they feed soul rather than starve it.*

PEAKS AND VALES

I have called this talk "Peaks and Vales," and I have been aiming to draw apart these images in order to contrast them as vividly as I can. Part of separating and drawing apart is the emotion of hatred. So I shall be speaking with hatred and urging strife, or *eris*, or *polemos*, which Heraclitus, the first ancestor of psychology, has said is the father of all.

The contemporary meaning of *peak* was developed by Abraham Maslow, who in turn was resonating an archetypal image, for peaks have belonged to the spirit ever since Mount Sinai and Mount Olympus, Mount Patmos and the Mount of Olives, and Mount Moriah of the first patriarchal Abraham. And you will easily name a dozen other mountains of the spirit. It does not require much explication to realize that the peak experience is a way of describing pneumatic experience, and that the clamber up the peaks is in search of spirit or is the drive of the spirit in search of itself. The language Maslow uses about the peak experience—"self-validating, self-justifying and carries its own intrinsic value with it," the godlikeness and God-nearness, the absolutism and intensity—is a traditional way of describing spiritual experiences. Maslow deserves our gratitude for having reintroduced *pneuma* into psychology, even if his move has been compounded by the old confusion of pneuma with psyche. But what about the *psyche* of psychology?

Vales do indeed need more exposition, just as everything to do with soul needs to be carefully imagined as accurately as we can. *Vale* comes from the Romantics: Keats uses the term in a letter, and I have taken this passage from Keats as a psychological motto: "Call the world, if you please, the vale of soul-making. Then you will find out the use of the world."

Vale in the usual religious language of our culture is a depressed emotional place—the vale of tears; Jesus walked this lonesome valley, the valley of the shadow of death. The very first definition of *valley* in the *Oxford English Dictionary* is a "long depression or hollow." The meanings of *vale* and *valley* include entire subcategories referring to such sad things as the decline of years and old age, the world regarded as a place of troubles, sorrow, and weeping, and the world regarded as the scene of the mortal, the earthly, the lowly.

There is also a feminine association with vales (unlike peaks). We find this in the Tao Te Ching, 6; in Freudian morphological metaphors, where the wooded river valley teeming with animal life is an equivalent for the vagina; and also we find a feminine connotation of the valley in mythology. For valleys are the places of the nymphs. One of the etymological explanations of the word *nymph* takes these figures to be personifications of the wisps and clouds of mist clinging to valleys, mountainsides, and water sources. Nymphs veil our vision, keep us shortsighted, myopic, caught—no long-range distancing, no projections or prophecies as from the peak.

This peak/vale pairing is also used by the fourteenth Dalai Lama of Tibet. In a letter (to Peter Goullart) he writes:

The relation of height to spirituality is not merely metaphorical. It is physical reality. The most spiritual people on this planet live in the highest places. So do the most spiritual flowers. . . . I call the high and light aspects of my being *spirit* and the dark and heavy aspect *soul.*

Soul is at home in the deep, shaded valleys. Heavy torpid flowers saturated with black grow there. The rivers flow like warm syrup. They empty into huge oceans of soul.

Spirit is a land of high, white peaks and glittering jewel-like lakes and flowers. Life is sparse and sounds travel great distances.

There is soul music, soul food, soul dancing, and soul love. . . .

When the soul triumphed, the herdsmen came to the lamaseries, for soul is communal and loves humming in unison. But the creative soul craves spirit. Out of the jungles of the lamasery, the most beautiful monks one day bid farewell to their comrades and go to make their solitary journey toward the peaks, there to mate with the cosmos. . . .

No spirit broods over lofty desolation; for desolation is of the depths, as is brooding. At these heights, spirit leaves soul far behind. . . .

People need to climb the mountain not simply because it is there but because the soulful divinity needs to be mated with the spirit. . . . [abbreviated]

May I point out one or two little curiosities in this letter. They may help us to see further the contrast between soul and spirit. First, did you notice how important it is to be *literal* and not "merely metaphorical" when one takes the spiritual viewpoint? Also, this viewpoint requires the *physical sensation* of height, of "highs." Then, did you see that it is the most *beautiful* monks who leave their brothers, and that their mating is with the cosmos, a mating that is compared with snow? (Once in our witch-hunting Western tradition, a time obsessively concerned with protecting soul from wrong spirits—and vice versa—the devil was identified by his icy penis and cold sperm.) And finally, have you noticed the two sorts of *anima symbolism*: the dark, heavy, torpid flowers by the rivers of warm syrup and the virginal petaled flowers of the glaciers?

I am trying to let the *images* of language draw our distinction. This is the soul's way of proceeding, for it is the way of dreams, reflections, fantasies, reveries, and paintings. We can recognize what is spiritual by its style of imagery and language; so with soul. To give *definitions* of spirit and soul—the one abstract, unified, concentrated; the other concrete, multiple, immanent—puts the distinction and the problem into the language of spirit. We would already have left the valley; we would be making differences like a surveyor, laying out what belongs to whom according to logic and law rather than according to imagination.

From the viewpoint of soul and life in the vale, going up the mountain feels like a desertion. The lamas and saints "bid farewell to their comrades." As I'm here as an advocate of soul, I have to present its viewpoint. Its viewpoint appears in the long hollow depression of the valley, the inner and closed dejection that accompanies the exaltation of ascension. The soul feels left behind, and we see this soul reacting with anima resentments. Spiritual teachings warn the initiate so often about introspective broodings, about jealousy, spite, and pettiness, about attachments to sensations and memories. These cautions present an accurate phenomenology of how the soul feels when the spirit bids farewell.

If a person is concurrently in therapy and in a spiritual discipline—Vedanta, breathing exercises, transcendental meditation, etc.—the spiritual teacher may well regard the analysis as a waste of time with trivia and illusions. The analyst may regard the spiritual exercises as a leak in the psychic vessel, or an escape into either physicality (somatizing, a sort of sophisticated hysterical conversion) or into metaphysicality. These are conditions that grow in the same hedgerow, for both physicalize, substantiate, hypostasize, taking their concepts as things. They both lose the "as if," the metaphorical Hermes approach, forgetting that metaphysics too is a fantasy system, even if one that must unfortunately take itself as literally real.

Besides these mutual accusations of triviality, there is a more essential question that we in our analytical armchairs ask: *Who* is making the trip? Here it is not a discussion about the relative value of doctrines or goals; nor is it an analysis of the visions seen and experiences felt. The essential issue is not the analysis of content of spiritual experiences, for we have seen similar experiences in the county hospital, in dreams, in drug trips. Having visions is easy. The mind never stops oozing and spurting the sap and juice of fantasy, and then congealing this play into paranoid monuments of eternal truth. And then are not these seemingly mind-blowing events of light, of synchronicity, of spiritual sight in an LSD trip often trivial—seeing the universe revealed in a buttonhole stitch or linoleum pattern—at least as trivial as what takes place in a usual therapy session that picks apart the tangles of the daily domestic scene?

The question of what is trivial and what is meaningful depends on the archetype that gives meaning, and this, says Jung, is the self. Once the self is constellated, *meaning* comes with it. But as with any archetypal event, it has its undifferentiated foolish side. So one can be overwhelmed by displaced, inferior, paranoid meaningfulness, just as one can be overwhelmed by eros and one's soul (anima) put through the throes of desperate, ridiculous love. The disproportion between the trivial content of a synchronistic event on the one hand, and on the other, the giant sense of meaning that comes with it, shows what I mean. Like a person who has fallen into love, so a person who has fallen into meaning begins that process of self-validation and self-justification of trivia which belong to the experience of the archetype within any complex and form part of its defense. It therefore makes little difference, psychodynamically, whether we fall into the shadow and justify our disorders of morality, or the anima and our disorders of beauty, or the self and our disorders of meaning. Paranoia has been defined as a disorder of meaning—that is, it can be referred to the influence of an undifferentiated self archetype. Part of this disorder is the very systematization that would, by defensive means of the doctrine of synchronicity, give profound meaningful order to a trivial coincidence. . . .

Thus the relation of the soul analyst to the spiritual event is not in terms of the doctrines or of the contents. Our concern is with the person, the Who, going up the mountain. Also we ask, Who is already up there, calling?

This question is not so different from one put in spiritual disciplines, and it is crucial. For it is not the trip and its stations and path, not the rate of ascent and the rung of the ladder, or the peak and its experience, nor even the return—it is the person in the person prompting the whole endeavor. And here we fall back into history, the historical ego, our Western-Northern willpower, the very willpower that brought the missionaries and trappers; the cattlemen and ranchers and planters; the Okies and Arkies; the orange growers, winegrowers, and sectarians; and the gold rushers and railroaders to California to begin with. Can this be left at the door like a dusty pair of outworn shoes when one goes into the sweet-smelling pad of the meditation room? Can one close the door on the person who brought one to the threshold in the first place?

The movement from one side of the brain to the other, from tedious daily life in the supermarket to supraconsciousness, from trash to transcendence, the "altered state of consciousness" approach—to put it all in a nutshell—denies this historical ego. It is an approach going back to Saul who became Paul, conversion into the opposite, knocked off one's ass in a flash.

The accommodation between the high-driving spirit on the one hand and the nymph, the valley, or the soul on the other can be imagined as the puer-psyche marriage. It has been recounted in many ways—for instance, in Jung's *Mysterium Coniunctionis* as an alchemical conjunction of personified substances, or in Apuleius's tale of Eros and Psyche. In the same manner as these models, let us imagine in a personified style. Then we can feel the different needs within us as volitions of distinct persons, where puer is the Who in our spirit flight, and anima (or psyche) is the Who in our soul.

Now the main thing about the anima is just what has always been said about the psyche: it is unfathomable, ungraspable. For the anima, "the archetype of life," as Jung has called her, is that function of the psyche which is its actual life, the present mess it is in, its discontent, dishonesties, and thrilling illusions, together with the whitewashing hopes for a better outcome. The issues she presents are as endless as the soul is deep, and perhaps these very endless labyrinthine "problems" *are* its depth. The anima embroils and twists and screws us to the breaking point, performing the "function of relationship," another of Jung's definitions, a definition that becomes convincing only when we realize that relationship means perplexity.

This mess of psyche is what *puer* consciousness needs to marry so as to undertake "the battle of the sexes." The opponents of the spirit are first of all the hassles under its own skin: the morning moods, the symptoms, the prevarications in which it gets entangled, and the vanity. The puer needs to battle the irritability of this inner "woman," her passive laziness, her fancies for sweets and flatteries—all that which analysis calls *autoeroticism*. This fighting is a fighting *with*, rather than a fighting off or fighting against, the anima, a close, tense, devoted embracing in many positions of intercourse, where puer madness is met with psychic confusion and deviation, and where this madness is reflected in that distorted mirror. It is not straight and not clear. We do not even know what weapons to use or where the enemy is, since the enemy seems to be my own soul and heart and most dear passions. The puer is left only with his craziness, which, through the battle, he has resort to so often that he learns to care for it as precious, as the one thing that he truly is, his uniqueness and limitation. Reflection in the mirror of the soul lets one see the madness of one's spiritual drive, and the importance of this madness.

Precisely, this is what the struggle with the anima, and what psychotherapy as the place of this struggle, is all about: to discover one's madness, one's unique spirit, and to see the relationship between one's spirit and one's madness, that there is madness in one's spirit, and there is spirit in one's madness.

The spirit needs witness to this madness. Or to put it another way, the puer takes its drive and goal literally unless there is reflection, which makes possible a metaphorical understanding of its drive and goal. By bearing witness as the receptive experiencer and imager of the spirit's actions, the soul can contain, nourish, and elaborate in fantasy the puer impulse, bring it sensuousness and depth, involve it in life's delusions, care for it for better or for worse. Then the individual in whom these two components are marrying begins to carry with him his own reflective mirror and echo. He becomes aware of what his spiritual actions mean in terms of psyche. The spirit turned toward psyche, rather than deserting it for high places and cosmic love, finds ever-further possibilities of seeing through the opacities and obfuscations in the valley. Sunlight enters the vale. The word participates in gossip and chatter.

The spirit asks that the psyche help it, not break it or yoke it or put it away as a peculiarity or insanity. And it asks the analysts who act in psyche's name not to turn the soul against the puer adventure but rather to prepare the desire of both for each other. . . .

Once the spirit has turned toward the soul, the soul can regard its own needs in a new way. Then these needs are no longer attempts to adapt to Hera's civilizational requirements, or to Venus's insistence that love is god, or to Apollo's medical cures, or even Psyche's work of soul-making. Not for the sake of learning love only, or for community, or for better marriages and better families, or for independence does the psyche present its symptoms and neurotic claims. Rather these demands are asking also for inspiration, for long-distance vision, for ascending eros, for vivification and intensification (*not* relaxation), for radicality, transcendence, and meaning—in short, the psyche has spiritual needs, which the puer part of us can fulfill. Soul asks that its preoccupations be not dismissed as trivia but seen through in terms of higher and deeper perspectives, the verticalities of the spirit. When we realize that our psychic malaise points to a spiritual hunger beyond what psychology offers and that our spiritual dryness points to a need for psychic waters beyond what spiritual discipline offers, then we are beginning to move both therapy and discipline.

The puer-psyche marriage results first of all in increased interiority. It constructs a walled space, the thalamus or bridal chamber, neither peak nor vale, but rather a place where both can be looked at through glass windows or be closed off with doors. This increased interiority means that each new puer inspiration, each hot idea, at whatever time of life in whomever, be given psychization. It will first be drawn through the labyrinthine ways of the soul, which wind it and slow it and nourish it from many sides (the "many" nurses and "many" maenads), developing the spirit from a one-way mania for "ups" to *polytropos,* the many-sidedness of the hermetic old hero, Ulysses. The soul performs the service of indirection to the puer arrow, bringing to the sulfuric compulsions of the spirit the lasting salt of soul. ("Peaks and Vales," 57-60, 62-64, 66-68)

SOUL AND SPIRIT

Here we need to remember that the ways of the soul and those of the spirit only sometimes coincide and that they diverge most in regard to psychopathology. A main reason for my stress upon pathologizing is just to bring out the differences between soul and spirit, so that we end the widespread confusions between psychotherapy and spiritual disciplines. There is a difference between Yoga, transcendental meditation, religious contemplation and retreat, and even Zen, on the one hand, and the psychologizing of psychotherapy on the other. This difference is based upon a distinction between spirit and soul.

Today we have rather lost this difference that most cultures, even tribal ones, know and live in terms of. Our distinctions are Cartesian: between outer tangible reality and inner states of mind, or between body and a fuzzy conglomerate of mind, psyche, and spirit. We have lost the third, middle position which earlier in our tradition, and in others too, was the place of soul: a world of imagination, passion, fantasy, reflection, that is neither physical and material on the one hand, nor spiritual and abstract on the other, yet bound to them both. By having its own realm psyche has its own logic—psychology—which is neither a science of physical things nor a metaphysics of spiritual things. Psychological pathologies also belong to this realm. Approaching them from either side, in terms of medical sickness or religion's suffering, sin, and salvation, misses the target of soul. . . .

The spiritual point of view always posits itself as superior, and operates particularly well in a fantasy of transcendence among ultimates and absolutes.

Philosophy is therefore less helpful in showing the differences than is the language of the imagination. Images of the soul show first of all more feminine connotations. *Psyché*, in the Greek language, besides being soul, denoted a night moth or butterfly and a particularly beautiful girl in the legend of Eros and Psyche. Our discussion in the previous chapter of the anima as a personified feminine idea continues this line of thinking. There we saw many of her attributes and effects, particularly the relationship of psyche with dream, fantasy, and image. This relationship has also been put mythologically as the soul's connection with the night world, the realm of the dead, and the moon. We still catch our soul's most essential nature in death experiences, in dreams of the night, and in the images of *lunacy*.

The world of spirit is different indeed. Its images blaze with light, there is fire, wind, sperm. Spirit is fast, and it quickens what it touches. Its direction is vertical and ascending; it is arrow straight, knife sharp, powder dry, and phallic. It is masculine, the active principle, making forms, order, and clear distinctions. Although there are many spirits, and many kinds of spirit, more and more the notion of *spirit* has come to be carried by the Apollonian archetype, the sublimations of higher and abstract disciplines, the intellectual mind, refinements, and purifications.

We can experience soul and spirit interacting. At moments of intellectual concentration or transcendental meditation, soul invades with natural urges, memories, fantasies, and fears. At times of new psychological insights or experiences, spirit would quickly extract a meaning, put them into action, conceptualize them into rules. Soul sticks to the realm of experience and to reflections within experience. It moves indirectly in circular reasonings, where retreats are as important as advances, preferring labyrinths and corners, giving a metaphorical sense to life through such words as *close, near, slow,* and *deep.* Soul involves us in the pack and welter of phenomena and the flow of impressions. It is the "patient" part of us. Soul is vulnerable and suffers; it is passive and remembers. It is water to the spirit's fire, like a mermaid who beckons the heroic spirit into the depths of passions to extinguish its certainty. *Soul is imagination,* a cavernous treasury—to use an image from St. Augustine—a confusion and richness, both. Whereas spirit chooses the better part and seeks to make all one. Look up, says spirit, gain distance; there is something beyond and above, and what is above is always, and always superior.

They differ in another way: spirit is after ultimates and it travels by means of a *via negativa*. "*Neti, neti,*" it says, "not this, not that." Strait is the gate and only first or last things will do. Soul replies by saying, "Yes, this too has place, may find its archetypal significance, belongs in a myth." The cooking vessel of the soul takes in everything, everything can become soul; and by taking into its imagination any and all events, psychic space grows.

I have drawn apart soul and spirit in order to make us feel the differences, and especially to feel what happens to soul when its phenomena are viewed from the perspective of spirit. Then, it seems, the soul must be disciplined, its desires harnessed, imagination emptied, dreams forgotten, involvements dried. For soul, says spirit, cannot *know*, neither truth, nor law, nor cause. The soul is fantasy, all fantasy. The thousand pathologizings that soul is heir to by its natural attachments to the ten thousand things of life in the world shall be cured by making soul into an imitation of spirit. The *imitatio Christi* was the classical way; now there are other models, gurus from the Far East or Far West, who, if followed to the letter, put one's soul on a spiritual path which supposedly leads to freedom from pathologies. Pathologizing, so says spirit, is by its very nature confined only to soul; only the psyche can be pathological, as the word *psychopathology* attests. There is no *pneumopathology*, and as one German tradition has insisted, there can be no such thing as *mental illness (Geisteskrankheit)*, for the spirit cannot pathologize. So there must be spiritual disciplines for the soul, ways in which soul shall conform with models enunciated for it by spirit.

But from the viewpoint of the psyche the humanistic and Oriental movement upward looks like repression. There may well be more psychopathology actually going on while transcending than while being immersed in pathologizing. For any attempt at self-realization without full recognition of the psychopathology that resides, as Hegel said, inherently in the soul is in itself pathological, an exercise in self-deception. Such self-realization turns out to be a paranoid delusional system, or even a kind of charlatanism, the psychopathic behavior of an emptied soul. (*Re-Visioning*, 67–70)

How does psychology contribute to the age of psychopathy? Or how do the spiritual disciplines do this? The spiritual disciplines do this, in my mind, because they are not really interested in receiving other people. They're interested, for example, in doctrine and they're interested in techniques for achieving certain states of spiritual advancement and the doctrine for that advancement. They're interested in various processes of the mind. They are not concerned with noticing people's nature, which they do not value for itself. Feelings, relationships, perceptions, images, fantasies, dreams—all that sort of differentiation at the psychological level—are things to be gotten through and gotten rid of.

An imageless consciousness or freedom, or a white light—this is what's desired. And in spiritual disciplines a person's doctrine is very important. It's important to know the doctrine and all the rules, all the saints, or all the teachers. The *nature* of the teacher is not considered important. So many of the teachers are found to be scandalous; they're screwing forty women at one time, or they have forty Cadillacs or $40 million. . . .

I have a world view of *attachment*. We live in a *gemeinschaft*. We are not solitary. If people choose to go that way, the way of detachment, I wish they would go far away to Mt. Athos or Tibet, where they don't have to be involved in the daily soup. Attachment to the world, continuity with the world, is very important. I think that the spiritual disciplines are part of the disaster of the world. They foresake the world to its pollution, to its toxicity, to its corruption. And they have a defended philosophy that keeps them there.

I think it's an absolute horror that someone could be so filled with what the Greeks called *superbia*, to think that his personal, little, tiny self-transcendence is more important than the world and the beauty of the world: the trees, the animals, the people, the buildings, the culture. What is the psychological pull of this transcendence? What is happening in the psyche that could make a person so incredibly self-centered? So self-centered to say, "Good-bye brothers, good-bye children, good-bye wife, good-bye flowers, good-bye everything. I'm off to the snowy heights. I want an imageless white liberation and freedom from the cycle of birth and rebirth." And what in the world is going on in the psyche that this delusional system can so take hold? I think one has fallen to the archetype of spirit. ("On Soul and Spirit," 10)

ALCHEMICAL SOLUTIONS

Salt is the mineral substance or objective ground of personal experience making experience possible. No salt, no experiencing—merely a running on and running through of events without psychic body. Thus salt makes events sensed and felt, giving us each a sense of the personal—my tears, my sweat and blood, my taste and value. The entire alchemical opus hangs on the ability to experience subjectively. Hence it is said in *The Golden Tract:* "He who works without salt will never raise dead bodies." The matters are only macrocosmic and chemical, out there, dead unless one works with salt. These intensely personal experiences which give taste and flavor to events are nonetheless common to all—both mine and yet common as blood, as urine, as salt. In other words, salt acts like the ground of subjectivity ("That which is left at the bottom of our distilling vessel is our salt—that is to say our earth."). It makes possible what psychology calls felt experience. So, we must turn to this same ground to mine our salt.

Felt experience takes on a radically altered meaning in the light of alchemical salt. We may imagine our deep hurts not merely as wounds to be healed but as salt mines from which we gain a precious essence and without which the soul cannot live. The fact that we return to these deep hurts, in remorse and regret, in repentance and revenge, indicates a psychic need beyond a mere mechanical repetition compulsion. Instead, the soul has a drive to remember; it is like an animal that returns to its salt licks; the soul licks at its own wounds to derive sustenance therefrom. We make salt in our suffering and, by working through our sufferings, we gain salt, healing the soul of its salt-deficiency. . . .

Salt requires a pinch, feeling the pinch of the event that stings; lead seems to require time, waiting it through. What results from the salt cure is a new sense of what happened, a new appreciation of its virtue for soul. . . .

Salt may also be mined from whatever is stable. As the principle of stability whose alchemical sign was a square, salt can be mined from the rocks of concrete experience, those fixities which mark our lives with defined positions. These places are not merely solid facts— my degree, my property, my car accident, my war record, my divorce; these are also places where psychic body is salted away and stored. These rocks, when recognized and owned, belong to the history of my soul, where it has been salted down by the fixities of experience, giving a certain crystallization to my nature and keeping me from inflammations and volatilizations. . . .

Though we do not make it by fire, we do make salt by means of dissolutions. Salt is soluble. Weeping, bleeding, sweating, urinating bring salt out of its interior underground mines. It appears in our moistures, which are the flow of salt to the surface. "During the work the salt assumes the appearance of blood" (*CW* 14, §337). Moments of dissolution are not mere collapses; they release a sense of personal human value from the encrustations of habit. "I too am a human being worth my salt"—hence my blood, sweat, and tears. . . .

Viewed from the perspective of salt, early traumas are moments of initiation into the sense of being a *me* with a subjective personal interior. We tend to fixate on *what* was done to us and *who* did it: resentment, revenge. But what psychologically matters is *that* it was done: the blow, the blood, the betrayal. Like the ashes which are rubbed into the wounds at initiation rites to purify and scarify, the soul is marked by its trauma. Salt still is touched to the body in Christian Baptism, and eaten still at Jewish Pessach in ritual remembrance of trauma. A trauma is a salt mine; it is a fixed place for reflection about the nature and value of my personal being, where memory originates and personal history begins. These traumatic events initiate in the soul a sense of its embodiment as a vulnerable experiencing subject.

The paradigmatic story of "looking back" is that of Lot's wife. (Lot and Lot's wife were even used as alchemical terms for salt— *Johnson's Dictionary*.) Because Lot's wife could not refrain from looking back at the destruction of Sodom from which they had been saved, she was turned to a pillar of salt. Jewish commentators on the tale say that her mother-love made her look behind to see whether her married daughters were following; and Christian comments on

Luke 17:32 also see the source of her move in remembrances of family and relatives, personal subjectivities of feeling. Evidently, family fixations are also salt mines. The disappointments, worries, smarts of mother-complex love—the evening with the photograph album, the keepsakes—are ways the psyche produces salt, returning to events in order to turn them into experiences.

The danger here is always fixation, whether in recollection, childhood trauma, or in a literalized and personalized notion of experience itself: "I am what I have experienced." Paracelsus defined salt as the principle of fixation (II:366).   ("Salt," 117–120)

The coolness of the image, whether of the moon or of the under-world, and the cool detachment by which we see through to the image, can become seized, as if from without, by the *calor inclusus* or innate heat of love lurking within it. So there will be within each moment of silver—creative fantasy, mental thought, mirrored re-flection—a propensity to burn with sulfur. Perhaps the less activated this innate heat of love within imagining (i.e., the less manifest the copper or the more humid and viscous the sulfur), the more the silver of the psyche is subject to sudden scorching of its outer skin, by which I understand the exteriorizing and literalizing of the innate sulfur into desires which no longer can see themselves as images (the blackening of the silver). Hence the importance of recognizing, as we are trying to do in this chapter, all that silver implies. We would activate it so that it not blacken, our images not be burned by their innate vitality.   ("Silver (I)," 28)

Alchemical psychology remarkably condenses the two traits of the lion heart—the conformity of its thought and its objectifica-tion—into the alchemical substance, sulfur, the principle of "combustibility," the *magna flamma*. "Where is the sulfur to be found?" asks Kramer, a fourteenth-century English Benedictine. "In all substances, all things in the world—metals, herbs, trees, animals, stones, are its ore."

Everything that suddenly lights up, draws our joy, flares with beauty—each bush a god burning: this is the alchemical sulfur, the flammable face of the world, its phlogiston, its aureole of desire, *enthymesis* everywhere. That fat of goodness we reach toward as consumers is the active image in each thing, the active imagination of the anima mundi that fires the heart and provokes it out.

At the same time that sulfur conflagrates, it also coagulates; it is that which sticks, the mucilage, "the gum," the joiner, the stickiness of attachment. Sulfur literalizes the heart's desire at the very instant that the *thymos* enthuses. Conflagration and coagulation occur together. Desire and its object become indistinguishable. What I burn with attaches me to it; I am anointed by the fat of my own desire, captive to my own enthusiasm, and thus in exile from my heart at the very moment I seem most to own it. We lose our soul in the moment of discovering it: "Sweet Helen," says Marlowe's Faustus, "make me immortal with a kiss./Her lips suck forth my soul: see where it flies!" Hence Heraclitus had to oppose *thymos* and *psyche*: "Whatever *thymos* wishes, it buys at the expense of soul."

Psychology now calls this love in the heart of the lion compulsive projection. The alchemical basis of this kind of projection is actually the sulfur in the heart that does not recognize it is imagining. The objective *himma* is literalized into the objects of its desire. Imagination is thrown outward, ahead of itself; and the task is less to take back these kinds of projections—who takes them back and where are they put—but more to leap after the projectile reclaiming it as imagination, thereby recognizing that himma demands that images always be experienced as sensuous independent bodies. There are styles of projection: it is not a unitary mechanism. Cordial projection requires an equally leonine mode of consciousness: pride, magnanimity, courage. To desire and to see through desire—this is the courage that the heart requires.

As Jung says: "Sulphur represents the active substance of the sun . . . the motive factor in consciousness, on the one hand will and on the other compulsion" (*CW* 14, §151). Compulsion becomes will through courage; it is in the heart that the operations upon sulfur are performed. We shall come back to these operations in the second part. For now it is enough to recognize compulsive projection to be a necessary activity of the sulfur, as the way in which this heart thinks, where thought and desire are one.

Our lion rages and our sulfur burns. Our saint is eaten by lions. We cannot let loose our aesthetic outrage in its simple form. Alchemical psychology recognized this need for work on the lion.

Alchemical psychology considered the black and red sulfurs, and the green lion, in desperate need of subliming. One well-known method cuts off the green lion's paws, depriving it of its reach into the world. Yet it stays alive as a *succus vitae* in the heart, for "green is the color of the heart and of the vitality of the heart," as we know from Corbin. The color of the himma must be green like the natural driving sulfur that is also the green/red copper goddess Venus. This ardent green has to be enlightened, the sulfur chastened: a whitening of the heart.

To make white the heart is an *opus contra naturam*. We expect the heart to be red as its natural blood, green as its hopeful desire. This heart operation originates in the dilemma presented by sulfur: the imagination captive in its sulfur that both burns and coagulates at the same instant, imagination held fused into its desire and its desire fused with its object. The himma blinded, unable to distinguish between feeling and image, image and object, object and subject, true imagining and illusion.

Alchemy often speaks of subliming to a sulfur white as snow. This is not only an operation of calming and cooling, the "Doves of Diana." In fact sublimation requires going with the fire, like curing like, raising the temperature to a white heat so as to destroy all coagulations in the intensity of the desire, so that *what* one desires no longer matters, even as it matters most, mattering now sublimed, translucent, all flame.   (*Thought of the Heart*, 7–9, 45–46)

Divertissement

WIT PILAFFS

One day I was visited by a young Viennese woman, Frau H., wife of a rice merchant of my acquaintance, who complained of an embarrassing disturbance in her laugh life. Frequently, and ever-increasingly, when she broke into laughter, she would wet her pants. Sitting in her salon at home, or gaily bantering with friends at a café, flirting and joking, she would suddenly rise up and race off, only to arrive at her intended goal too late to avert the inevitable catastrophe. (It was the case of Frau H., in fact, that led me for the first time in my practice to place the patient on a couch, in a supine position, thereby hoping to relieve pressure on the bladder and save my carpets.)

The reader will readily assume that the symptom has its origins in childhood bed-wetting during sleep. But this path toward understanding defies the logic of the unconscious. For uproarious laughter does not usually accompany wetting one's bed, even in sleep, and only the most infantile *Schlemozzle* would find laughter in wetting the bed in childhood.

The symptom encroached evermore upon my patient's intimate life. Formerly gay and carefree, with happy eyes, she came to my consulting room grimly wrapped in a strange garment, which she believed could be opened the more quickly in an emergency. Every nerve in her face defended against even the slightest potential for humor.

She could no longer attend the comic opera, she said, missing as well the sardonic comedies of our famous Wiener, Schnitzler. In fact, she refused all theater save for Racine. Her husband was condemned to telling her only lugubrious tales of business dealings, and recently she had taken to wearing padding in her underclothes. Her laugh life was seriously disturbed.

I must here break into the narrative to inform the reader that her symptom, though I had then not yet met it in my practice, was epidemic in Vienna during the so-called Belle Epoque. The bustling life of the coffee houses, the hurriedness of the music halls and the fast pace of the *Weingartens* was not just due to the legendary Viennese wit and merriment. For accompanying this wit and merriment was an incontinent urge to pee that went with one's laugh. A ceaseless flow in and around the tables was of laughing ladies hastening to and from their *Toiletten*.

Here, then, was a symptom that threw together two involuntary reactions of the nervous system. What on the level of the psyche, I asked myself, corresponded with these involuntary nervous reactions? What, in other words, was the unconscious association of peeing and laughing?

The *pilaff*, as I later termed this syndrome, provided the impetus for my long study on humor, *Wit and Its Relation to the Unconscious,* in 1905. There I was able to record for my own amusement, under the guise of a "scientific" analysis, of course, my favorite anecdotes and stories, which were to keep me laughing into late old age.

Crucial to all such cases is what I wrote there: "Strictly speaking, we do not know what we are laughing about."

We do know, however, that repression is the soul of wit, and that sudden laughter represents the breakthrough of the deeply repressed. The common denominator of the pilaff, then, is a holding back of the repressed. Amelioration of the symptom is thus only possible, as I learned from this case, by lifting the repression in stages and by gradually easing into the joke.

Frau H. had hitherto always "burst" into laughter, or she would "break" into laughter or be overcome by spasms of it. She had fallen prey to the quick wit of one-liners, or *quickies* as she called them. She had to learn through analysis to move slowly from wit to humor.

Unlike wit, humor extends over an entire situation satisfying one deeply; it is not concentrated at a single point of explosive discharge. Her defense against all humor had only increased its tendency to appear the more urgently. She learned in analysis to sublimate her holding back into delay, a sublimation that allowed ripples of pleasure and small bubbles of joy to precede the climactic punch line which could be delayed interminably as she simmered her laughter slowly.

I termed this *the forepleasure principle.* This refers to laughter in anticipation of joking, laughter that there is a joke going on, or laughter for its own sake. This case taught me that the content of the repression is nothing other than the laugh itself, a fact I have ever and again confirmed. No, it is not the genital aspect of the laughable that is repressed but the laughable aspect of the genitals. What is repressed is laughter itself and what cures must therefore also be the return of the repressed, the repressed laugh.

One is reduced to laughter, I see now, and not the other way around. The error of my wit book was in my attempt to reduce laughter to something else: sexual libido. Laughter is the irreducible, all human: all people have it. There are even taboos on it; but that is another subject.

The charming young woman, having refound her "irrepressible" joy in life, discovered in analysis the art of the forepleasure principle, drawing out the jokes into ever more witty refinements, and seeing in advance what was coming down the *Strasse,* so to speak. Now she could imagine the endings and not need to arrive there so quickly, enjoying instead minor flourishes and delicious titillations along the way.

Years later I learned that she left the rice merchant and Vienna, too, and had a noteworthy career in American vaudeville on the Steel Pier in Atlantic City.

The following pilaff recipes, then, all the product of this patient's analysis, with occasional pleasurable trips to the kitchen to work them out, will be tried by the patient cook. Remember, in your patience is your soul. There are no rice shortcuts, I have found. A diet of minute rice is as cloying as having to listen to a string of one-liners. One may laugh, but not well. Let the pilaff cook. Let the pun rise. (*Cookbook,* 78–83)

THE PRIMAL MEAL

It is the privilege of age to correct the follies of youth—even one's own. Years ago I discovered that children's fantasies interpreting their parents' intercourse as a sadistic act determined the course of their future neuroses. These *primal fantasies*, as I termed them, circling about the disappearance of parents and the subsequent whispers and strangulated moans from behind closed doors, could so delay dinner, burn the roast, or let the soup get cold, that a child's instinctual gratifications could suffer nearly irreversible damage.

The correction I am now able to bring after decades of silent attention to the fantasies of my patients is not directed at the primal fantasies themselves. The core of the theory has been confirmed in case after case: neurotics suffer from reminiscences. But the focus of this suffering is not, as I thought then, the bed. It is the table! It is not the imagined sadism of the primal scene that harms the child, but the actual sadism of the primal meal.

These reminiscences are usually covered by screen memories of the family romance: the little loving clan gathered around the table, smiling mother spooning warm *Knödels*, bearded father bowed in grace, the children giggling, little kicks and pinches between the chairs, perhaps some *Schmarotzer* of a dear impoverished uncle making jokes.

Then, as the analysis proceeds, the truth is laid bare. The repressed reminiscence returns: one sits again, three years old face-to-face with strained spinach and mashed meat congealing on the plate under the brutal command: "Stop playing around and eat!" The crucial factor here is that of distancing. The small child has no distance between his face and the food: his head is barely six inches from his plate. The sadistic torture of this position is made all the worse by parents with long necks and long arms who ignore the injustice of the child's inferior size. All the while the child is told that only if one eats can one grow.

We thus see how the imagined sadism of the bedroom—that the parents may be murdering each other—is actually a wish to escape from the terror of the primal meal, and the desire to watch big people in the bedroom actually a conversion of the memory of being watched by big people at the table.

Of the various neurotic symptoms that can be traced back to the primal meal, none is more devastating than carrot envy. The child staring into his soup fixes his or her gaze on a piece of carrot submerged there. "Must I eat that, all of that? It is so big!"

He or she then looks into the soups of siblings, rivalrously discovering that they have what seems a smaller carrot, or better yet, none at all. Intense carrot envy ensues, which emerges in adolescence as a curiosity about all carrot-shaped objects, their size and length—and absence.

But let us return to the primal meal itself and the command: "Stop playing around and eat!"

Here are sown the seeds for that long-lasting opposition between playing around and eating. *Essen ohne Freud,* we call it, a joylessness in food; for playing around has become the alternative to a good dinner. Don Juanism, coupled with the fast-food habit *(consummatio rapida),* can be expected as a consequence.

(This condition, I am told by Minna, is witnessed in modern cinema, where it is the fashion for the flirtatious heroine in restaurant scenes to toy with her food, and for the conquering hero never to pause to see what is in the icebox or make himself a little sandwich. I do not favor the cinema myself; not only because there is never enough time to get there with all that we have to do for dinner, but because when one has seen as many screen memories as I have, who needs celluloid?)   (*Cookbook,* 27–28)

THE DOUBLE-BLEULER

The origins of this instrument are said to go back to the *bain-marie,* or Mary's bath, of early alchemy, where it was used to provide a prolonged gentle heat for dissolving immersed substances. "Mary" was the legendary Maria Prophetessa of Egypt, another name for Miriam, the sister of Moses. Because the alchemists also referred to Maria as Mary the Jewess, the history of refined cooking indeed commences in the art of the Jewish mother.

But the Double-Bleuler we use is a Swiss piece of equipment: a smaller, thinner pot sits concealed inside a sturdier one of solid reputation, whose bottom is well covered, so as to prevent the contents inside from direct contact with the heat. Martha uses it for melting chocolate that might otherwise burn or for sauces that tend to curdle or separate.

The Double-Bleuler takes its name from old Eugen Bleuler's famous theory of ambivalence. He coined the term in 1910 for those double tendencies of the will and emotion in schizophrenia, when, as he said, the "patients want at the same time to eat and not to eat."

Others more privy to Bleuler, the man, maintain that the concept of two pots under one lid refers to his own character. He was a very concealing man, so thick-skinned and stiff that, as I said once, "it's like embracing a piece of linoleum."

But I know those Swiss! The Double-Bleuler is just clever Swiss shorthand for Eugen and his little son Manfred, who grew up in the Burghölzli Clinic among his father's patients. The *klein* Bleuler also became a psychiatrist, but was not as big as his father. Always, with Swiss equipment, one has to be careful: they like to give things a mystique sometimes that is neither necessary nor deserved.   (*Cookbook*, 83–84)

WONDERBREAD,
OR THE FUTURE OF AN ILLUSION

My theory of bread lay all but dormant on a shelf for half a century. It rose slowly into consciousness after its first infusion with Breuer's yeast in 1881, derived from that famous encounter with the passion of his patient, Anna O. When she flung her arms around his neck, why did he run away? What impairment of passion had so affected his instinctual body that this normal and altogether genuine show of affection struck him with a fear unto death? On that decisive morning so many years ago what had he had for breakfast? Toast?

Prolonged inquiry (carried out with the greatest caution so as not to evoke hysteria in the Breuer family) established that he had taken, as usual, a continental breakfast consisting of a Gipfel or two and other little rolls of refined flour. His course of action in the consulting room had been prepared unconsciously at the break of day: Breuer was fatefully reenacting the instinctual renunciation going on daily in the bakeries and homes of an entire civilization: its religious addiction to white bread.

Bread was also Anna's incurable symptom. Breuer reported: "She allowed me to feed her, so that she very soon began to take more food. But she never consented to eat bread. After her meal she invariably rinsed out her mouth." Clearly, Anna's symptom was an attempt at cure, a *cri de coeur:* she wanted her instincts back. Wanting a healthy body instead of all her crazy symptoms, her unconscious mind knew that the kind of bread Breuer ate was a source of illness. She would not touch it.

In our German language the association between bread and body is only too plain. The same word sound means body *(Leib)* and loaf *(Laib).* So, an overrefined loaf equals an instinctless body. Both doctor and patient were afflicted by a disease in the culture—its daily breads. If a whole culture suffers, can an individual be spared? No psychoanalytic wonder cure can cure this plague of wonderbread.

Only after I had passed through several death crises myself and reached the other side of my seventies did I dare link civilization's bread neurosis to religion outright. None other than Jesus says (John 6:51) "I am the living bread . . . the bread . . . is my flesh." In fact, Jesus and his *compan*ions (the word derives from *panis,* "bread," and means that they ate bread with each other) do a lot of talking about bread. It makes the serious student of the Bible wonder if all the emphasis on Jesus the carpenter or his cronies the fishermen is not but a disguise for the fact that they were really in the bread business, producing loaves out of thin air for a multitude of customers.

Thus the refining process in the flour mills, which castrates the wheat of its germinating seed, is a secondary elaboration of our culture's theology whose God of salvation has no mature genitality. Simply put, bread will be soppy on earth so long as sappiness rules in heaven. Those dead white loaves turned out on endless belts (the technology of eternity), attended by acolytes and ministrants in white, can never age, never stale, only chemically decompose. The limp, doughy bodies, embalmed with gaseous bubbles (for yeast takes its own natural time) and injected with a cryptic litany of esoteric additives, their outer faces cosmeticized with caramel (for such bread does not darken in heat or form a crust), emerge risen and ethereal in minutes (it is instant resurrection), each body covered with its plastic Veil of Turin, a slippery, soggy, sentimental sublimation, all passion spent.

When Nietzsche said "God is dead," he had just been served a slice of wonderbread by his sister, and, his mouth crammed with an unswallowable gulp of the stuff, she misheard what he was trying to say. Never imagining that a diseased mind like her brother's could make an intelligent comment about what he was eating, she transcribed his remark on the demise of bread as yet another of his attacks on deity. Poor Nietzsche. He was never understood.

In the same way, some decided that my book on wonderbread (*The Future of an Illusion*) was a deliberate attack on the illusion of salvation in "white Christian civilization." That good Swiss Protestant, Pastor Pfister (see "Veal Oskar Pfister") wrote a refutation. But these critics, as always with my work, missed the point: I was not out to get salvation, I was only trying to save bread.

My investigation into bread, therefore, had to go all the way. This meant into its roots in religion, for wonderbread is merely the end product of a long cultural evolution, a religious evolution. The bread that was the god (primitive identification), and the breaking of the loaf that was the god's body (totemism) and then the sharing of that broken bread in a communal meal commemorated with different Christian masses (sacrifice of the father imago) became sublimated over time into the neurosis of civilization, resulting in that little tasteless wafer, a mere macaroon or meringue without savor or crumb; bleached, stamped, boxed, and slipped onto the id-less penitent's tongue in uniform sterile portions that next became uniform slices of "bread for the masses."

The illusion we now call *bread* has no future. Nor does the civilization that comes wrapped with it. As long as the prayer goes forth daily to Mister Muffin Man in the Sky to give us this day our daily bread, our flour mills will go on grinding and bleaching, our loaves knowing neither ferment nor crust, and our sandwiches dwelling forever in the house of gumminess and goo.

No, the bagel is not the answer. Nor is Vienna bread. No matter how they twist it into ever new-fangled Freudian shapes, these are just fancier versions of the same white civilized flour.

I offer no recipe for bread. Why should an old man? Have I not done enough already? But advice I do have: if you would live as long as I, if you want a future that is not an illusion, get yourself a nice loaf of Jewish rye. Enjoy!   (*Cookbook*, 174–177)

FANTASIAS

The horizon of the psyche these days is shrunk to the personal, and the new psychology of humanism fosters the little self-important man at the great sea's edge, turning to himself to ask how he feels today, filling in his questionnaire, counting his personality inventory. He has abandoned intellect and interpreted his imagination in order to become one with his "gut experiences" and "emotional problems"; his soul has become equated with these. His fantasy of redemption has shrunk to "ways of coping"; his stubborn pathology, that *via regia* to the soul's depths, is cast forth in janovian screams like swine before Perls, dissolved in a closed Gestalt of group closeness, or dropped in an abyss of regression during the clamber up to maslovian peaks. Feeling is all. Discover your feelings; trust your feelings. The human heart is the way to soul and what psychology is all about.
(*Re-Visioning*, 181)

Commerce and advertising know about the delight of moistening. . . . We do buy moisture: plants all over the house, waterfalls in the restaurants, each receptionist under her tree, gallons in the flush toilets and shower heads, bigger bathrooms, spas, and pools, liquid diets, free drinks, sappy teenagers gurgling sodas, cats purring over moist foods, flow charts not dry statistics, melt, soft drinks, even abstract art is runny and drippy—and of course the ultimate article of faith: the trickledown economy to increase cash flow to build the affluent society.

A common manner of moistening the soul is by dreaming. Dreaming is a nightly dip, a skinny dip, into the pool of images and feelings. . . . Dreams solve problems because all dreams are wet: they dissolve the mental constraints of the day world in the flow of imagination. And they affect our humor because they are full of humor themselves.
("Moisture," 203)

The great pile of interpretative ideas about feces, what shit is supposed to "mean" (the crap about shit): the gift of love to the parent; creative expression beginning with smearing and coloring; the control of wealth and the origins of conscience; the death within; the birth of the non-I, making possible separation and objectivity; the negative self of values hidden in the most vile and rejected; the shadow that follows after one, at one's behind; as well as the scatological rites of all nations, and the inexhaustibility of outhouse humor—all this is an embarrassment of riches. Just this suggests an archetypal background in the richness of Hades, in Pluto's wealth. Of course, the underworld is also made of excrements, for they are a richness for continual fantasy images. From this viewpoint, *feces* is not translatable into another term. As residue of residues, feces suggests an essence permanently present and continually forming anew. Its appearance in dreams reflects an underworld to which we daily bend in homage, never to be rid of.   (*Dream and the Underworld*, 185)

A PROCESSIONAL EXIT

Though this has been a groundwork of irreplaceable insights, they are to be taken neither as foundations for a systematic theory nor even as a prolegomenon for any future archetypal psychology. Soul-making needs adequate ideational vessels, and it equally needs to let go of them. In this sense all that is written in the foregoing pages is confessed to with passionate conviction, to be defended as articles of faith, and at the same time disavowed, broken, and left behind. By holding to nothing, nothing holds back the movement of soul-making from its ongoing process, which now like a long Renaissance processional slips away from us into memory, offstage and out of sight. They are leaving—even the bricoleur and the rogue Errant who put together the work and charted its course; there goes Mersenne in his monk's dress, and Lou, and Hegel; the Cartesians depart, and the transcendent refusers of pathology, and Heroic Ego who had to bear such brunt; now Anima in all her marvelous veils moves off southward smiling; going too are Freud and Jung, side by side, psychologized, into the distance, and the mythical personages from Greece, the Greek words and Latin phrases, the footnoting authorities, the literalistic enemies and their troop of fallacies; and when the last image vanishes, all icons gone, the soul begins again to populate the stilled realms with figures and fantasies born of the imaginative heart.   (*Re-Visioning,* 229)

7

Pathologizing:
The Wound and the Eye

Because of its family ties to medicine, psychotherapy typically thinks of affliction as the enemy, something to overcome. James Hillman's interest in the phenomena of the soul, in contrast, includes a respectful and unusual appreciation for psychological suffering. The soul, he says, naturally pathologizes. It presents itself variously in abnormality, twistedness, pain, exaggeration, and mess. Hillman does not romanticize abnormality, but he authenticates it as native and essential to the soul.

In many attempts at health and normalcy Hillman sees the heroic ego at work. This is the figure eager to wage wars on poverty, disease, drugs, and any and all kinds of trouble. As an alternative to this heroic fantasy, Hillman recommends the less active and less inspiring posture of inferiority. By trying so hard to transcend, the hero represses feelings of inferiority, which can return as grand failures. Rather than cure these manifestations of the soul at their first appearance, Hillman advises that they be held close and investigated for their intentions.

This slant on pathology encourages curiosity and interest in the ways of the soul. One becomes a "naturalist of the psyche." This loving interest in the soul and its quirks forms the beating heart of Hillman's work. It arises from the ashes of heroics and offers a portrait of the psychologist as one involved in an ecology of soul.

Hillman speaks, too, of society's pathology as something to hold in contemplation, for the gods are in social dis-ease just as they are in the problems of individuals. Social problems waken the rescuing hero who cannot feel content until he has solved all problems, because his very existence depends on slaying monsters, cleaning stables, and saving cities. Hillman offers two alternatives. One is to follow the chronic disorder and social pathologizing into its depth, leading to genuine culture, to arts and ideas engendered by pathology. Elsewhere Hillman encourages the citizen to trust his outrage, desires, and fears as accurate echoes of conditions in the world soul. Emotions bond us to the world's suffering and prevent us from political and social anesthesia.

Hillman's imaginal approach to pathology may appear quietistic and passive. In contrast to the modern social activist or high-tech soldier in the war against disease, aesthetic contemplation may seem rather mild. But, in fact, imagination requires its own kind of muscle and capacity for endurance. It is easy to fall into literalistic solutions, no matter how much physical effort they entail. Far more demanding is the ability to break out of one's narrow paradigms and world views, to acquire insight into fantasies trapped in everyday assumptions.

Without imagination, all human activity is riddled with unconsciousness and acts out myths that have not been fully appropriated. It takes courage to "own" the myth that has captivated your life. In a similar way, heroic efforts to subdue symptoms are not nearly as bold as skillful imagination teasing out bits of insight from the opaque symptoms that try our souls. Yet, as Hillman says, in our symptoms is our soul.

SYMPTOMS

In order to approach the psychology of pathology afresh, I am introducing the term *pathologizing* to mean the psyche's autonomous ability to create illness, morbidity, disorder, abnormality, and suffering in any aspect of its behavior and to experience and imagine life through this deformed and afflicted perspective.

Pathologizing is present not only at moments of special crisis but in the everyday lives of all of us. It is present most profoundly in the individual's sense of death, which he carries wherever he goes. It is present also in each person's inward feeling of his peculiar "differentness," which includes, and may be even based upon, his sense of individual "craziness." For we each have a private fantasy of mental illness; "crazy," "mad," "insane"—all their substitutes, colloquialisms, and synonyms—form a regular part of our daily speech. As we cast our internal deviance from us with these exclamations about others, we are at the same time acknowledging that we each have a deviant, odd second (or third) personality that provides another perspective to our regular life. Indeed, pathologizing supplies material out of which we build our regular lives. Their styles, their concerns, their loves, reflect patterns that have pathologized strands woven all through them. The deeper we know ourselves and the other persons of our complexes, the more we recognize how well we, too, fit into the textbook sketches of abnormal psychology. Those case histories are also our own biographies. To put it in sociological language: nearly every individual in the United States of America has been, now is, or will have been in the hands of professional soul care of one kind or another, for a shorter or longer period, for one reason or another. . . .

Symptoms, not therapists, led this century to soul. The persistent pathologizings in Freud and in Jung and in their patients—pathologizings that refused to be repressed, transformed, or cured, or even understood—led this century's main explorers of the psyche ever deeper. Their movement through pathology into soul is an experience repeated in each of us. We owe them much, but we owe our pathologizing more. We owe our symptoms an immense debt. The soul can exist without its therapists but not without its afflictions.

Pathologized images do indeed bring guilt, and not only because of the long historical tradition linking sin and illness. The guilty feelings are more than historically caused; they are psychologically authentic because affliction reaches us partly through the guilt it brings. Guilt belongs to the experiences of deviation, to the sense of being off, failing, "missing the mark" (*hamartia*). It is indeed questionable whether guilt and pathologizing could be so severed from each other that we could feel pathologized and vulnerable without at the same time feeling guilty.

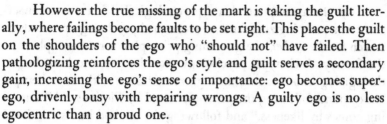

Tx

However the true missing of the mark is taking the guilt literally, where failings become faults to be set right. This places the guilt on the shoulders of the ego who "should not" have failed. Then pathologizing reinforces the ego's style and guilt serves a secondary gain, increasing the ego's sense of importance: ego becomes superego, drivenly busy with repairing wrongs. A guilty ego is no less egocentric than a proud one.

But we can let go of this style of guilt, seeing through it as a defensive business that prevents archetypal fantasies from coming through. For from the archetypal point of view, the matter is less that one feels guilty than *to whom:* to which person of the psyche and within which myth does my affliction belong, and does it bespeak an obligation? Which figures in which complexes are now laying claim? From this perspective the guilt brought by pathologizing takes on radical importance. It leads out of the ego and into a recognition that through a pathologized experience I am bound to archetypal persons who want something from me and to whom I owe remembrance.

A sickened image of course vitally afflicts us, for pathologizing touches our sense of life. It both vitiates and vitalizes, a quickening through distortion. The sense of vital affliction we feel leads us into a natural response. Because the fantasy or dream image is so concretely vivid and we feel it so vitally, we match it with a concrete, medical-style move. But we forget that the image is part of dream speech and that the sense of affliction, too, is as necessary a part of that speech as the feeling aspect of the metaphor. The affliction reflects a *pathos*, a being moved, or movement, now taking place in the psyche. Categories of positive and negative, health and disease, do not apply. Instead we assume that something essential for the psyche's survival, its very life, and death, is being expressed in this manner and cannot be expressed with the same subtle and vital impact in any other way. We would save the phenomena just as they are, untreated, uncured. The fantasies of sickness are assumed from the outset and in entirety to be part of the psyche's depth—and we are depth psychologists by virtue of these pathologized enigmas which provide the subjective stuff of psychological reflection. Though pathologizing uses the language of natural events, this does not imply that we are to take these events naturalistically.

※

On the assumption that a psychological sickness is an enactment of a pathologizing fantasy, archetypal psychology proceeds to search for the *archai,* the governing principles or root metaphors of the fantasy. Archetypal psychology would attempt to lead the pathologizing into meaning through resemblance with an archetypal background following the principle stated by Plotinus, "All knowing comes by likeness," and following the method he also initiated called *reversion (epistrophé)*—the idea that all things desire to return to the archetypal originals of which they are copies and from which they proceed. Pathologizings, too, would be examined in terms of likeness and imagined as having the intentionality of returning to an archetypal background. . . .

It is to this mythical realm that I return all fantasies. The authentication of the fantasies of sickness is not in nature but in psyche, not in literal sickness but imaginal sickness, not in the psychodynamics of actual configurations past or present, but in mythical figures which are the eternal metaphors of the imagination, the universals of fantasy. These mythical figures, like my afflictions, are "tragical, monstrous, and unnatural," and their effects upon the soul, like my afflictions, "perturb to excess." Only in mythology does pathology receive an adequate mirror, since myths speak with the same distorted, fantastic language.

Pathologizing is a way of mythologizing. Pathologizing takes one out of blind immediacy, distorting one's focus upon the natural and actual by forcing one to ask what is within it and behind it. The distortion is at the same time an enhancement and a new clarification, reminding the soul of its mythical existence. While in the throes of pathologizing, the psyche is going through a reversion into a mythical style of consciousness. Psychoanalysts have seen this but condemned it as regression to magical, primitive levels. But the psyche reverts not only to escape reality but to find another reality in which the pathologizing makes new sense.

Archetypal psychology can put its idea of psychopathology into a series of nutshells, one inside the other: within the affliction is a complex, within the complex an archetype, which in turn refers to a god. Afflictions point to gods; gods reach us through afflictions. Jung's statement—"the gods have become diseases; Zeus no longer rules Olympus but rather the solar plexus, and produces curious specimens for the doctor's consulting room" (*CW* 13, §54)—implies that gods, as in Greek tragedy, *force themselves symptomatically into awareness.* Our pathologizing is their work, a divine process working in the human soul. By reverting the pathology to the god, we recognize the divinity of pathology and give the god his due. . . .

A complex must be laid at the proper altar, because it makes a difference both to our suffering and perhaps to the god who is there manifesting, whether we consider our sexual impotence, for example, to be the effect of the Great Mother's son who may be served thereby, or Priapus who, neglected, is taking revenge, or Jesus whose genitality is simply absent, or Saturn who takes physical potency and gives lascivious fantasy. Finding the background for affliction calls for familiarity with an individual's style of consciousness, with his pathologizing fantasies, and with myth to which style and fantasy may revert.

To study the complex only personally, or to examine only personally the psychodynamics and history of a case is not enough, since the other half of pathology belongs to the gods. Pathologies are both facts and fantasies, both somatic and psychic, both personal and impersonal. This view of pathology brings with it a view of therapy such as we find in the Renaissance with Paracelsus, who said:

The physician must have knowledge of man's other half, that half of his nature which is bound up with astronomical philosophy; otherwise he will be in no true sense man's physician, since Heaven retains within its sphere half of all bodies and all maladies. What is a physician who knows nothing of cosmography?

Cosmography here refers to the imaginal realm, the archetypal powers bearing the names of the planets and the myths portrayed by the constellations of the stars. Neglect of this "half," the imaginal or psychic component, the god in the disease, fails the human. To deal fully with any human affair, one must devote half one's thoughts to what is not human. "Maladies" lie also in the archetypes and are part of them.

If gods reach us through afflictions, then pathologizing makes them immanent, opening the psyche for them to enter; thus pathologizing is a way of moving from transcendental theology to immanent psychology. For immanence is only a doctrine until I am knocked back through symptoms by these dominant powers, and I recognize that in my disturbances there really are forces I cannot control and yet which want something from me and intend something with me.

Of all my psychological events my pathologizing seems at times to be the only happening that is peculiarly mine. Afflictions give me the convincing delusion of being different. My hopes and fears, and even my loves, may all have been put upon me by the world's directions, or by my parents as residues and options of their unlived lives. But my symptoms point to my soul as my soul points to me through them.

Yet the symptoms and quirks are both me and not me—both, most intimate and shameful and a revelation of my deeps, steering my fate through character so that I cannot shrug them off. Yet they are *not* of my intention; they are visitations, alienations, bringing home the personal/impersonal paradox of the soul: what is "me" is also not "mine"—*I* and *soul* are alien to each other because of soul's domination by powers, daimones, and gods.

The pathological experience gives an indelible sense of soul, unlike those we may get through love or beauty, through nature, community, or religion. The soul-making of pathology has its distinct flavor, salty, bitter; it "skins alive," "wounds," "bleeds," making us excruciatingly sensitive to the movements of the psyche. Pathology produces an intensely focused consciousness of soul, as in undergoing a symptomatic pain—sobering, humbling, blinding. It gives the hero a little twinge of heel, the soft spot that reminds the ego of death, of soul. Do you remember Zooey's remark (in Salinger's story) when his sister asks him about his symptom? "*Yes*, I have an ulcer, for Chrissake. This is Kaliyuga, buddy, the Iron Age. Anybody over sixteen without an ulcer's a goddamn spy." In my symptom is my soul.   (*Re-Visioning*, 57, 70–71, 83–84, 99–100, 104–106)

Let us suppose that *pathologizing too were interwoven in the cosmos of each event* just as its beauty, its virtue and its truth; pathologizing necessary and intrinsic, a shadowy fourth omitted by Plato though lived by Socrates. Its particular function (not its telos) depending on its particular context. In one instance affliction may signal disease, at another inform of danger; or, it may heighten awareness or narrow it; promote fantasies of freedom, surcease and oblivion; constellate hopelessness; motivate courage; induce sympathy; or bring to mind the sage who asks about purpose. Pathologizing as intrinsic to cosmos of course implies that no event is without this shadow, *that pathologizing is cosmic,* that essential to the arrangement of whatever is, as the Buddha said, is decay. Each thing, including Blake's grain of sand, can hurt and be hurt, for each thing to be true, good and beautiful must also be pathological. ("Cosmos," 300)

THE MYTH OF NORMALCY

The soul sees by means of affliction. Those who are most dependent upon the imagination for their work—poets, painters, fantasts—have not wanted their pathologizing degraded into the "unconscious" and subjected to clinical literalism. (*The unconscious,* and submitting the pathologized imagination to therapy, found favor with less imaginative professions: nurses, educationalists, clinical psychologists, social workers.) The crazy artist, the daft poet and mad professor are neither romantic clichés nor antibourgeois postures. They are metaphors for the intimate relation between pathologizing and imagination. Pathologizing processes are a source of imaginative work, and the work provides a container for the pathologizing processes. The two are inextricably interwoven in the work of Sophocles and Euripides, Webster and Shakespeare, Goya and Picasso, Swift and Baudelaire, O'Neill and Strindberg, Mann and Beckett—these but an evident few.

The wound and the eye are one and the same. From the psyche's viewpoint, pathology and insight are not opposites—as if we hurt because we have no insight and when we gain insight we shall no longer hurt. No. Pathologizing is itself a way of seeing; the eye of the complex gives the peculiar twist called *psychological insight.* We become psychologists because we see from the psychological viewpoint, which means by benefit of our complexes and their pathologizings.

Normal psychology insists that this twisted insight is pathological. But let us bear in mind that normal psychology does not admit pathologizing unless dressed in its patient's uniform. It has a special house called abnormal. And let us also bear in mind that the ego's normative view of the psyche is a cramped distortion. If we studied soul through art, biography, myth; or through the history of wars, politics and dynasties, social behavior and religious controversy; then normal and abnormal might have to switch houses. But normal academic psychology eschews these fields and compiles its statistics so often from undergraduates who have not yet had the chance to experience the range of their madness.   (*Re-Visioning*, 107)

The figures of myth—quarreling, cheating, sexually obsessed, revenging, vulnerable, killing, torn apart—show that the gods are not only perfections so that all abnormalities can fall only on humans. The mythemes in which the gods appear are replete with behavior that, from the secular standpoint, must be classified under criminal pathology, moral monstrosity, or personality disorders.

When we think mythologically about pathologizing, we could say, as some have, that the "world of the gods" is anthropomorphic, an imitative projection of ours, including our pathologies. But one could start as well from the other end, the *mundus imaginalis* of the archetypes (or gods), and say that our "secular world" is at the same time mythical, an imitative projection of theirs, including their pathologies. What the gods show in an imaginal realm of myth is reflected in our imagination as fantasy. Our fantasies reflect theirs, our behavior only mimetic to theirs. We can imagine nothing or perform nothing that is not already formally given by the archetypal imagination of the gods. If we assume that the necessary is that which occurs among gods, i.e., that myths describe necessary patterns, then their pathologizings are necessary, and ours are necessary to the mimesis of theirs. Since their *infirmitas* is essential to their complete configuration, it follows that our individual completion requires our pathologizings.

If so, we are as much in harmony with the archetypal realm when afflicted as when in beatific states of transcendence. Man is as much in the image of the gods and goddesses when he is ludicrous, enraged, or tortured, as when he smiles. Since the gods themselves show *infirmitas*, one path of the *imitatio dei* is through infirmity. Furthermore, it is this *infirmitas* of the archetype that can be nurse to our self-division and error, our wounds and extremities, providing a style, a justification, and a sense of significance for ours. . . .

What I am asking you to entertain is the idea of the sickness in the archetype—and this is not the same as the archetype of sickness. That latter approach to abnormality is that of a single scapegoat archetype, a morbid principle like Thanatos, a sickness daimon, a devil or shadow, who carries the evil so that the others may remain supremely ideal. That approach enucleates the core of pathologizing intrinsic to each archetypal figure and necessary to that figure's way of being. Whereas our approach tries to understand pathologizing as an inherent component of every archetypal complexity, which has its own blind, destructive, and morbid possibility. Death is fundamental to each pattern of being, even if the gods do not die. They are *athnetos* which implies that the *infirmitas* they present is also eternal. Each archetype has a way of leading into death, and thus has its own bottomless depth so causing our sicknesses to be fundamentally unfathomable.

To express this *infirmitas* of the archetype theologically we would say that original sin is accounted for by the sin in the originals. Humans are made in the images of the gods, and our abnormalities image the original abnormalities of the gods which come before ours, making possible ours. We can only do in time what gods do in eternity. Our infirmities will therefore have to have their ground in primordial infirmity, and their infirmities are enacted in our psychopathologies. If those concerned with the plight of religion would restore it to health and bring its God back to life, a first measure in this resuscitation would be to take back from the devil all the pathologies heaped on his head. If God has died, it was because of his own good health; he had lost touch with the intrinsic *infirmitas* of the archetype.

❧

The great passions, truths, and images are not normal middles, not averages. Tongue-tied Moses who kills, has horns and a black desert wife; Christ turning miracles, lacerated on the Cross; ecstatic Muhammad; Hercules and the heroes, even Ulysses; and the extraordinary awesome goddesses—all these are unpredictable extremes that bespeak the soul in extremis. And these mythical figures show *infirmitas:* possessions, errors, wounds, pathologizings. In Vico's terms, metaphorical truth is more than life, other than life, even while it presents the ideal standards for life. The very ideality is partly expressed through pathologized enormities.

I am not pleading for a baroque romanticism or Gothic horror, a new cult of the freakish to shock the bourgeois. Such is merely the other side of normalcy. Rather I wish us to remember Plato's *Timaeus:* reason alone does not rule the world or set the rules. Turning to the middle ground for norms, norms without enormity, are delusions, false beliefs, that do not take into account the full nature of things. Norms without pathologizings in their images perform a normalizing upon our psychological vision, acting as repressive idealizations which make us lose touch with our individual abnormalities. The normalcy fantasy becomes itself a distortion of the way things actually are.   ("Abnormal Psychology," 3–5, 25–26)

DEPRESSION

Depression. Because Christ resurrects, moments of despair, darkening, and desertion cannot be valid in themselves. Our one model insists on light at the end of the tunnel; one program that moves from Thursday evening to Sunday and the rising of a wholly new day better by far than before. Not only will therapy more or less consciously imitate this program (in ways ranging from hopeful positive counseling to electroshock), but the individual's consciousness is already allegorized by the Christian myth and so he knows what depression is and experiences it according to form. It must be necessary (for it appears in the crucifixion), and it must be suffering; but *staying* depressed must be negative, since in the Christian allegory Friday is never valid per se, for Sunday—as an integral part of the myth—is preexistent in Friday from the start. The counterpart of every crucifixion fantasy is a resurrection fantasy. Our stance toward depression is a priori a manic defense against it. *Even our notion of consciousness itself serves as an antidepressant:* to be conscious is to be awake, alive, attentive, in a state of activated cortical functioning. Drawn to extremes, consciousness and depression have come to exclude each other, and psychological depression has replaced theological hell.

In Christian theology the heavy sloth of depression, the drying despair of melancholy, was the *sin* of *acedia* (as it was called in church Latin). It is just as difficult to manage today in therapeutic practice because our culture on the New Testament model has only the one upward paradigm for meeting this syndrome. Even though the Christ myth is supposedly no longer operative, tenacious residues remain in our attitudes toward depression.

Depression is still the Great Enemy. More personal energy is expended in manic defenses against, diversions from, and denials of it than goes into other supposed psychopathological threats to society: psychopathic criminality, schizoid breakdown, addictions. As long as we are caught in cycles of hoping against despair, each productive of the other, as long as our actions in regard to depression are resurrective, implying that being down and staying down is sin, we remain Christian in psychology.

Yet through depression we enter depths and in depths find soul. Depression is essential to the tragic sense of life. It moistens the dry soul, and dries the wet. It brings refuge, limitation, focus, gravity, weight, and humble powerlessness. It reminds of death. *The true revolution begins in the individual who can be true to his or her depression.* Neither jerking oneself out of it, caught in cycles of hope and despair, nor suffering it through till it turns, nor theologizing it—but discovering the consciousness and depths it wants. So begins the revolution in behalf of soul. (*Re-Visioning*, 98–99)

The blue transit between black and white is like that sadness which emerges from despair as it proceeds toward reflection. Reflection here comes from or takes one into a blue distance, less a concentrated act that we do than something insinuating itself upon us as a cold, isolating inhibition. This vertical withdrawal is also like an emptying out, the creation of a negative capability, or a profound listening—already an intimation of silver. . . .

Sadness is not the whole of it. A turbulent dissolution of the nigredo can also show as blue movies, blue language, *l'amour bleu*, bluebeard, blue murder, and cyanotic body. When these sorts of pornographic, perverse, ghastly, or vicious animus/anima fantasies start up, we can place them within the blue transition toward the albedo. Then we will look for bits of silver in the violence. There are patterns of self-recognition forming by means of horror and obscenity. The soul's *putrefactio* is generating a new anima consciousness, a new psychic grounding that must include underworld experiences of the anima itself: her deathly and perverse affinities. The dark blue of the Madonna's robe bears many shadows, and these give her depths of understanding, just as the mind made on the moon has lived with Lilith so that its thought can never be naive, never cease to strike deep toward shadows. Blue protects white from innocence. . . .

The transit from black to white via blue implies that blue always brings black with it. (Among African peoples, for instance, black includes blue: whereas in the Jewish-Christian tradition blue belongs rather to white). Blue bears traces of the *mortificatio* into the whitening. What before was the stickiness of the black, like pitch or tar, unable to be rid of, turns into the traditionally blue virtues of constancy and fidelity. The same dark events feel different. The tortured and symptomatic aspect of mortification—flaying oneself, pulverizing old structures, decapitation of the headstrong will, the rat and rot in one's personal cellar—give way to depression. As even the darkest blue is not black, so even the deepest depression is not the *mortificatio* which means death of soul. The *mortificatio* is more driven, images locked compulsively in behavior, visibility zero, psyche trapped in the inertia and extension of matter. A *mortificatio* is a time of symptoms. These inexplicable, utterly materialized tortures of psyche in *physis* are relieved, according to the procession of colors, by a movement toward depression, which can commence as a mournful regret even over the lost symptom: "It was better when it hurt physically—now I only cry." Blue misery. So, with the appearance of blue, feeling becomes more paramount and the paramount feeling is the mournful plaint (Rimbaud equates blue with vowel *O*; Kandinsky with the sounds of the flute, cello, double bass and organ). These laments hint of soul, of reflecting and distancing by imaginational expression. Here we can see more why archetypal psychology has stressed depression as the *via regia* in soul-making. The ascetic exercises that we call *symptoms* (and their *treatments*), the guilty despairs and remorse as the nigredo decays, reduce the old ego-personality, but this necessary reduction is only preparatory to the sense of soul which appears first in the blued imagination of depression.

It is the blue which deepens the idea of reflection beyond the single notion of mirroring, to the further notions of pondering, considering, meditating.

The colors which herald white are spoken of as Iris and the rainbow, as many flowers, and mainly as the brilliance of the peacock's tail with its multiple eyes. According to Paracelsus, the colors result from dryness acting on moisture. Believe it or not, there is more color in the alchemical desert than in the flood, in less emotion than in more. Drying releases the soul from personal subjectivism, and as the moisture recedes that vivacity once possessed by feeling can now pass over into imagination. Blue is singularly important here because it is the color of imagination *tout court*. I base this *apodicticus* not only on all we have been exploring: the blue mood which sponsors reverie, the blue sky which calls the mythic imagination to its farthest reaches, the blue of Mary who is the Western epitome of anima and her instigation of image making, the blue rose of romance, a *pothos* which pines for the impossible *contra naturam* (and *pothos*, the flower, was a blue larkspur or delphinium placed on graves). . . .

The nature of this achievement can be garnered from the accounts of those we have summoned. They suggest that the alchemical *unio mentalis* is the interpenetration of thought and image, of perceived world and imaginal world, a state of mind no longer concerned with distinctions between things and thought, appearance and reality, or between the spirit that develops theory and the soul that builds fantasy. We have colored this *unio mentalis* "blue," because the blue we have been encountering transfigures appearances into imaginal realities and imagines thought itself in a new way. Blue is preparatory to and incorporated in the white, indicating that the white becomes earth, that is, fixed and real, when the eye becomes blue, that is, able to see through thoughts as imaginative forms and images as the ground of reality.   ("Blue," 34–36, 39, 43)

Τhe Renaissance writers—and I think now of *Letters* by Petrarch, *Letters* by Ficino, *Letters* by Michelangelo—are filled with anima: depression, weakness, sickness, complaint, love of different kinds, helplessness. They aren't able to do what they want to do. Of course, these men were extremely active: Ficino never stopped his work despite all his complaints about being paralyzed and being unable to do anything anymore. Michelangelo thought he was old when he was forty and then he went on living beyond eighty. The soul builds its endurance, its *stamina* as Rafael Lopez calls it, through hopelessness and depression. I think the Italians have an enormous sense of anima, just because they know immediately what its moods feel like. It's only that you needn't take all those moods and all those weaknesses and helplessnesses and so on as literal. One thing you do learn in therapy is how, when you have a depression, it belongs to you, but you don't identify with the mood. You live your life in the depression. You work with the depression. It doesn't completely stop you. It only stops you if you're manic. Depression is worst when we try to climb out of it, get on top of it.

To feel something thoroughly does not mean to be it thoroughly. It is a mistake, a big bad mistake, to take feelings utterly

literally. Psychotherapy has got itself caught in this worship of feelings. If we took ideas that literally, we would say a person was
paranoid, but we take feelings as if they were the truth of who and
what we are. Look, when you get depressed, it belongs to you and
you can't help but feel it thoroughly (unless you take pills or go into
a manic defense), but you don't have to be identified with the mood.
You can live your day in a depressed style. Things slow down, there
is a lot of sadness. You can't see over the horizon. But you can notice
all this, recognize it, and go on—my God, thousands of people live
like this, regularly or in periods. You can find ways of talking from
it, seeing the world through it, connecting to people without covering it. It's amazing how others can respond to your depression *if you
don't identify with it:* a sigh immediately produces a sigh in the other
person. Did you ever think what a relief to be with someone who
knows how to live in the depression without being it. That's a master
to learn from, like old people sometimes can be. Depression lets you
live down at the bottom. And to live down at the bottom means
giving up the Christian thing about resurrection and coming out of
it; "light at the end of the tunnel." No light fantasy; and then the
depression at once becomes less dark. No hope, no despair. That
message of hope only makes hopelessness darker. It's the greatest
instigator of the pharmaceutical industry ever!

(Inter Views, 19–21)

This concern with depth leads us in practice to pay special attention to *whatever is below.* This has been so since the beginning of
psychoanalysis, and its notions of suppression, subconscious, and
shadow. These are terms for what we see in images: burials, the dead,
ancestors; workers in refuse, sewers, plumbers; criminals and out-
casts; the lower body, its garments and its functions; lower forms of
life that we "look down upon," from apes to bugs; the underside of
the world, the floor of the sea, the downstairs and cellars, and, in fact,
anything whatsoever that can be turned over in the sense of *hyponoia*
to reveal a deeper significance. The emotions that go with these
images of bottoming are reluctance, loathing, sadness, mourning,

inhibition, enclosure, lethargy, or that sense of depth that presses on us as depression, oppression, suppression. Our downward imagination has entered the earth. Bottom's dream.

(*Dream and the Underworld*, 139–140)

Crucial to this move into internal space is realizing that it must be black and must be empty, otherwise the antidote cannot appear in the poison. Rigid self-centered focusing without escape into future hopes is precisely the melancholy method, a process of archetypal self-correction.

The very agitation and circling thoughts that accompany the narrowing solitude and interior imaginal monologue are the peripheral activities that go along with every centering. The contradictories of center and circumference appear in the paradox of *agitated depression*—handwringing, pacing, insomnia. The intensely focused desert saint is assailed by chattering distractions; the old king wanting to be left alone to his books at the same time is out busily defending his far-flung borders. (It's only when we are in a centering fantasy that we worry about "the ten thousand things.") The structure obsessively works at its inner opposition. The body symbol is still the head. . . .

When a psychotherapist finds it beneficial for a person depressed to "go into the depression," or for older people to occupy themselves with thoughts, visions, and the strange otherness in their dreams he is expressing what Ficino, child of Saturn that he was, presented as a cogent method. Senex consciousness is finally at rest in the imaginal realm of the *archai*, which are *dei ambigui* of endless complications and contradictions. Melancholy drives us to where we can think and imagine no further, to the inmost void which is also the furthest limits of the mind. These are the borderlands, a borderline condition of emotional ambivalence which, as Freud wrote, is a root factor in melancholia. But now, from what we gather of Ficino's approach to what might be regarded as the psychotic bottom of depression, there is no rage to end the internal contradictions by choosing one or the other. The opposite impulses present themselves as indistinguishable. At this border, one side is the same as the other. Fantasy here transcends the opposites as a problem. Images are merely themselves, not arraigned for judgments, positions and oppositions. There is nothing to affirm or deny.

("Negative Senex," 98–99)

WOUNDS

By recognizing a basic cry we may evoke this child in the pathology; it is as if there were a basic cry in persons that gives direct voice to the abandoned content. For some persons it is: "Help, please help me"; others say, "take me, just as I am, take me, all of me without choice among my traits, no judgment, no questions asked"; or "take me, without my having to do something, to be someone." Another cry may be "hold me," or "don't go away; never leave me alone." We may also hear the content saying simply, "Love me." Or we can hear, "teach me, show me what to do, tell me how." Or, "carry me, keep me." Or the cry from the bottom may say, "Let me alone, all alone; just let me be."

Generally the basic cry speaks in the receptive voice of the infant, where the subject is an object, a *me* in the hands of others, incapable of action yet poignantly enunciating its knowledge of its subjectivity, knowing how it wishes to be handled. Its subjectivity is in the crying by means of which it organizes its existence. So, as well, we hear it in the basic cry a person addresses to his environment, turning his entourage into helpers, or lovers, or constant companions (a *thiasos*) who will nurse, dance attendance, or teach, or accept all blindly, who will never let him alone, or the reverse, from whom he flees in continual rejection. And the cry says how a person is unable to meet his needs himself, unable to help himself, or let himself alone.

It is worth insisting here that the cry is never cured. By giving voice to the abandoned child it is always there, and must be there as an archetypal necessity. We know well enough that some things we never learn, cannot help, fall back to and cry from again and again. These inaccessible places where we are always exposed and afraid, where we cannot learn, cannot love, and cannot help by transforming, repressing or accepting are the wildernesses, the caves where the abandoned child lies hidden. That we go on regressing to these places states something fundamental about human nature: we come back to an incurable psychopathology again and again through the course of life yet which apparently does go through many changes before and after contact with the unchanging child.

Here we strike upon the psychological relationship between what philosophy calls becoming and being, or the changing and the changeless, the different and the same, and what psychology calls growth on the one hand and on the other psychopathy: that which cannot by definition reverse or alter but remains as a more or less constant lacuna of character throughout life. In the language of our theme we have the eternal vulnerability of the abandoned child, and this same child's evolving futurity.

In this conundrum we usually pick up one side or the other, feeling ourselves different, changing, evolving, only to be smashed back by the shattering recurrence of a basic cry which in turn leads to the belief of being hopelessly stuck, nothing moving, just the same as always. The history of psychotherapy has also been driven back and forth by this apparent dilemma. At times degeneration theory (inheritance and constitution, or an idea of predestination) declare character is fate and that we can but move within predetermined patterns. At other times, such as today in American humanistic developmental psychology, the category of growth through transformation covers all psychic events.

Neither position is adequate. Like the metaphorical child of Plato's *Sophist* who, when asked to choose, opts for "both," the abandoned child is both that which *never grows*, remaining as permanent as psychopathy, and also that futurity springing from vulnerability itself. The complex remains, and the lacunae; that which becomes different are our connections with these places and our reflections through them. It is as if to change we must keep in touch with the changeless, which also implies taking change for what it is, rather than in terms of development. Evolution tends to become a "means of disowning the past" (T. S. Eliot); what we want to change we wish to be rid of. ("Abandoning," 19–20)

Building the psychic vessel of containment, which is another way of speaking of soul-making, seems to require bleeding and leaking as its precondition. Why else go through that work unless we are driven by the despair of our unstoppered condition? The shift from anima-mess to anima-vessel shows in various ways: as a shift from weakness and suffering to humility and sensitivity; from bitterness and complaint to a taste for salt and blood; from focus upon the emotional pain of a wound—its causes, perimeters, cures—to its imaginal depths; from displacements of the womb onto women and "femininity" to its locus in one's own bodily rhythm. . . .

We have said that each symptom brings the archetypal condition of woundedness. Although the wound may be experienced through a symptom, they are not the same. A symptom belongs to diagnosis, pointing to something else underlying. But the wound, as we have been imagining it, takes one into the archetypal condition of woundedness and gives even the smallest symptoms their transcending importance. Every symptom would turn us into its fantasy, so that skin spots make us lepers, diarrhea makes us little babies, and a sprain turns us into old derelicts on the bench. The *magnificatio* that wounding brings is a way of entering archetypal consciousness, that is the awareness that more is going on than my reason can hold. One becomes an open wound, hurting all over, as consciousness is transfigured into the wounded condition. We experience affliction in general, afflictedness as a way of being-in-the-world. The wound announces impossibility and impotence. It says: "I am unable." It brutally brings awareness to the fact of limitation. The limitation is not imposed from without by external powers, but this anatomical gap is an inherent part of me, concomitant with every step I take, every reach I make.

Because limitation is so difficult and painful for the puer structure, its statement, "I am unable," is exhibited by the painfulness of the wound. He stands before you, still radiant and cheery, as innocent as ever, all the while grossly demonstrating his incapacity by the thick plaster cast on his leg. A puer-man, psychically, hides his wound, since it reveals the secret that weakens this mode of consciousness. It fears feeling its own inability. For, when the wound is revealed at the end of the story, it kills one as a puer. The wound is one's mortality. Each complex has its symptom, its Achilles' heel, its opening into humanity through a vulnerable and excruciatingly painful spot, be it Samson's hair or Siegfried's heart.

Therapy must touch this spot; it must move from the beautiful wounded condition into the actual present hurt. The archetype, remember, generalizes, because archetypes are universals. So drive the nail home! Go into the crippling, maiming, bleeding; probe the specific organ—liver, shoulder, foot or heart. Each organ has a potential spark of consciousness, and afflictions release this consciousness, bringing to awareness the organ's archetypal background, which, until wounded, had simply functioned physiologically as part of unconscious nature. But now nature is wounded. The organ is now inferior. Deprivation of natural functioning gives awareness of the function. We realize for the first time its feeling, its value, its realm of operations. Limitation through the wound brings the organ to consciousness—as if we know something only as we lose it, in its limitation and decay; as if the knowledge death gives is the knowledge of what a psychic thing *is* in itself, its true meaning and importance for the soul. A "dying" consciousness is released by the wound.

This dying awareness, or awareness of dying, may heal the wound, for the wound is no longer so necessary. In this sense, a wound is the healing of puer consciousness and, as healing takes place, the wounded healer may begin to constellate. We must admit, after all, to a curious connection in fact between puer persons and the vocation to therapy.

The *wounded healer* does not mean merely that a person has been hurt and can empathize, which is too obvious and never enough to heal. Nor does it mean that a person can heal because he or she has been through an identical process, for this would not help unless the process had utterly altered consciousness. Let us remember that the *wounded healer* is not any human person, but a personification presenting a kind of consciousness. This kind of consciousness refers to mutilations and afflictions of the body organs that release the sparks of consciousness in these organs, resulting in an *organ- or body-consciousness*. Healing comes then not because one is whole, integrated, and all together, but from a consciousness breaking through dismemberment.   ("Ulysses' Scar," 115–117)

CULTURAL DISORDER

Culture takes place in closed, even closeted places, involving the alchemical *putrefactio,* or decadence as the body of fermentation. Generation and decay happen together; and they are not always easy to distinguish. What goes with civilization are irrigation systems, monuments, victories, historical endurance, wealth, and power as a cohesive force with common purpose. Civilization works; culture flowers. Civilization looks ahead, culture looks back. Civilization is historical record; culture a mythic enterprise.

They may interrelate, but they also seem able to do without each other. Civilization without culture is all around us. Culture without civilization? I think of the Tierra del Fuego Indians found by Westerners in the eighteenth century, with hardly fire, clothes, shelter, tools or vessels, always starving, always sick, yet whose vocabulary was more numerous than Shakespeare's or Joyce's, and whose culture was altogether myths of every sort.

Culture, as I have been speaking of it, looks backward and reaches back as a nostalgia for invisibilities, to make them present and to found human life upon them. The cultural enterprise attempts to peel, flail, excite individual sensitivity so that it can again—notice the *again*—be in touch with these invisibles and orient life by their compass. The key syllable in culture is the prefix *re.*

To build an argument upon a pun, the back wards display the backwards toward which culture reaches. For here is a display of recurring forms that do not change through time and which repeat in every age and society. (All societies, by the way, have some sort of psychopathology.) This universality and chronicity is expressed by both the physical view, backward as "genetic defectives" and the moral view, backward as sin, fall, or eternal damnation. If the gods have become diseases, then these forms of chronic disorder are the gods in disguise; they are occulted in these misshapen, inhuman forms, and our seeing through to them there—in all forms of chronic disorder in ourselves and our city—is a grounding act of culture. The education of sensitivity begins right here in trying to see through the manifestations of time into the eternal patterns within time. We may regard the discontents of civilization as if they are fundamentals of culture.

It may be surprising to associate the diseased with the divine and culture with deformity. We do so want the gods to be pristine, models in marble on Olympus, pure as driven snow. But they are not without their shadows, their afflictions and infirmities. As they are beyond time (*athnetos*, "immortal"), so these shadows of disorder that they portray in their myths reappear in those human events that are not affected by time, that is, in chronic disorders. Since we are created in their images, we can only do in time what they do in eternity. Their eternal afflictions are our human infirmities.

So, my point is coming clearer: it is in dealing with the back ward that culture grows. I do not mean going off to apprentice oneself in an asylum, to become a therapist—although I understand what students are asking for by wanting to enter a training program. Not merely to help people—that's the welfare reason. Rather it is to move from civilization toward culture. By being present with the chronic castaways of civilization, they become present to the timeless incurable aspect of the soul. I may make this yet clearer to you if you think again of your own backward back ward. Nursing and sitting with it, dwelling upon it, tracing the invisible mystery in it, letting compassion come for your own chronic disorder—this all slows down your progress, moves you from future thinking to essential thinking about our nature and character, upon life's meaning and death's, upon love and its failure, upon what is truly important, and upon the small things in words, manners, act, necessitated by the limitations of your inescapable disorder. We begin to hear differently, watch differently, absorb more sensitively. Confronted with the unbearable in my own nature, I show more trepidation—which is after all the first piece of compassion. In regard to others, my manners alter, my language more attuned and precise, I become more sophisticated and artful—as a cat steps, a bird perceives, a dog follows invisibles in the air. I look to arts for understanding, to ritual for enactments, and to the lives of men and women of the past and how they came through. I need something further than community and civilization for they may be too human, too visible. I need imaginal help from tales and images, idols and altars, and the creatures of nature, to help me carry what is so hard to carry personally and alone. Education of sensitivity begins in the back ward, culture in chronic disorder.

Finally, if you allow me one more paragraph, I come to appreciate the chronic itself. More than slowing down, more than an occasion for tolerance or instruction in survival, I come to see that things chronic are things that have nothing to do with civilized time, either future time when it will be better, or present time and adjustment, disguise, or complaint—but rather the timeless structures of being which accompany us, keep company with us, in forms that do not change and do not go away, seemingly so out of place, out of step with civilization and its courageous march toward its inevitable destruction. For civilizations do eventually decline and perish. Cultures, by existing always in decay, in disorder, may continue beyond the civilizations that seem to hold them. In the shadows of the gods are the very gods themselves, their myths in the midst of what survives because it will not go away.   ("Chronic Disorder," 19–21)

8

Psychoanalysis
in the Street

James Hillman's essays put the world on the couch for a brief psychoanalysis, demonstrating that there is nothing in the world that is not imaginal. So, he finds soul in odd places. First, rather than only sift through the details of an individual life, he goes into the streets and searches the soul of culture. Second, rather than staying in the sunshine, he ventures into the dark recesses where soul can hide.

A corollary of this proposition that the world is a suitable candidate for psychoanalysis is the opportunity for psychological relief for ourselves. If buses and highways are neurotic, then maybe we can find some therapy for our lives by treating things around us that are in distress. Obviously, this calls for a psychologizing of things, seeing through the bland literalism of the commonplace to the fantasies contained therein. The world can be treated like any other patient.

Hillman has an unusual ability to unveil soul values in the shadow of culture. It is easy, as he says of America, to picture ourselves as a peaceable people and then act violently. It is more difficult but revealing to examine warfare imaginally, to look for the myth in war without prejudice to its validity or morality. The same is true of money. It is easy to speak from that place in us that refuses to be contaminated by money, but psychoanalysis cannot hide in fantasies of purity. It has to enter whatever mess is presented in order to find its myth and necessity. Only when we see the myth can we find our way into it.

Implied in Hillman's psychology of the world is a radically different way of dealing with social problems. It is a postmodern approach, closer to traditions of magic, incantation and ritual than modern analysis and treatment plans. If alcohol is the problem, then we must find out what the soul wants from alcohol, or what kind of alcohol it wants, or what alcohol wants by infusing itself into the psyche. Is it an alchemical substance, like the moisture a city seeks in constructing a man-made lake?

The temptation always is to deal with social ills from the spirit: find out what is going on, develop a plan of attack, and get it under control. Hillman's way is to take the labyrinthine way of the soul, to find a cure by entering into the symptom with unrelenting imagination. Therefore, Hillman's essays on the world's soul are full of surprising twists, new ways of picturing the most mundane matters, and inversions of values. His point is to open imagination to fantasies that in fact are present and operative yet hidden to a literalistic point of view. It is the task of a psychologist to bring imagination rather than explanation to the many problematical aspects of everyday life. Hillman opens a two-way gate. On one hand, he invites planners, designers, and social and political activists to regard themselves also as imaginative psychologists, even as therapists of soul. On the other, he counsels the professional therapist to move into the street where, Hillman claims, today's major unconsciousness now lies.

EDUCATION

Education of children, as Jung said in his lecture on this subject in 1924, begins with the education of parents and teachers, and it begins in lower education, not higher; in retarded, not advanced; with lowering our sights and their standards, down on all fours, with finger paints, with drums, with bare feet; with slower days not longer hours; with tasting, not testing; with nonsense instead of jargon. Too much Rousseau and the sentimental education? Too much Rudolf Steiner, free schools, and hippy-happy kindergartens? Don't get me wrong: I am talking about *us*, adults—not what children should be doing.

If nonsense rhymes and finger paints seem too childish, look at what we do now with the child—pouting resentments and junk food, passive-aggressive sport violence in front of the television, buckets of popcorn, buckets of beer. The adult household with its apple toys, home as a radio shack, a fantasy island or closet of collectibles, its game rooms, its gimmicks and gadgets for building bodies as the imagination cheapens and blow-dries. Mary Kay and supermarket paperbacks. Meanwhile, growth, originality, and initiative, those primordial forces of the child, are consumed by that hyperactive omnipotence fantasy called *development*—whether personal, mystical, or financial, the project of oneself in space.

Nonsense rhymes and finger paints mean that I am not recommending the replacement of trashy child*ish*ness with higher forms of child*like*ness, such as Bachelard's reveries toward childhood, Jung's divine child, Blake's innocence and delight, the Platonic child of wonder in the cosmos. A therapeutic education must beware of the ennobling course. Therapy is an education that works with equivalences, not conversions. It's a business of straight barter. We can't turn sinners into saints or dimes into dollars without shortchanging the shadow. So, in exchange for fingering the push buttons, finger-painting; instead of television's nonsense language game, Lewis Carroll; instead of Kodachrome, Easter eggs. The primitive barter of stupidity for simplicity—beginning where it's at.

Education, however, cannot stop where it starts. By definition, education must *lead out*. It leads simple fantasy into imagination. The fingers themselves and the tongue, twisting along in its syllabic chant, want more than repetitions. The fingers and tongue find novelty by sophisticating fantasy into imagination.

We have come to that old conundrum, the difference between fantasy and imagination, and we can locate this difference now in the mother-child tandem. Fantasy is the activity of the motherless child; imagination is mothered fantasy: it is purposive, responsive, thoughtful. It mothers because it is child focused—focused on the imagination. The key word of imagining is therefore not free but *fecund*, and its aim therefore is not exploring only but furthering, and the elation of fantasy is contained by consistency and carefulness. Child and mother, both. To be led out to this *both*, we must make another psychological equivalence, exchanging the actual child as focus of education for focus upon imagination of the adult. We take childhood back in. This recovery of childhood from children gives them their chance at poise, dignity, and sobriety, their desire for reason and for duty, as we return to the closet of our childishness. This move is primary because the fantasy of educating imagination has all been put on actual children—what they should do for us. They have had to do what we as adults are not allowed (except in asylums and in that national asylum, California, the golden state of childhood), leaving us with an undernourished, deprived, mute, abused, and violent childishness, fit for Pacman, *Star Wars*, and *Halloween*—amusements of the adulterated mind. . . .

Daily encounters with the city of the world are imaginative moments to the child's mind. To the imagination, events are stories, people are figures, things and words are images. To the imagination, the world itself is a mother, a great mother. We are nestled in its language, held by its institutions, nourished by its things. The great mother complex that so afflicts our Western psyche—its dread and fascination with matter, its denial of dependency that we call *free will*, the oral craving of consumer economics as cure for depression—cannot be resolved by personal therapy alone. Personal therapy as cure, and that notion of cure itself, is an apotropaic defense against her—banning the city from the consulting room. The little mother of the consulting room can take care of us for a while, but outside lies the great wide world, and only the great wide world can cure us—not *of* the Great Mother, but by means of her, for the word *cure* comes from *cura,* "care." Like cures like because likes care for each other. The city itself mothers us once we recover the child of imagination.

We need but remember that the city, the *metro-polis,* means at root a streaming, flowing, thronging mother. We are her children, and she can nourish our imaginations if we nourish hers. So, the *magna mater* is not the *magna culpa.* The actual blame for it all—the whole caboodle of downtown and the budget, of illiteracy and re-armament, ethical decay and ecological poison, the cause of the withering of our institutions—government, schools, family, trades and services, publishing and language—is the neglect of the city. And the city can be restored as mother by the child of imagination. Without that child we cannot imagine further our civilization or further our civilization's imagination, so that civilization itself becomes a bad mother, offering no ground or drink to the soul. Of course the individual mother feels a failure. The experience of bad mothering is given with the civilization itself when the education of imagination is neglected. ("Bad Mother," 179–181)

Why have we as a nation become more and more illiterate? We blame television and the computer, but they are not causes. They are results of a prior condition that invited them in. They arrived to fill a gap. When imaginative ability declines, other ways to communicate appear. These ways work even though they too are dyslexic in structure: simultaneity of bits, odd juxtapositions, messages that do not move linearly from left to right. Yet television and personal computers communicate.

Evidently, reading does not depend solely on the ordering of words or the ordering of letters in the words. Indeed, poets use dyslexic structures deliberately. Reading depends on the psyche's capacity to enter imagination. Reading is more like dreaming, which, too, goes on in silence. Our illiteracy reflects our educative process away from the silent grounds of reading: silent study halls and quiet periods, solitary homework, learning by heart, listening through a whole class without interruptions, writing an essay exam in longhand, drawing from nature instead of lab experiments. This long neglect of imaginational conditions that foster reading—*Sputnik* and the new math; social problems and social relatedness; me-centered motivation; the confusion of information with knowledge, of opinion with judgment, and trivia with sources; communications as messages by telephone calls and answering machines rather than as letter writing in silence; learning to speak up without first having something learned to say; multiple choice and scoring as a test of comprehension—has produced illiteracy.

The human person as a data bank does not need to read more than functionally. A data bank deciding yes or no on the basis of feedback (i.e., reinforcement) need not imagine beyond getting, storing, and spending. Just get the instructions right; never mind the content. Learn the *how* rather than the *what* with its qualities, values, and subtleties. Then the human agent becomes an incarnated credit card performing the religious rituals of consumerism. You need only be able to sign your name in the space marked *X*, like an immigrant, like a slave, or a . . .

Or a psychopath. Descriptions of psychopathy, or sociopathic personalities, speak of their inability to imagine the other. Psychopaths are well able to size up situations and charm people. They perceive, assess, and relate, making use of any opportunity. Hence their successful manipulations of others. But the psychopath is far less able to imagine the other beyond a fantasy of usefulness, the other as a true interiority with his or her own needs, intentions, and feelings. An education that in any way neglects imagination is an education into psychopathy. It is an education that results in a sociopathic society of manipulations. We learn how to deal with others and become a society of dealers.

("Right to Remain Silent," 150–151)

WORK

We moralize work and make it a problem, forgetting that the hands *love* to work and that in the hands is the mind. That "work ethic" idea does more to impede working . . . it makes it a duty instead of a pleasure. We need to talk of the work instinct, not the work ethic, and instead of putting work with the superego we need to imagine it as an id activity, like a fermentation, something going on instinctively, autonomously, like beer works, like bread works. . . .

I have a fantasy, for example, that I have a farm, and it doesn't matter whether I'm correcting proofs or writing footnotes or reading some tiresome paper or other or editing somebody else's work . . . whatever I am doing, it's like a farm, and I have to feed the chickens and hoe the potatoes and chop the wood and do the accounts and pull the weeds. And every one of those jobs is necessary, and none is more important than the other one. So the new white page, the important new thought you are developing is not more important than the many little things that happen to be in your way or along your way. But they also happen to be the way itself. I don't have a monocentric image of work as if each person had one special task. If I ask myself, What's your task in life? I'm going to get a single answer. Questions like this come out of the ego so they only can have one answer—or a choice among single answers. Ego questions are setups—you can never answer them psychologically, with a polytheistic answer. So there isn't just one special task, like a calling or vocation. Vocation is a very inflating spiritual idea. One to one. God to me. Notice how our idea of Renaissance man is a polytheistic fantasy. He does all kinds of things. But vocation addresses the ego and makes it a specialist—then you "believe in yourself"—and that's another trap of that devil, belief—because who is believing in whom? I am believing in myself—all ego, and then I have a mission. Now that fantasy of the farm is polytheistic, and who is to say what is *the* important thing on a farm: the man who buys eggs from me would like more eggs and sees the time I spend chopping wood a waste. "Have a secretary do it. You have the best eggs around. Produce more, and even better ones." Specialization: the best eggman around; and that's monotheism and mission and early death! . . .

My farm is a *psychological* fantasy, and therefore it tends to distribute the value into the actual tasks rather than having a *spiritual* farm where the tasks would be laid out in a hierarchy. *Importance* on my farm is not some overarching idea of a great canvas or a thousand-page history of psychology; importance appears in the way you do each thing.

❧

I merely want to speak of working as a *pleasure,* as an instinctual gratification—not just the "right to work," or work as an economic necessity or a social duty or a moral penance laid onto Adam after leaving Paradise. The hands themselves *want* to do things, and the mind loves to apply itself. Work is irreducible. We don't work for food gathering or tribal power and conquest or to buy a new car and so on and so forth. Working is its own end and brings its own joy; but one has to have a fantasy so that work can go on, and the fantasies we now have about it—economic and sociological—keep it from going on, so we have a huge problem of productivity and quality in our Western work. We have got work where we don't want it. We don't want to work. It's like not wanting to eat or to make love. It's an instinctual laming. And this is psychology's fault: it doesn't attend to the work instinct. (*Inter Views,* 163–168)

MONEY

Money is a *psychic reality,* and as such gives rise to divisions and oppositions about it, much as other fundamental psychic realities—love and work, death and sexuality, politics and religion—are archetypal dominants which easily fall into opposing spiritual and material interpretations. Moreover, since money is an archetypal psychic reality, it will always be inherently problematic because psychic realities are complex, complicated. Therefore, money problems are inevitable, necessary, irreducible, always present, and potentially if not actually overwhelming. Money is devilishly divine.

One of Charles Olson's *Maximus* poems sets out this archetypal view most compactly:

> *the under part is, though stemmed, uncertain is, as sex is, as moneys are,*
> *facts to be dealt with as the sea is . . .*

This is an extraordinary statement. "Facts to be dealt with as the sea is." The first of these facts is that money is as deep and broad as the ocean, the primordially unconscious, and makes us so. It always takes us into great depths, where sharks and suckers, hard-shell crabs, tight clams and tidal emotions abound. Its facts have huge horizons, as huge as sex, and just as protean and polymorphous.

Moreover, money is plural: moneys. Therefore I can never take moneys as an equivalent for any single idea: exchange, energy, value, reality, evil, and whatever. It is many stemmed, it is uncertain, polymorphous. At one moment the money complex may invite Danaë who draws Zeus into her lap as a shower of coins, at another moment the gold may invite Midas. Or, Hermes the thief, patron of merchants, easy commerce. Or it may be old moneybags Saturn who invented coining and hoarding to begin with. As on the original coins the Greeks made, there are different gods and different animals—owls, bulls, rams, crabs—each time the complex is passed from hand to hand.

Money is as protean as the sea god himself; try as we might with fixed fees, regular billings, and accounts ledgered and audited, we never can make the stems of money balance. The checkbook will never tally, the budget will never stay within bookkeeping columns.

We invent more and more machinery for controlling money, more and more refined gauges for economic prediction, never grasping what Olson tells us: the facts of money are like the facts of the sea. Money is like the id itself, the primordially repressed, the collective unconscious appearing in specific denominations, that is, precise quanta or configurations of value, i.e., *images*. Let us define money as that which possibilizes the imagination. Moneys are the riches of Pluto in which Hades's psychic images lie concealed. To find imagination in yourself or a patient, turn to money behaviors and fantasies. You both will soon be in the underworld (the entrance to which requires a money for Charon).

Therapy draws back. Do you know of the study done on therapeutic taboos? Analysts were surveyed regarding what they feel they must never do with a patient. It was discovered that touching and holding, shouting and hitting, drinking, kissing, nudity and intercourse were all less prohibited than was "lending money to a patient." Money constellated the ultimate taboo.

For money always takes us into the sea, uncertain, whether it comes as inheritance fights, fantasies about new cars and old houses, marriage battles over spending, ripping off, tax evasion, market speculations, fear of going broke, poverty, charity—whether these complexes appear in dreams, in living rooms, or in public policy. For here in the facts of money is the great ocean, and maybe while trawling that sea floor during an analytical hour we may come up with a crazy crab or a fish with a shekel in its mouth.

Just as animals were spirits or gods in material forms, so too is money, a kind of third thing between only spirit and only the world, flesh, and devil. Hence, to be with money is to be in this third place of soul, psychic reality. And, to keep my relation with the unclean spirits whether the high daimones or the low daimones, I want some coins in my purse. I need them to pay my way to Hades into the psychic realm. I want to be like what I work on, not unlike and immune. I want the money changers where I can see them, right in the temple of my pious aspirations. In other words, I try my darndest to keep clear about the [Christian] tradition I have just exposed because I think it a disastrous one for psychotherapy, and of course also for the culture as a whole.

The cut between Caesar and God in terms of money deprives the soul of world and the world of soul. The soul is deflected onto a spiritual path of denial and the world is left in the sins of *luxuria*, avarice, and greed. Then the soul is always threatened by money, and the world needs the spiritual mission of redemption from the evil caused by the Weltbild that cuts Caesar from God. That money is the place where God and Caesar divide shows that money is a "third thing" like the soul itself, and that in money are both the inherent tendency to split into spirit and matter and the possibility to hold them together. . . .

If money has this archetypal soul value, again like the ancient coins bearing images of gods and their animals and backed by these powers, money will not, cannot, accept the Christian depreciation, and so Christianity time and again in its history has had to come to terms with the return of the repressed—from the wealth of the churches and the luxury of its priests, the selling of indulgences, the rise of capitalism with Protestantism, usury and projections on the Jews, the Christian roots of Marxism, and so on. . . .

That we cannot settle the money issue in analysis shows money to be one main way the mothering imagination keeps our souls fantasizing. So, to conclude with my part of this panel, Soul and Money: yes, soul *and* money; we cannot have either without the other. To find the soul of modern man or woman, begin by searching into those irreducible embarrassing facts of the money complex, that crazy crab scuttling across the floors of silent seas.

("Soul and Money," 35–38, 43)

TRANSPORTATION

Let me show you how the practice of psychotherapy operates. When a problem is brought into the consulting room, we listen to it very carefully, attempting to hear through it for fantasies. . . . Let's begin with our patient, transportation.

Possibly some of the cure of our patient lies in the transformation of our notions of a region from a geometry of space and a mechanics of acceleration to a topography of places, a city as clustering places. Where space tends to propel us into future fantasies (space-age *utopias,* a word which means "nowhere"), places tend to remind us of history, of ethnic and earthy differences that cannot be homogenized into the universal sameness of our contemporary utopias, the nowhere everywhere of our shopping centers and roads to and from them.

City originally refers to community, a fellowship of persons in places. But our patient has come to speak of it as a center, "center city." *Center* too is a geometrical notion. It is not a geography, for the word comes directly from *kentron,* the Greek for that prick point made by a compass in tracing a circle. Its earlier verb form means a spoke, a stick for striking, a goad or spur to make a horse or ox "getta going." "Stimulus" and "instigate" are the exact Latinate translations.

So the city conceived as a center, is where it happens, downtown that's where the action is, where we are stimulated and spurred, and the center beats us forward like beasts of burden, even if paradoxically the actual center city is a static place of parking lots and windswept fronts. My first recommendation to the patient is remove from all roads all signs saying "city center"; let nothing be called "central"—it is sure to be choked by its own hurry and exhaust(ion).

Our maps tend to show cities as centers, as focal points—big round circles and bold capital letters, so that our map thinking soon draws imaginary lines—like the interstate highway system—connecting the centers. The location of the center in its *region,* its actual placing in physical geography, is abstracted by the larger vision of centers surrounded by empty spaces, dotted by peripheral minor satellites, much like an astronomer's chart of the heavens.

Cities conceived as centers—rather than as named places, personalities, embedded in physical earth—influence even our eating habits which further complicate our transportation problem. The loss of regional embeddedness makes us forget that cities rise from the earth, from land with local produce. Map thinking favors long-haul trucking, neglecting what belongs right here at hand. Instead, food from a thousand miles, unrelated to season and locality—and taste.

These constructs so important to the way we conceive transportation also create a world with little place for slowness. It has been banned from the city to the country. For classic and medieval man, nature was demonic; now the city is demonic. We flee from it via express lanes and nonstop flights to take us to where we can slow down and stop. In order to reimagine transportation we would as well have to re-vision the city as a place of rest and leisure, of nature's elements, water, fire, and earth, refuge, paths in the shade, temple gardens . . . we might then be less eager to get away.

In conclusion now, most of our "case study" has involved the idea of *motion*. This is surely the deepest fantasy in the transportation problem. Motion has been essential to the Western idea of God who has been defined as the self-moved mover, and the Western idea of nature which defined the universe by laws of motion (for "Greek and modern are agreed that the most universal characteristic of this world is motion"). The idea is essential to the soul which since Aristotle has been considered the motion of the human person. We are either quick or dead.

We are forced to recognize that transportation awakens profound fantasies about motion, and that transportation plans are attempts to rationalize motion. Driving to center city, covering space with speed, my foot on the accelerator, puts me automatically into the fantasy of motion as an *actual experience* that before our automotive age was imagined only in terms of gods, stars, and atoms. I, the modern secular ego, is the self-moved mover, which is precisely what the word *automobile* means. Moreover, these wheels, including the steering wheel, reflect the ancient Celtic and Mediterranean symbol of the wheel of death. As long as I am driving, the wheel is in my hands; no matter the facts of death on the roads, my fantasy assures me I have death in my control. To meet our patient's complaint, to restructure the relations between private driving and public service, means coming to terms with this gigantic fantasy of our godlike power over motion and death.

This fantasy that identifies the control of motion with the control of individual fate makes it so difficult to conceive transportation as a service required by a community, much like justice and education, fire protection and public safety, water and sewage, lighting and cleaning. Instead, we imagine transportation from a private viewpoint, as if it should pay its way, part of free enterprise, competitive. Where street lighting, street signs, and street repair may belong to our community life and be supported by taxes, we resist paying for public conveyances through these same public streets. Public transportation seems to infringe upon our identity as self-moved individual—so that we pay for the *automobile* fantasy with every sort of tax without protest. But we are unwilling to invite, and to pay for, public transport, the collectivity of the omnibus, the tracks and schedules of trains, which take the wheel of fate out of my hands.

My ending note is dark. But our depth psychological tradition is not known for optimism. We don't point ways out of problems; rather we search for ways more deeply into them. In this case I have tried to show the inherent link between the city transportation problem and an egocentric conceptual model that constructs a world in which the problem fits and is inevitable. Our patient cannot cure one isolated symptom, transportation, without a deeper change in character structure, which means our view of ourselves in the universe. If we would move the transportation problem, we must also shift the fantasies in which it is embedded. This shift begins by attacking the strategic problem on a tactical level—localized qualitative improvements. I am suggesting a place-age imagining of *values* rather than a space-age thinking of projections, thinking spatially in terms of lines, speed, and numbers. Then we have begun a shift of perspectives not only from space to place, but as well from city center to community, public to persons, homogeneity to differences, geometry to geography, from quick and easy to slow and interesting, from private driver to civic passenger, that sense of transciency which accepts that the wheel on which we turn can never truly be in our own hands. (*Transportation*, unnumbered)

SEX

Men are not talking to each other about sex, at least not heterosexual men. Women talk—in detail!—yet the few men who talk about sex talk only with their women partners. With each other, sex talk becomes adolescent boastings and action-packed machismo. How can a man learn, or teach, about what really happens and might happen if he keeps secretive and dumb about genital intimacy?

Dumb sex is cultural. Our white American speech doesn't provide good words for genitals and intercourse—and hardly any phrases about places, rhythms, touches, and tastes.

Listen to the marvelous language of foreign erotica: jade stalk, palace gates, ambrosia! Compare these with cock, prick, dick, nuts, balls; with suck, jerk, blow, yank; and with gash, bush, frog, slit, clit, hole. A Chinese plum is to be deliciously enjoyed; our cherries are to be taken, popped, or broken. Suppose we were to call him, as he once was named, Jolly Roger or Little Johnny Jump-up, or happy warrior, smiling wand, black magic, or Purusha who is smaller-than-small and bigger-than-big.

Our Puritan prose cannot encompass the sexual imagination to which great temples are built in India. Our imagination reinforces the image of lovemaking as a heroic performance, that hard-rock fantasy of sex. Yet performance heroism makes impotence all the more threatening—and inevitable. This hard language at the core of our sex talk makes us ignore that times of lassitude and gentle reluctance are also divine, for in these moments, imagination swells the body with reverie and longing.

Confidence in male prowess doesn't require talking big or even being big as much as letting our flaccid sexual speech become more redolent and swollen. Purpling. This means talking more concretely and with more pleasure about sexual fantasies. For the sexual acts themselves depend on imagination.

I find three dominant modes of imagining sexuality now. One is the heroic; screwing, scoring, chasing, shooting. Another is the romantic fantasy of fusion, where the two become one, riding the rhythm so that the cock belongs to both, or to no one. But this fusing can turn suddenly into terror and be felt as loss of phallos: She took it; consumed it. Romantic enchantment becomes bewitchment by female power.

A third mode holds desire within mysteries of initiation, invoking the dark gods—both in their wild animal and little child shapes. A kind of neobaroque theater of the sublime—a strange beauty of terror, awe, and play together—the sexual body and the emotions of love meet at the risky edge, promising neither heroic victories nor completely satisfying unions. Here is a wider devotion to the animistic or animalistic powers on which sexuality always depends and urges toward; not secular humanism, but the mysteries.

("Sex Talk," 76)

WAR

You will recall, if you saw the film *Patton*, the scene in which the American general, who commanded the Third Army in the 1944-45 drive across France into Germany, walks the field after a battle: churned earth, burnt tanks, dead men. The general takes up a dying officer, kisses him, surveys the havoc, and says: "I love it. God help me I do love it so. I love it more than my life."

❋

I believe we can never speak sensibly of peace or disarmament unless we enter into this love of war. Unless we enter into the martial state of soul, we cannot comprehend its pull. This special state must be ritualistically entered. We must be "inducted," and war must be "declared"—as one is declared insane, declared married or bankrupt. So we shall try now to "go to war" and this because it is a principle of psychological method that any phenomenon to be understood must be empathetically imagined. To know war we must enter its love. No psychic phenomenon can be truly dislodged from its fixity unless we first move the imagination into its heart. . . .

My method of heading right in, of penetrating rather than circumambulating or reflecting, is itself martial. So we shall be invoking the god of the topic by this approach to the topic. . . .

Besides the actual battles and their monuments, the monumental epics that lie in the roots of our Western languages are to a large proportion "war books": the *Mahabarata* and its *Bhagavad Gita*, the *Iliad*, the *Aenead*, the Celtic *Lebor Gabala*, and the Norse *Edda*. Our Bible is a long account of battles, of wars and captains of wars. Yahweh presents himself in the speeches of a war god and his prophets and kings are his warriors. Even the New Testament is so arranged that its final culminating chapter, Revelations, functions as its recapitulative coda in which the Great Armageddon of the Apocalypse is its crisis.

In our most elevated works of thought—Hindu and Platonic philosophy—a warrior class is imagined as necessary to the well-being of humankind. This class finds its counterpart within human nature, in the heart, as virtues of courage, nobility, honor, loyalty, steadfastness of principle, comradely love, so that war is given location not only in a class of persons but in a level of human personality organically necessary to the justice of the whole.

❧

Love and war have traditionally been coupled in the figures of Venus and Mars, Aphrodite and Ares. This usual allegory is expressed in usual slogans—make love not war, all's fair in love and war—and in usual oscillating behaviors—rest, recreation and rehabilitation in the whorehouse behind the lines, then return to the all-male barracks. Instead of these couplings which actually separate Mars and Venus into alternatives, there is a venusian experience within Mars itself. It occurs in the sensate love of life in the midst of battle, in the care for concrete details built into all martial regulations, in the sprucing, prancing and dandying of the cavaliers (now called *boys*) on leave. Are they sons of Mars or of Venus?

In fact, we need to look again at the aesthetic aspect of Mars. Also there a love lies hidden. From the civilian sidelines, military rites and rhetoric seem kitsch and pomposity. But look instead at this language, these procedures as the sensitization by ritual of the physical imagination. Consider how many different kinds of blades, edges, points, metals and temperings are fashioned on the variety of knives, swords, spears, sabers, battle-axes, rapiers, daggers, lances, pikes, halberds that have been lovingly honed with the idea of killing. Look at the rewards for killing: Iron Cross, Victoria Cross, Medal of Honor, Croix de Guerre; the accoutrements: bamboo baton, swagger stick, epaulets, decorated sleeves, ivory-handled pistols. The music: reveille and taps, drums and pipes, fifes and drums, trumpets, bugles, the marching songs and marching bands, brass, braid, stripes. The military tailors: Wellington boots, Eisenhower jackets, Sam Brown belts, green berets, red coats, "whites." Forms, ranks, promotions. Flags, banners, trooping to the colors. The military mess—its postures, toasts. The manners: salutes, drills, commands. Martial rituals of the feet—turns, steps, paces, warriors' dances. Of the eyes—eyes front! Of the hands, the neck, the voice, ramrod backbone, abdomen—"Suck in that gut, soldier." The names: Hussars, Dragoons, Rangers, Lancers, Coldstream Guards, and nicknames, bluejacket, leatherneck, doughboy. The great walls and bastions of severe beauty built by Brunelleschi, da Vinci, Michelangelo, Buon-talenti. The decorated horse, notches in the rifle stock, the painted emblems on metal equipment, letters from the front, poems. Spit and polish and pent emotion. Neat's-foot oil, gunsmith, swordsmith; the Shield of Achilles on which is engraved the whole world.

Our American consciousness has extreme difficulty with Mars. Our founding documents and legends portray the inherent nonmartial bias of our civilian democracy. You can see this in the Second, Third and Fourth constitutional amendments which severely restrict military power in the civilian domain. You can see this in the stories of the Massachusetts Minutemen versus European mercenaries and redcoats, and in the Green Mountain boys and the soldiers of the Swamp Fox—civilians all. And you can see it in the casual individualistic Texans at San Jacinto versus the Mexican officers trained in the European mold.

Compared with our background in Europe, Americans are idealistic: war has no place. It should not be. War is not glorious, triumphal, creative as to a warrior class in Europe from Rome and the Normans through the Crusades even to the Battle of Britain. We may be a violent people but not a warlike people—and our hatred of war makes us use violence against even war itself. Wanting to put a stop to it was a major cause of the Los Alamos project and Truman's decision to bomb Hiroshima *and* Nagasaki, a bomb to "save lives," a bomb to end bombs, like the idea of a war to end all wars. "The object of war," it says on General Sherman's statue in Washington, "is a more perfect peace." Our so-called double-speak about armaments as "peacemakers" reflects truly how we think. War is bad, exterminate war and keep peace violently: punitive expeditions, preemptive strikes, send in the Marines. More firepower means surer peace. We enact the blind god's blindness (Mars *Caecus* as the Romans called him, and Mars *insanus, furibundus, omnipotens*), like General Grant in the wilderness, like the bombing of Dresden, overkill as a way to end war. . . .

The rhetoric of Mars in war journals, poems and recollections speaks of attachment to specific earthly places, comrades, things. The transcendent is in the concrete particular. Hemingway writes that after World War I: "abstract words such as glory, honor, cour-age . . . were obscene beside the concrete names of villages, the numbers of roads, the names of rivers, the regiments and dates." How rare for anyone to know the date of Alamogordo (or even where it is), the date of Hiroshima, of the first hydrogen bomb explosion, or the names of people or places or units engaged. Gone in abstraction. Glenn Gray writes: "Any fighting unit must have a limited and specific objective. A physical goal—a piece of earth to defend, a machine-gun nest to destroy, a strong point to annihilate—more likely evokes a sense of comradeship."

Martial psychology turns events into images: physical, bounded, named. Hurtgen Forest, Vimy Ridge, Iwo Jima. A beach, a bridge, a railroad crossing: battle places become iconic and sacred, physical images claiming the utmost human love, worth more than my life.

Quite different is the transcendent experience of the nuclear fireball. The emotion is stupefaction at destruction itself rather than a heightened regard for the destroyed. Nuclear devastation is not merely a deafening cannonade or firebombing carried to a further degree. It is different in kind: archetypally different. It evokes the apocalyptic transformation of the world into fire, earth ascending in a pillar of cloud, an epiphanic fire revealing the inmost spirit of all things, as in the Buddha's fire sermon:

All things, O priests, are on fire . . . the mind is on fire, ideas are on fire . . . mind consciousness is on fire.

Or like that passage from the *Bhagavad Gita* which came to Oppen-heimer when he saw the atomic blast:

If the radiance of a thousand suns
Were burst at once into the sky
That would be like the splendour of the Mighty One.

The nuclear imagination leaves the human behind for the worst sin of all: fascination by the spirit. *Superbia.* The soul goes up in fire. If the epiphany in battle unveils love of this place and that man and values more than my life yet bound with this world and its life, the nuclear epiphany unveils the apocalyptic god, a god of extinction, the god-is-dead god, an epiphany of nihilism.

Apocalypse is not necessary to war. Let me make this very clear: apocalypse is not part of the myths of Mars. Mars asks for battle, not wipeout, not even victory. (*Nike* belongs to Athena, not Ares.) Patton supposedly said: "I like making things happen. That's my share in Deity." Apocalypse is inherent not in the martial deity, but in the Christian deity. Fascination with a transcendent Christ may be more the threat to the Christian civilization than the war god himself. Are not civilizations saved by their gods also led to destruction by those same, their own, gods?

There is one more distinction, one that may be of the most therapeutic significance. If nuclearism produces "psychic numbing," stupefaction, stupidity, Mars works precisely to the contrary. He intensifies the senses and heightens fellow feeling in action, that energized vivification the Romans called *Mars Nerio* and *Mars Moles,* molar, massive, making things happen. Mobilization. Mars gives answer to the hopelessness and drifting powerlessness we feel in the face of nuclear weapons by awakening fear. Phobos, his Greek companion or son, and rage, *ira,* wrath. Mars is the instigator, the primordial activist. To put the contrast in eschatological terms, Mars is the god of beginnings, the sign of the ram. March is his month, and April, *Mars Apertus,* opening, making things happen. Apocalypse may lift veils, but it closes down into the truly final solution, after which there is no reopening, no *recorso.* Broken the wheel.

To hold the bomb as image in the mind requires an extraordinary extension, and extraordinary daring, in our imagining powers, a revolution of imagination itself, enthroning it as the main, the greatest reality, because the bomb, which imagination shall contain, is the most powerful image of our age. Brighter than a thousand suns, it is our omnipotent god term (as Wolfgang Giegerich has expounded), our mystery that requires constant imaginative propitiation. The translation of bomb into the imagination is a transubstantiation of God to *imago dei,* deliteralizing the ultimate god term from positivism to negative theology, a god that is all images. And, no more than any other god term can it be controlled by reason or taken fully literally without hideous consequences. The task of nuclear psychology is a rituallike devotion to the bomb as image, never letting it slip from its pillar of cloud in the heaven of imagination to rain ruin on the cities of the plain.

("Mars," 118–120, 123–125, 128–130, 134–135)

TERRORISM

If you had been in a concentration camp in the forties and the doctors took out your womb, that would be a war crime, wouldn't it? All right, and now more than half of the women over forty in the United States have their wombs removed. Imagine that! Every other woman over forty you pass in the street in the United States has no uterus. Hysterectomies are performed more than appendectomies and tonsillectomies. It's America's favorite operation. This is terrifying, terrible—it's not forced on the women as in a concentration camp. They come willingly: it's "good for you." Or take Germany today: one out of seven people—that means millions—take sleeping pills of some kind *every* night. This is *Fahrenheit 451; 1984*, . . . don't you see?

Of course, today we don't live in concentration camps, literally, with barbed wire and SS guards. But if we go on imagining those camps of the forties as the *only kind* of terror, then we miss the actual horrors that are perpetrated every day—whether with toxic dumps and industrial pollutants or with drug prescriptions or with those hysterectomies. Even if the women collude with their surgeons and want the operation, it is still a horror. The clitoridectomies in some African societies or the binding of Chinese feet in the Mandarin culture were horrors, terrors in fact, even if the women "wanted" these operations. Terror doesn't depend only on whether what's done to you is "voluntary" or not—that's a big part of it, of course, and I'm not denying that in the 1940s in Germany cruelty and force were used. Cruelty and force can happen in ways that are not felt as cruelty and force—but still they are cruelty and force. For instance, we know from studying what goes on in schizogenetic families that the terror is there even if it's not perceived. At least then, in the 1940s, we weren't already so anesthetized, already so unconscious that the victims didn't sense what was happening. Maybe it's worse today since we don't even sense it. Instead we have this huge displacement on abortion, the right to life. Never mind the fetus; what about the women over forty? What about what's happening—the terror of which we are unconscious—in our everyday anesthetized lives! And this is only the medical aspect, and a tiny bit of it.

Look at the world of buildings: look at all that has been blown up and torn down, everything solid and well made and with memory—now if that happened in the forties, and it did happen—Dresden, Coventry, Rotterdam, Warsaw, all over—it was called bombing and destruction, and we mourned the loss of our cities. Now we call it development, and the people who do it are called "developers" and "planners." This is Orwell: *1984.* Then it was terror: now, of course, people aren't firebombed and killed, but the civilization—the world of things that are their repositories of memory and beauty and love—these are gone, and I think this is a terror, an unconscious terror, an even worse terror to live in a city that has been destroyed and yet looks marvelous and new. The soul feels its loss but it can't tell what's wrong. It's schizogenetic. We are getting two signals at once, because the actual destruction that is terrible is given wonderful names like "development," "urban renewal"—and then we wonder why the cities with their marvelous buildings and developments are full of crime, as if it were the fault of social factors or unemployment or fatherless families. Well, the crime begins in those buildings, on the drawing boards and planning commissions. One crime begets another. . . .

Of course I'm exaggerating. That's the best way to enter into the extremist mentality: not by taking the opposite stance of reasonable good sense. If you become classic with me, sure enough I'll become romantic. Right now we are attempting to enter the anarchist fantasy, the nihilist fantasy of terrorism. And I'm trying to place it as a reaction to a world soul that is in terror, from all that has been done to its materialization in things. Not just by developers and planners, but by Christianity and Descartes and Newton and by science and the universities . . . our whole tradition has declared matter and material things to be evil and dead to begin with. You've studied philosophy; you know how much serious time is spent proving the reality of the external world. Imagine having to prove what every animal knows! You know that our main tradition says the world has no qualities whatsoever—no color, no taste, no texture, no temperature—and some of that tradition even denies its existence if we aren't there to perceive it. Ascetic world denial, world destruction going on every day in our philosophy classes. Terrorism and nihilism are already in our Western worldview, so the terrorists are the incarnation of the nihilism that is inherent to our system of thinking. . . .

I remember a student of religion telling me about his T.M., his meditation. Somebody in the seminar said, "What about the political world?" He said, "That doesn't matter. Computers can run the political world, the whole country, much more efficiently, and that frees us to pursue enlightenment with meditation." Do you see the complete harmony between central dictatorship, fascism, political callousness, and the self-centeredness of the spiritual point of view? It opened my eyes: I saw the present cults of meditation not so gentle, not so harmless as they like to be, but a vicious bunch of totalitarians. They can't see the individual—which you see only if you look for soul, look with soul. They can't see an individual person, let alone an individual thing. And the terrorist shooting a man coming out his front door, shooting him in the knees, is not seeing that man at all. He is in his spiritual meditation, he is actually a religious fanatic. . . .

They are like those mystics who have wiped out imagination to live in the dark night of the spirit, and their *via negativa* shoots you in the knees—the knees, the very place of kneeling, of genuflection, bending before images. We have to tie terrorism to its roots in our religious consciousness. A terrorist is the product of our education that says that fantasy is not real, that says aesthetics is just for artists, that says soul is only for priests, imagination is trivial or dangerous and for crazies, and that reality, what we must adapt to, is the external world, and that world is dead. A terrorist is a result of this whole long process of wiping out the psyche. Corbin said to me one time, "What is wrong with the Islamic world is that it has destroyed its images, and without these images that are so rich and so full in its tradition, they are going crazy because they have no containers for their extraordinary imaginative power."

(*Inter Views*, 138–142)

We may therefore read the conventional descriptions of the paranoid soul (which I have extracted mainly from the *Diagnostic and Statistical Manual of Mental Disorders* and other standard works used by practitioners in the United States) as also descriptions of the soul of the paranoid state.

"Pervasive and unwarranted suspiciousness and mistrust." "Individuals are hypervigilant and take precautions against perceived threat." "Perceive an unusually wide range of stimuli." "Tend to avoid blame even when it is warranted." "Avoidance of depression." "Question the loyalty of others." "Insist on secrecy." "Severe and critical with others." "Tendency to counter-attack." "Unwilling to compromise." "Intense, but suppressed anger." "Driving, ambitious, aggressive and unusually hostile and destructive." "Generate uneasiness and fear in others." "Often interested in mechanical devices, electronics, and automation." "Avoid group activities unless in a dominant position." "Avoid surprise by virtually anticipating it." "Dread . . . passive surrender." "Friends are constantly tested . . . until they withdraw or actually become antagonistic." "Inordinate fear of losing power to shape events in accordance with their own wishes." "Transformation of internal tension into external tension." "Continuous state of total mobilization." "Giving in to external domination and giving in to internal pressure involve a threat." "Fear of being tricked into surrendering some element of self-determination." "Generally uninterested in art or aesthetics." "Rarely laugh." "Lack of a true sense of humor." "What looks like comfortable familiarity . . . seems like an imitation. . . . It is not friendly; it is only designed to look friendly." "Keenly aware . . . of who is superior or inferior." "They disdain people seen as weak, soft, sickly, or defective."

To hear these descriptions as pertaining to the soul of the Soviet or the American state literalizes "political" into party politics, *parteiisch*, grasping only a part. Instead, we need to hear these descriptions as pertaining to politics and government as such so as to recognize the inherent paranoia in the soul of the state as such. The deepest problem of statecraft is how to govern the inherent paranoia of government so that its symptoms not exacerbate into corrupt tyranny and Byzantine paralysis, symptoms such as secret police, loyalty oaths and lie detection, electronic surveillance, fear of weakness, systemized defenses and predictions (domino theory), and the absence of those soul qualities, humor, aesthetics and softness replaced by grand eschatological ideals: order, peace, humanity, fraternity, rights and God.

Given this inherent unconscious paranoia, there will be a need for a projected fantasized enemy and fantastical defenses against the fantasized enemy. Situations will always be valued by constructs of strength and weakness, winning and losing. Demand for unconditional surrender and the fear of it will be paramount. Treaties based on compromise will be all but impossible to negotiate. A nation in league with others will be forced—whenever it becomes unable to dominate the group—to veto or withdraw. The potential for open hostility is ever present and will be denied. Official denial will be essential to maintaining a government "above suspicion" and true to its idealizations. There will be little interest in art or aesthetics, and when government should intervene then the aesthetic tends to be suborned as state art in service of national resolve. Even the most solicitously conducted foreign relations will tend to generate uneasiness and fear in others. Defense against depression will motivate ever-increasing defenses. The disdain for the weak, sickly and defective will bring to the fore that contemporary, though ever-recurring, conflict between security and compassion (guns vs. butter, swords vs. plowshares), between the burden of armaments for defense and the burden of welfare for the failing. Owing to the fear of dependency, self-sufficiency will be idealized into an isolation called *splendid*.

Above all else will be mistrust and expectations of deceit between the governed and their government, requiring watchdog committees, bureaus of investigation, advocacies of every sort of reform, since paranoid suspicion is inherent to the very soul of state. Not only will the state mistrust the foreign (xenophobia), but within its borders also the alien, the subculture and the minority—unless it be "strong," thereby necessitating minority pressure groups and division of the body politic into rivalrous single-issue or monomanic constituencies. The more rigidly demanding government is of the governed, and vice versa, the more suspicions of corruption abound, particularly suspicions regarding "security," and the more information gathering and storing become prized and litigation the mode of decision. For, the negative relation with mercurius results in that basic proposition of all paranoia: whatever is hidden is harmful (hence revelation equals security), requiring continuous scanning, hypervigilance toward the food we eat, the reports we hear, the contracts we sign. Exposé and cover-up become the *modus operandi*—our theological paradigm of revelation and concealment in the political sphere.

Despite the promulgation of the nation-state by the nation-state, its inherent paranoia fosters mistrust in the very institutions which are its pillars including the validity of the city and the calling of politics. The welfare of the citizens and the institutions which serve the common good become secondary, owing to the primary confusion of welfare with security, the common good with national strength, or "military needs." (It should be evident that I am referring not only to the contemporary world, but to the nation-states from Assyria through Rome, and others analyzed by Toynbee.) When the noble institutions of political life, such as political rhetoric, the providential role of leadership, public office and public service, fall prey to paranoid systematization, then the great images of justice, prudence, equity, community, and the like, dangle down from heaven unreceived, the containing shapes for the archetypal powers in disarray. All the while, obsessed by its delusional need for security, the paranoid state takes recourse in defense mechanisms of projection and reaction-formation, that is, increased scanning for enemies, terrorists and defectors (defectives), with policies sponsored not by initiative which is paralyzed by ambivalence (immobility combined with bellowing), but which are rationalized as "purely" defensive reactions to threat.

Threat belongs to what Jung calls the end of the *aeon* (*CW* 9, ii, p. ix); The Book of Revelations announces apocalyptic catastrophe. We live in a *Zeitgeist* of threat, in a soul state and political state of paranoia. This has been scripturely revealed and is being confirmed politically in the Soviet state of mind (ever homaging the twenty million who died defending against the last Western invasion) and the American (ever defending against penetration into the body politic by emissaries of the Evil Empire—colored pinko, terrorists and spies). Threat of catastrophe justifies the measures taken against threat, thereby making the menace ever more literal. ". . . the fear of catastrophe is most likely to elicit the syndrome." Worse: the syndrome requires catastrophe to fulfil its own prophecy. The vicious circle of paranoid psychology is the present political reality.

("Paranoia," 49–52)

EROS

and Eros who is love, handsomest,
who breaks the limb's strength,
who in all gods, in all human beings
overpowers the intelligence,
and all their shrewd planning.
—HESIOD, *Theogony*

9

Mythology
as Family

The soul searches everywhere for the myths that will nourish it. For millennia people have looked at trees, springs, caves, mountains, wheels, tall buildings, strong men, lovely women, and animals of all kinds and have found the sparks of myth. Fantasy weaves around these things and ripens into myth. Later, scholars sometimes try to explain myth by reducing it to the originating object, but they get it backward. It is myth that is significant to human experience, not the object that sparked fantasy.

It's difficult to apply this mythological viewpoint to the family. We have been thoroughly educated into thinking of the family as a literal sociological and psychological entity. Nevertheless, the family that is the concern of many of James Hillman's essays is the mythic, archetypal family.

It's possible to look at anything through the image of family. The image itself continually draws on our actual experience of family, but it is not about the actual family. The family serves as metaphor, as a special lens through which we can see certain relations and patterns. Even in actual families, images of family members do not always coincide with literal expectations. A father or brother in a family may evoke maternal qualities, the mother a paternal tone, and so on.

Our daily language often reflects this fantasy family. Industries and corporations speak of a family of companies or products. Unions and other organizations call themselves brotherhoods and sisterhoods. We speak casually of mother figures and father figures. Hillman's writing on the family examines subtle aspects of this metaphoric family.

Hillman's earlier essays explored family members as myth: the abandoned child, the hero's mother, the senex, the puer. These family personalities were seen as types or figures for ways of being.

One of the problems in thinking about family mythology is the tendency to forget that even as we think we are always in a particular myth. Even psychological analysis is done through a particular mythic pair of eyes. It is easy to fall into the senex when condemning youth as irresponsible and self-destructive. Some people naturally slip into a maternal complex whenever they encounter a child. A puer might easily discuss the senex with apparent objectivity and yet, from the puer viewpoint, make subtle negative judgments about conservatism or slowness.

Hillman helps us get some distance on these unconscious habits derived from the mythical figures of family. For example, he warns against an element of emptiness in the puer's charm, and he suggests that senex melancholy might be a way toward imagination.

These essays on family members also attempt to move us out of conventional and therefore unreflected biases. Hillman does not accept the commonly presented view that consciousness is a young male hero battling for independence from a smothering mother. He does not see the child as a phase we grow out of, or as a shadowless source of creativity. He criticizes fantasies of personal growth and warns that we cannot enjoy the benefits of the eternal child unless we also tolerate the childishness and dependence that come along with it.

Hillman also closely studies relations among the members of the archetypal family. He looks for polarities that suggest what is sometimes called a split archetype. From a certain point of view, puer and senex are part of the same archetypal formation. For instance, one solution to senex rigidity and authoritarianism in an organization or in government might involve accomodating some puer elements, some experimentation and re-visioning, rather than valuing only order and tradition.

Implied, however, in Hillman's approach is an avoidance of compensatory moves. He has frequently warned against the dangers of compensation in any oppositionalist view of the psyche. Therefore, in a case of a destructive senex complex, it might be better to deepen and enrich the senex element than to compensate by trying to force carefree spontaneity. It is the troublesome family member that needs closer attention, not some other figure.

In his essay on Oedipus, Hillman does not follow Sigmund Freud literally, but he acknowledges Freud's great contribution in raising family to the level of myth. By re-visioning Freud's mythic reading of the family story, Hillman takes his portrait of the archetypal family even further. Along the way, he develops shadow aspects of the family with a precision one rarely finds in psychologies of shadow. For example, he points out specific psychological values of the negative father. The destructive, withholding father destroys idealized images in the son or daughter and also initiates the children into their own shadows. Negativity is neither denied nor repressed; it is shown to have an important place in the relations of the family members.

Even incest is treated as a matter for the gods, as a mythic phenomenon. Incest brings out so many reactive feelings, so many fantasies of blame and rescue, that it is difficult to perceive the deep fantasies there. But Hillman sees incest as an eternally present, archetypal transgression of limited, restrained consciousness, a transcending of the limits we place on desire out of too narrow an appreciation of eros.

As soon as a child is born it is immediately woven into a mythical order of baby girl, or little brother, or special and divine child, or ugly duckling. And, every mother or father is absorbed into the larger figure of mythical parent, which gives to the actual mother or father such fearful authority and expectations of safety and comfort. If we look plainly, we see literal fathers, mothers, and children. But if we were to look with imagination, we would find the mythic family.

Hillman's psychology of the family challenges the literalistic longing in us for simple solutions. The family we experience is the imagined family. That imaginal family, weaving its way into many aspects of life, requires attention. In what kind of imagination is the person who abuses a child? What effect does the chairperson's mythic family have on the workings of an organization? Where is the mythic family in a compulsion to drink, to eat, or not to eat?

Family, as a whole or in its many members, is an entire symbol system in itself. It is a far-reaching, deeply placed mythology. No wonder Freud saw the family as the fundamental myth of adulthood. Hillman serves the family myth by drawing it farther from its base in the actual family to the realm of pure metaphor.

FAMILY

We are born into a family and, at the last, we rejoin its full extension when gathered to the ancestors. Family grave, family altar, family trust, family secrets, family pride.

Our names are family names, our physiognomies bear family traits and our dreams never let us depart from home—father and mother, brother and sister—from those faces and those rooms. Even alone and only ourselves, we are also always part of them, partly them. . . .

Where does family fit in the modern myth of individual independence? That myth says home is what you leave behind. Moving on means moving out. You can't go home again—unless after failure or divorce. Women want careers, downtown, where the action is. Men long for something more, undefined, but most surely *not* more family. Marriages and family founding, especially foundings of large families, are more and more countered by separations, living apart, single-parent households, divorces. Generations divided; children in day care; elders in Arizona. The place where one is most likely to be killed is at home, both perpetrator and victim, family members.

Yet family has been battered by more than these sociological developments. It has taken an even worse beating from the notion of development itself. Nothing has abused the family more than our psychological theories of development, with their myth of individual independence.

Family, so goes the developmental tale, is only the beginning, a necessary evil, which like all beginnings must be left behind. An adult has grown up, declared his independence, and his life and liberty are dedicated to the pursuit of his own happiness. In the United States a newborn infant is believed to be so symbiotically fused with its mother that every effort must be made to develop its ability to separate, to stand on its own as early as it can. In Japan a newborn infant is believed to be so utterly alien that every effort must be made to enfold it within the human community as early as possible. Two opposed trajectories of development. Neither is right or wrong. Both are living myths, *myths* because they are lived unconsciously as truths and have long-term consequences.

Psychoanalysis has swallowed whole the myth of individual development away from family. Everyone who buys an hour of analysis buys into this myth called "strengthening the ego." The first steps of any current treatment in mental hygiene (brain washing?) uncover the family romance, as it is called, which, in the widest sense, refers to the damaging fantasies arising from an individual's relations within the family. Notice here the focus on the independent ego; the family represents merely the limits imposed by genetic nature or environmental nurture, a restrictive influence on personal growth. Other cultures would not imagine the individual over and against family. Where other cultural myths dominate, an individual is always perceived as a family member. Our myth, however, insists that ego is strengthened and full personality achieved away from familial ties and pressures.

Psychology has even invented secondary embellishments to make its myth of individual independence more compelling. (Otherwise a person might naively suppose that the family pulls and pressures are what other cultures regard as filial bonds, kinship love, family pride, parental sacrifice.) Therefore, psychology has discovered an entire demonology within family: the irremediable envy of sibling rivalry between brothers and sisters, castration threats by fathers, disguised cannibalism by sons, devouring mothers and schizogenetic mothers, as well as omnipotent, amoral, polymorphously perverse children. These are only some of the denizens of the deeps in family life. Of course, therefore, maturing, coping and handling have come to mean freedom from family. And of course psychology finds itself justified to go right into the home to exorcise by means of family therapy the creatures that its myth has created.

Is it too much to assert that the most devastating effect of Western psychology is neither the reductive sexualization of the mind nor the pseudoreligion of self-centeredness, but rather its deliberate rupture of the great chain of generations, which it has accomplished by means of its myth of individual development toward independence? Not honor your father and mother, but blame them and you will come out strong. . . .

The overwrought, exhausting difficulties that consume family life indicate that something important is going on. Any big emotion signals value; the task is to discover the gold in the sludge. Let's see what we can recover from [four] typically emotional moments in family life.

False identity: During childhood, traits of personality are identified and one's identity begins to form partly in accordance with the perceptions of others. "Gilly's a real tomboy, a stringbean who only has time for animals." (Will Gilly ever marry? Will she become a lesbian or a veterinarian?) "Billy can't keep out of trouble. I can't trust him out of my sight." (Will Billy ever hold down a decent job? Might he end up in prison?) "Milly was the quietest baby, always smiling and such a charmer." (Will Milly stay home with her parents, keeping them happy, or get pregnant at fifteen?)

From these sorts of family fantasies two contradictory clichés emerge: "No one knows you better than your family," and "My family can't see me at all." The division of "goods" between Gilly, Billy and Milly keeps them in family-determined roles that seem, as time goes on, to be false identities. Was I really a tomboy or was I only living out what my mother wanted to be herself? Am I really a charmer or was I only placating my father?

Discovering whether these perceptions are true or false, that illusion of finding a real identity independent of the family fantasy, is far less rewarding than is the recognition that within the family a personal myth begins to take shape, the myth that forms one's identity. By identity here I mean identifiable reactions, habits, styles. One finds oneself inside a myth, which is neither true nor false, but simply the precondition for fitting one into the family drama as a recognizable character.

Moreover, if there are no pronounced family fantasies, the drama doesn't work, and we flounder about in that strangely loveless limbo that psychology calls an "identity crisis." Family love expresses itself by means of these fantasies of "what I want you to become" and "what I am proud of you for." These fantasies of identity show that someone is noticing traits, habits, styles. Whether a person lives into the myth or rebels against it, there must first be a myth.

Relatives and in-laws: Most lives are spent among likes—similar budgets, similar age spreads, and gaps, similar tastes and vocabularies. The people whom we choose to be with do not truly force us beyond our usual psychological boundaries. In the family, however, just where you might expect to be with those most like you, you encounter instead a collection of the strangest folk! At any large family gathering there come together the most extraordinary behaviors and most incompatible opinions, yet all this is in the same clan.

Voltaire supposedly said, "Nothing human is alien to me." Relatives and in-laws provide the opportunity of extending our human understanding to what strikes us as alien, indeed. Where else, how else would one ever spend an evening with a man from Orange County who pays dues to the Klan, or with a math professor who interprets signals from outer space, or a junkyard dealer who did time in the state penitentiary. And the manners, the clothes, the bodies!

This is more than "alien," Voltaire. This is downright outlandish, freakish. Here we realize that large family affairs, rather than being scenes of convention, are actually performances of high comedy, outrageously funny, which also serve to encourage one's own peculiarities.

After all, as an in-law and relative yourself, you too appear, and are, rather freakish to the others. The attentiveness you pay to the in-laws and relatives at such reunions works both ways, for rarely are you yourself heard out so patiently, with such curiosity. Family seems to evoke a profound curiosity in each of its members about the others, especially the more distantly related or more peculiarly entwined. Gossip abounds; people spill the beans and try to catch up on what has happened "since we last met"—a catching up that goes beyond recording births and deaths. Shadows come rushing out of the closet and join the party without moral opprobrium. A large family reception receives, *in magnificentia et gloria*, all shadows; all events, whether good news or bad, associated with family members, are magnified and glorified, thereby extending the size of the family's heart. The measure of a family's magnanimity is not what it gives to charity but rather its capacity to shelter the shadows of its members. Charity begins at home. We each feel this heart extending when, for instance, a little pride arises over the naming as "best insurance salesman in the county" a seemingly unremarkable young man who is, nonetheless, married to your great niece. . . .

Family meals: The sign "Home Cooking" might still bring in some customers, but for many the family table was the place of trauma. Studies in family disorders accuse the evening meal of being the major focus of household tension. Here, at table, family fights over money, politics or morals are most likely to break out, and later eating patterns—the rhythms of chewing, swallowing, breathing and talking; the intermissions between silence and noise; the very notion of what constitutes "good" food—take on their definitive forms. Here, too, gross food disorders like anorexia and bulimia often appear first. Whether the atmosphere at meals be boisterous and competitive, or chaotic with phoning and television, or gravely formalized, tension is always on the menu.

Tension at the start of a meal belongs with the instinct of appetite. Just go to the zoo at feeding time and watch the animals pace and snarl, or ask a good Italian waiter about getting the *prima* (first course) on the table quickly. Meals are meant to start fast and conclude in digestive leisure. Tension therefore belongs to the moment of sitting down at table, and not only for animal reasons. Tension arises as an unconscious recognition of the sacramental nature of this family act. Grace overtly acknowledges this sacramental tension, and so do all the many rituals that go with family meals: fixed places and dinner "on time," the rituals of clean hands, of setting places and clearing the table, and the endless attempts to mollify the tension with light music, dimmer lights, and rules concerning what is appropriate to talk about at table. All this elaborate etiquette, and every family will have some rituals even if utterly disguised as "just dig in," attempts to propitiate the archetypal forces that gather invisibly around the family meals and are ready to explode civilized conventions at the most innocuous provocation.

Going back home: Whether from prison camp after a war or just taking the bus home for Thanksgiving, homecoming is fraught with dreadful anticipation. Opening the front door releases overwhelming emotions—and also the counterforce of repression against those emotions that so often characterizes the stifled atmosphere of returning.

Here we must remember that going home is always going *back* home. Returning is essentially a regressive act in keeping with an essential function of family: to provide shelter for the regressive needs of the soul. Everyone needs a place to crawl and lick his wounds, a place to hide and be twelve years old, inept and needy. The bar, the bed, the boardroom and the buddies do not meet the gamut of needs, which always limp along behind the myth of independent individuality. Something always remains undeveloped and this piece needs to "go back home" as country-and-western lyrics often enough affirm.

Going back may mean sleeping till two in the afternoon, or taking refuge in the bathroom, crying with mom in the kitchen, or just complaining as do the grandparents who fall ill during every visit. Going home, at whatever age, offers going back, regression. And the fight against family during these return trips is therefore a displacement of the fight against regression. We don't want to admit the weaknesses in our characters and the hungers in our desires. We don't want to admit that we have not "grown up," and so blame the family both for bringing out our worst and then for not indulging it enough. Meanwhile: that strange sense of consciousness ebbing away, going down the family drain.

The debilitating energy loss strikes everyone alike as if a communal power outage. Everyone caught in repeating, and resisting, old patterns. Nothing changed, after all these years! No one can get out even for a walk to break the spell, the whole family sinking deeper into the upholstery (and television has little to do with it and may even be, in such moments, the household god who saves). These moments attest to the capacity of family for sharing—French anthropology used to speak of a *participation mystique*—in a common soul or psychic state, and for containing the regressive needs of the soul.

No one is at fault, no one is kicked out, and no one can be helped. In the paralysis lies the profoundest source of acceptance. Grandpa can go on grumbling, brother attacking the administration, sister introvertedly attending her exacerbating eczema, and mother go on covering up with solicitous busy-ness. Everyone goes down the drain because family love allows family pathology, an immense tolerance for the hopeless shadow in each, the shadow that we each carry as permanent part of our baggage and that we unpack when we go back home.

These [four] bad moments are symptomatic of what lies at the root of family problems. Not the failure to "relate," not the breakdown of the old patriarchal model, not even the incurably freakish, especially depressive, pathologies that make their home at home, but rather the root lies in the archetypal nature of family itself. As an archetypal reality, the experience of family feels so often "unreal" because family is permeated through and through with eternal exaggerations, an impossible too-muchness or mythic dimension, which is the stuff of the symptoms we suffer and also the stuff of much of Western culture's stories, novels, and dramas. And this mythical exaggeration is at work in even the most conventionalized, urban, eat-and-run, unconnected, first-name parents, upward-mobile, areligious unit of consumers called *family*. Family is less a rational place than a mythical one, and the expectation of finding rational reality at home is precisely what makes us condemn it as "unreal." Attempts at unambiguous communication, reasonable discussion of problems and structuring a new paradigm, all overlook the fundamentals at the source of family life: the deep-seated and indestructible complexes of the psyche—once called daimones, ghosts and ancestors—whose place is in the home.

The notorious "nuclear" family of statistics, sermons and advertisements—two parents, two siblings, a family car and a pet—does not correspond with the Latin word from which family derives. "This famous word . . . is inseparable from the idea of land settlement, and is therefore essentially the house itself, with the persons living in it. . . . And thus the religion of the *familia* will be a religion of practical utility, of daily work, of struggle with perils. . . . It is not the worship of an idea of kinship" (W. W. Fowler, *The Religious Experience of the Roman People*, Macmillan).

Familia, familias to the Romans meant primarily "a house and all belonging to it," "a household establishment, family servants, domestics (not = family, i.e., wife and children)." Neither parentage nor descent, not even bloodkinship within the clan (for which the Romans had the word *gens*) determined the use of the word *family;* place did. By Romans, here, I mean the entire civilized Western world and its language that lives on in our Latinate roots.

Because *familia* connoted a physical house and all belonging to it as goods, fortune, inheritance, the more accurate part of the fantasy of the American nuclear family may be the estate car and the household pet. In fact, a domesticated animal was considered often a familiar. Living together in familiarity as a psychoeconomic organism—such is the meaning of family. Even the Greek word *oikonomia* (from which come economy and economics) means household management or keeping house. The family is a function of the house, rather than vice versa, where *house* is the concrete container of multiple familiarities and intimacies, the domesticated (from *domus* = "house") world of belongings—what belongs to us and to what we belong—and where "belonging" also means what is fitting, appropriate and customary.

This etymological revelation suggests a far broader sense of family, giving primary emphasis to the idea of a supportive psychic system under the same roof, whether farm, kibbutz, or a condominium block. This broader sense includes the notions of service and participation, a membership investing in and benefiting from a larger household. Filial piety and brotherly love seem irrelevant to this household, yet it does include all the things belonging to an estate: animals, goods and furnishings. Your family is your furniture in more than a metaphoric sense. Little wonder that such bitterness can erupt over dividing the family dishes after divorce or death; or that dreams of the old family car can continue to haunt long after the car itself was trashed.

Various gods and goddesses lived with the ancient family: Vesta at the hearth (*focus* is the Latin word) who must be acknowledged first and daily else the central bonding flame might go out; Janus at the gates so that one remembered the different faces required for inside and outside; the three different gods of the doorway (of the door, the hinges and the threshold) who prevented bad spirits from entering the domestic interior; the Lar or Lares who were the ever present and remembered ghosts of the household's dead. (Food fallen to the floor at a meal was at once taboo, belonging now to these familiars of the underworld.) And there were the Penates, or the wee ones of the cupboards, without whom Old Mother Hubbard might find not even a bone. The ancient home gave plenty of place to the invisibles that live in a family, propitiating and domesticating its daimones, which it acknowledged as rightfully belonging.

Above all these was Juno (Hera in Greece) who presided like a stately, powerful Roman matron over the psychic and material well-being of the household. In Juno was combined instinct and institution: marriage both as that coupling urge for permanent bonding and as a societal stability. The regular order of life within the household and within the bodies of the women in the household was regulated by the calendar; the first day of each month, the calends, was dedicated to Juno. Little houses made of clay were devotional objects in her cult, and heroes of myth—and most great Greek heroes were sent on their way because of Hera—were recognized as such not only by their deeds but also by the trophies they brought back home. Ulysses felt himself a failure because after a twenty-year absence he arrived home unclothed and without spoils. His family, by the way, included his old nurse and his old dog. Again, that emphasis upon ties beyond blood, and upon animals and things. . . .

The idea of family service, however, extends beyond the maintenance of its property, the heirlooms and records, keeping anniversaries and celebrations, beyond the daily labor devoted to the well-being of the household, those chores that belong to "homemakers." One also serves an invisible family, as if an archetypal force. With the passing of time a sense of its power grows within one's psyche, like the movements of its skeleton inside one's flesh, which keeps one in servitude to patterns entombed in our closest attitudes and habits. From this interior family we are never free. This service keeps us bonded to the ancestors. How we are able to live these habits and attitudes, and inherited propensities to specific diseases, our own morbidity, provides each person with an individual way of honoring "our fathers and our mothers."

I have been attempting to present family as supreme metaphor for our life on earth because it presents that force of human attachment to a dwelling place, of domestication of the savage and the nomad, of honoring the invisible, the demonic and the dead, of making intimate and familiar and "owned" the persons, animals and things of this world, taking them home to the hearth, ourselves as long-term caretakers in bondage to our fate on earth, playing out the comedy of human continuity.   ("Extending the Family," 6–11)

We cannot go home again, not even as repentant prodigals. Nor can we moderns, whose consciousness is characterized by uprootedness, exile, and an "antifamily" bias, attempt to restore a model of the nineteenth-century family by repeating it in our own lives. The reconstitution of family can be based on neither the former metaphor of parent and child nor the new one of a democratic "functional" family. To recreate family in our generation, eros and psyche must have the possibility of meeting in the home; this would favor soul-making and give an altogether different perspective to family relationships. This perspective looks less to the hierarchical connections of parent-child and the issues of early childhood, authority, and rebellion and more to the soul connection, as between brother and sister. Mother-son (Oedipus) and father-daughter (Electra) expose only half of the dual conjunction; where concern for soul is paramount, a relationship takes on more the nature of the brother-sister pair. Compare the *soror* in alchemy and the appellations of "Brother" and "Sister" in religious societies. Compare also the symbolic inter-relations in the *I Ching*, where six of the eight hexagrams are "sons" and "daughters," which, to one another, are brothers and sisters. Kinship libido, which, as Jung points out, is behind incest phenomena, would flow on the brother-sister model into the mutuality of soul-making rather than regressively toward parents. As J. E. Harrison says *(Prolegomena to the Study of Greek Religion)*, eros is also the dance, and the dance is not a hierarchical phenomenon. It takes place between partners. The implications for psychotherapy of the family problem are obvious: if soul-making is the aim, then the equality of the brother-sister relation must be paramount, else eros and psyche cannot constellate. Paternalism and maternalism become clinically unsound if soul-making is the aim. Clinics themselves still retain an unconscious predilection for the old model of family, but the obituary of this family form was written early in the century by Galsworthy and Proust, and by Mann in *Buddenbrooks.* An indication of the new model of family is presented in J. D. Salinger's work. In his Glass family, the brother-sister relations are primary, and the passionate interest and devotion to each other's psychic life provide an example—even a therapeutic example in *Franny and Zooey*—of soul-making through the constellation of eros and psyche in the home. Furthermore, a model of family where eros can meet psyche gives new opportunity to that woman who can no longer fill the nineteenth-century model of motherhood, that breasted, nourishing comforter. The woman of today who is sometimes called the anima, *puella,* or *betaira* type finds that her natural interest is in the relationships with her family as individual people, her interest constellating eros and psyche. *(Myth of Analysis,* 57–58, n. 56)

The infusion of Greek myth into the medical, academic, commercial and often Jewish Vienna of the 1890s, Freud's world and the world of his clientele, brought to family a transparency beyond bourgeois materialism and its hysteria. While Oedipus collapses into

Hansi down the street, there glimmers through little Hans the radiance of Oedipus, Sophocles, Greece, and the gods. As Freud says: "Hans was really a little Oedipus who wanted to have his father 'out of the way,' to get rid of him, so that he might be alone with his handsome mother and sleep with her."

Really, that is Freud's word.

What is *really* at work in the case is myth; what is really going on in family is myth: to feel myth in the daily world, just stay home with the family. Of course, it drives one crazy.

By returning family back to mythical figures, Freud performed an *epistrophé*. He reimagined our desires, our phobias, our childhoods. He relocated the human world in the mythical imagination. The world parents of creation myths became the parental world: the parental world became our culture's creation myth, at once personal, secular and historical. Parents gain supreme authority in the generation of the psychic cosmos. Whether actual, whether imagos, whether archetypal Mother and Father, parents become the great dominants. A father's terrifying authority arises—not because of introjected conventional religion which Freud abjured or because of patriarchal social norms—but because of myth: in the father is Laius and Apollo and the myth embroiling Laius, and in the mother is the queen, the throne, the city.

Ever since, psychoanalysis performs this *epistrophé*—if we read it in this light. Ever since, psychoanalysts are the myth preservers in our culture. They go on ritualizing the oedipal tale, go on affirming the cosmic power of parents and childhood for discovering identity. By divining the parental world each patient discovers a budding Oedipus in the soul. We believe we are what we are because of our childhoods in family, but this only because the actual family is "really" Oedipal, that is mythical. Even as actual, sociological, statistical family life dissolves, psychoanalysis retains the myth. Early years and repressed memories are so fateful, we believe, in our culture, because psychoanalysis dominates our cult of souls and Oedipus is the dominant myth practiced in the cult. Depth psychology believes in myth, practices myth, teaches myth. That myth hides from recognition and lies disguised in literal and secular case histories is appropriate to the very myth they teach—the tale of Oedipus, its disguises and pursuit of self-recognition. . . .

We emerge into life as creatures in a drama, scripted by the great storytellers of our culture. And as budding Oedipus we immediately transpose the stock figures of mom and dad, or the absent mom or dad as is mainly the situation today, or aunt or stepfather or day-care lady—whoever plays their stand-ins—into Jocasta and Laius, ennobling desire, parents, memory, forgetting, foretelling, early family scenes, early abandonments, abuses and mutilations, little boy and little girl wishes, and endowing these small, preinitiatory events with salient inevitable determinacy.

But none of this is literal. We must see this clearly: none of it can be taken at only this one level of historical fact. Not what happened in childhood, not your recollections of lust and hatred, not even what is recalled or not recalled and buried, nor your parents as such—all these emotions and configurations are ways in which we are remythologized. And that is why these emotions and configurations carry such importance. They are doors to Sophocles and Sophocles himself a door. Their importance rising not from historical events but mythical happenings that as Sallustius said never happened but always are, as fictions.

For the same reason Freud's basic theory still dominates, and will. It too is myth, wearing the costume appropriate to the nigredo consciousness of science's materialism. What holds us to Freud, provoking countless retellings and commentaries such as this one now, is not the science in the theory but the myth in the science. Freud wrote to Einstein in 1932:

It may perhaps seem to you as though our theories are a kind of mythology and, in the present case, not even an agreeable one. But does not every science come in the end to a kind of mythology like this? Cannot the same be said today of your own Physics?

And individual patients struggling with self-knowledge are so convinced by the fictions of childhood because they are Oedipus who finds who he is by finding out about his infancy, its wounds and abandonment. The entire massive apparatus of counseling, social work, developmental psychology—therapy in every form—continues rehearsing the myth, practicing the play in its practices.

("Oedipus," 266–269)

FATHER: SATURN AND SENEX

*S*enex is the Latin word for "old man." We find it still contained within our words *senescence, senile* and *senator*. In Rome the time of the senex was "from the latter half of the fortieth year onward." It could apply to old woman too. But as we shall inquire into this idea, senex will come to mean more than old person or old age. The imaginal notions condensed into this short term extend far beyond whatever personal ideas we might have of oldness, beyond our concerns with old age, old people and the processes of time in personal life. Perhaps, however, at this first level, where the senex affects our lives and aging we can grasp its import most easily. . . .

As natural, cultural and psychic processes mature, gain order, consolidate and wither, we witness the specific formative effects of the senex. Personifications of this principle appear in the holy or old wise man, the powerful father or grandfather, the great king, ruler, judge, ogre, counselor, elder, priest, hermit, outcast and cripple. Some emblems are the rock, the old tree, particularly oak, the scythe or sickle, the timepiece and the skull. Longings for superior knowledge, imperturbability, magnanimity express senex feelings as does intolerance for that which crosses one's systems and habits. The senex also shows strongly in ideas and feelings about time, the past, and death. Melancholy, anxiety, sadism, paranoia, anality, and obsessive memory ruminations reflect this archetype. Moreover, the main image of God in our culture—omniscient, omnipotent, eternal, seated and bearded, a ruler through abstract principle of justice, morality and order, a faith in words yet not given to self-explanation in speech, benevolent but enraged when his will is crossed, removed from the feminine (wifeless) and the sexual aspect of creation, up high with a geometric world of stars and planets in the cold and distant night of numbers—this image depicts a senex god, a god imaged through the senex archetype. *The high god of our culture is a senex god; we are created after this image with a consciousness reflecting this structure.* One face of our consciousness is inescapably senex. . . .

The temperament of the senex is cold, which can also be expressed as distance. Senex consciousness is outside of things, lonely, wandering, a consciousness set apart and outcast. Coldness is also cold reality, things just as they are, dry data, unchangeable cold hard facts. And coldness is cruel, without the warmth of heart and heat of rage, but slow revenge, torture, exacting tribute, bondage. As lord of the nethermost, Saturn views the world from the outside, from such depths of distance that he sees it all "upside down," and to this view the structure of things is revealed. He sees the irony of truth within the words, and the city from the cemetery, the bones below the game of skin. Thus the senex view gives the abstract architecture and anatomy of events, plots and graphs, presenting principles of form rather than connections, interrelations, or the flow of feeling.

The senex emblem of the skull signifies that every complex can be envisioned from its death aspect, its ultimate psychic core where all flesh of dynamics and appearances is stripped away and there is nothing left of those hopeful thoughts of what it might yet become, the "final" interpretation of the complex as its end. The end gives the pessimistic and cynical reflection as counterpart to puer beginnings.

⚜

The lead of Saturn is the downward and inward pull of gravity into subjectivity. The plumb line drops ever deeper, straight to the grave, and below, to time past and the underworld spirits. The inward and downward pull into oneself and one's death implies that the senex is the chief force at work in some descriptions of individuation. The end goal is often presented in senex imagery: isolation, unity, stones, cosmic systems and geometric diagrams, and especially the structured mandala and the Wise Old Man. Even "wholeness through integration" can reflect Saturn who ate all the other gods, swallowing his children. Furthermore, the method of arrival at these goals is also determined by senex fantasies: depression (not inflation), suffering (not laughter) and introversion and imagination require turning away from the world. At the same time the ego is to be stable, ordered and strong. There is a distinct stress on numbers as archetypal root structures, a belief in compensation as a psychic law (karma, retribution, revenge, and the balance of opposites belong to Kronos-Saturn), and a profound occupation with archaeology, history, religion, prophecy and outcast or occult phenomena.

⚜

The relation of Saturn to sexuality is also dual: on the one hand, he is patron of eunuchs and celibates, being dry, cold and impotent; on the other hand, he is represented by the dog and the lecherous goat. Certain kinds of sexual disorder could be controlled by means of lead, according to Albertus Magnus: "The effect of lead is cold and constricting, and it has a special power over sexual lust and nocturnal emissions . . ." Here, the senex constricts; yet it also imagines with the inordinate goatish desire of the "dirty old man." In either case, sexuality is at its extremes, transcending the normal and expected, so that these characteristics no longer refer to actual sexuality but to a fantasy of it. The dog and goat describe the impersonality of the desire, its commonplace and uninhibited earthiness, all eros-sentimentality shed. Impotence, on the other hand, prevents even the dog and goat level of connection, isolating the person and the drive itself to purely imaginal happenings. Impotence, like castration, is a pathological disturbance only when one expects sexuality to perform in the normative sense of generation and intercourse, sexuality in the service of life and love. But these are only two of its possible fantasies; sexuality may also be impotent for life and yet have potency in other aspects.

We must ask what is implied when sexuality is powerless to move externally, when it is contained altogether within; what is a man who is not a male, a force without an issue, a lifelessness of that which is generally considered the creative. Impotence as a death in the midst of life opens another avenue of sexual exploration so that senex consciousness offers the complex another kind of sexual possibility, another way of coming to terms with the meaning of its sexuality and of creativity. Without the senex and his inhibiting impotence, sexuality would exhaust itself in exteriority, the copulative delights, the ceaseless generations. . . .

The sexuality of the senex is given a pneumatic source. Its disorders, whether in the form of lechery or of impotence, become ultimately accountable through the *heightened power of imagination*. Senex consciousness presents a sexuality of the *vis imaginativa*, an appreciation of sexual behavior itself as one more form of fantasy. Impotence and lechery are aspects of the imagination first of all; they find their expression in sexuality but in other areas too. So we can look again at the castration of Uranus by his youngest son Kronos, not merely as an emblem of sexual impotence where the old king is dethroned when his fertility is replaced by the usurping heir. The tale tells as well that the reign of the old sky god as a myth maker and creator of imaginal possibilities is over when the sexual aspect of the *vis imaginativa* no longer functions.

If lechery and impotence both originate in the heightened imagination, we may detect in these apparently dissimilar phenomena a latent identity. Commonly, because old men are impotent they, of course, have dirty thoughts. Dirty thoughts are, commonly, inferior substitutes for the "real thing." But turned the other way around "real" sexuality dwindles in order to stimulate dirty thoughts. These fantasies are the sexualization of consciousness, the needed erotic stimulation to fertilize the imagination. The transition to a lecherous spirit and an impotent body is the transition from the normal to the *noetic,* where impotence may become the precondition for a potent imagination. A similar transition can occur through senile memory-loss which opens the way from the normal to the noetic memory, to the remembrance via early childhood of the archetypal as described in Plato's *Meno* and *Phaedo.*

To be filled therefore with lecherous fantasies means Saturn is near, and depression too; these fantasies offer access to this archetypal perspective and to all the complications that come with this senex structure. So, too, with impotence: Aphrodite may not want it, nor Zeus, nor Pan, but its appearance demands that sexuality be re-imagined now through the senex. As senex pertains not only to old people but to a structure of consciousness, so senex sexuality refers not only to the sexual behaviour of old people but to a kind of sexual consciousness, which provides the imaginal background for both impotence and lechery.

Despite the impotence, Saturn retains the attributes of Kronos; he is a fertility god. Saturn invented agriculture; this god of the earth and the peasant, the harvest and the Saturnalia, is ruler of fruit and seed. Even his castrating sickle is a harvesting tool. It would have to be Saturn who invents agriculture: only the senex has the patience equaling that of the soil and can understand the soil's conservation and the conservatism of those who till it; only the senex has the sense of time needed for the seasons and their chronic repetition; the ability to abstract so as to master the geometry of ploughing, the essence of seeds, the profitable counting, the dung, the loneliness and the affectionless objectivized sexuality. . . .

※

Dame Melancholy may also appear as the embodiment and vision of depression, where she brings wisdom, as she did to Boethius, who was betrayed and thrown into prison when not yet forty. There his suicidal melancholy conjured the feminine figure of Wisdom, who dictated to him his *Consolation of Philosophy*. Depression and the awakening of one's genius are inseparable, say the texts. Yet for most of us there is much depression and little genius, little consolation of philosophy, only the melancholic stare—what to do, what to do.

Psychological clichés claim that senex-consciousness is "cut off" from the feminine. But Kronos has mother and wife and daughters (Demeter, Hera, Hestia). Rather than dissociated femininity, this archetype shows a female counterpart—Lua, Dame Melancholy—which mirrors, and is thus indistinguishable from Saturn himself. His mother Ge (Mother Earth) repeats in his sister-wife Rhea, so that Saturn's agricultural, fertility and material functions are reflected by these feminine mirrors. The urge to "build cities" and "mint money," the deep-seated concretization of the senex impulse may very well be taken as an attribute of this mother-sister-wife complex. The *complicatio* of these earth goddesses in Kronos involve the senex in earthiness. Thus senex preoccupation with property, with the things and matters of the established order, its hoarding and its greed, derives not from the "excess of pneuma" and the "exaggerated irritability of the vis imaginativa," that is, Saturn's own native spirit, but rather from the feminine side of this structure, the earth and its materialism to which its ties are reinforced in triplicate.

By showing saturnine traits, senex femininity presents unpleasant, even maleficient, aspects of the anima. Here we meet her mad moodiness, her peculiar fascinations with the occult, or with power and possessions, or with the "way out" things of prisons, sewerage and magic. A state of mind occurs that seems obsessive, not anima and not feminine as we prettily conceive these notions. Senex femininity seems rather the witch side of the mother archetype. As if as we grow older not only do we whine and need helping, but use our infirmity for power. The old man has cut off not his mother, but his father; his mother he has married; they have become one. The senex anima can be so objectionable to ruling consciousness that a life may be, so to speak, dragged into the senex state. One turns against the moody consort and her materializations, attempting indeed to "cut off" the feminine, negating her effects by clinging to the relics of male authority, refusing the natural decomposition of the complexes, refusing that decay emanating through the earth-witch and depression, the senex bride and sister.

Or, to reawaken the puer aspect, the feminine may reappear as an object for complex-compelled falling in love. Enter: the girl of our dreams—Out: old woman, the decay and depression. The falling in love is a phenomenon not only of old age, but of an old attitude. It may occur at any time of life and be occasioned by the loss of any puer aspect. Then one is "ripe for it." It is less a *coniunctio* fantasy, nor even the renewal of the feminine, as much as it is prompted by the lost child and the re-connecting to the puer in oneself. So, the woman becomes Pandora—the first female brought into the all-male kingdom of Kronos—a magical, beautiful box of fantasies and hope for the complex to be rejuvenated, *senilis* to *juvenilis*. The fantasies bring forth Venus from the sea of unconscious emotions, suddenly ebbing and flooding again. Her birth is closely tied with the senex; she is his progeny, his sole creation. Without Kronos and the senex-despair of the complex, Aphrodite and her illusions might never float in off the foam. Venus rose from the sea after being conceived there from the genitals of Uranus that Kronos-Saturn, his son, cut off with his left hand and flung away. A senex act creates her of the seminal stuff of the father.

But these genitals are of the sky god. They are the "upper" aspect of sexuality, sexuality's *fantasy power*. So Venus is born from imaginal froth, the sea-foam of unconscious fantasy. When one attacks sexuality with senex-repression, severing the fathering fantasies of one's own loins, throwing it away left-handedly in the unconscious, it does not cease creating. Sexual fantasies inseminate below the waves, returning in the shape of Venus. Cut-off sexuality goes on living. The images return as the father's daughter: sweet, alluring, aphrodisiacal fantasies bred of the union of sexuality's "upper" genitals and the emotional depths.

Kronos's act fathered other daughters besides Aphrodite; her sisters were dark indeed: the Moira and the Erinyes. The latter—even called "daughters of Kronos"—were death-dealing deities; the former, chthonic powers of the fate portioned to all men and goddesses of death. These mythical sisters of Aphrodite (like the mythical servants of Aphrodite: Custom, Grief, Anxiety) reflect their parentage in senex-consciousness and its underworldly, otherworldly associations. Even the feminine delights that might be promised the old man through a young love come to him sternly and take him to his grave. Oedipus's daughters at the end bring not refreshment and renewal but ease his parting.

🌼

The need for a "second beginning" is often put in creation myths. The first start is wiped out, and the world begins again, after the flood. Gods and heroes have a second birth (Osiris, Dionysus) or two tales are told of their origin, and mystical man is twice born. Psychology has taken this ontological image about two levels of being and two structures of consciousness and laid it out in terms of progressive time: first half and second half of life. But these "halves" are less biological or psychological fact as they are a *mythical description of the two levels on which we live*. Some men live from a "twice-born" state early in their youth; others go through a midlife crisis moving from one to another; others may repeatedly live now one, now the other in alternations. *First half* and *second half* pertain to kinds of consciousness, not to periods.

So the senex may appear in dreams while we are still very young. It manifests as the dream father, mentor, old wise man, to which the dreamer's consciousness is pupil. When accentuated it seems to have drawn all power to itself, paralyzing elsewhere, and a person is unable to take a decision without first taking counsel with the unconscious to await an advising voice from an oracle or vision. Though this counsel may come from the unconscious, it may be as collective as that which comes from the standard canons of the culture. For statements of sagacity and meaning, even spiritual truths, can be bad advice. These representations—elders, mentors, analysts, and old wise men—provide an authority and wisdom that is beyond the experience of the dreamer, "helping" to keep him helplessly dependent. Therefore it tends to have him rather than he it, so that he is driven by an unconscious certainty, making him "wise beyond his years," ambitious for recognition by his seniors and intolerant of his own youthfulness. According to some research the senex figure comes more frequently in the dreams of women than those of young men, further indicating the distance between puer and senex in our present culture. Crucial in this discussion is that senex consciousness may be constellated at any age and in regard to any complex. . . .

("On Senex Consciousness," 146–149, 153, 155–158, 161–162, 164–165)

We find the senex in our solitary taking account, sorting through, figuring out; alone behind the wheel on the way to work; head under the shower, under the dryer; alone at the kitchen table looking down into black coffee, in bed staring into night—the senex mind tying together the unraveled fringes of the day, making order.

Here is our melancholy trying to make knowledge, trying to see through. But the truth is that the melancholy *is* the knowledge: the poison is the antidote. This would be the senex's most destructive insight: our senex order rests on senex madness. Our order is itself a madness.

The old king is crazy old King Lear, and the old wise man, a man mad as the prophet and the geometer, with his obsession of motionless Parmenidean order, mad as the old board chairman with his tables of organization and charts of aggrandizement. As we get older we get crazier, but the senex in our complexes has the foresight to see the mad outcome of each complex. "All true insight is foresight," said Coleridge (in a quote I cannot trace). Thomas Browne *(Religio Medici)* put the progressive madness in the complex in moral language:

But age doth not rectify, but incurvate our natures, turning bad dispositions into worser habits, and (like diseases), brings on curable vices; for every day as we grow weaker in age, we grow stronger in sin. . . . The same vice committed at sixteen, is not the same . . . at forty, but swells and doubles by the circumstances of our ages. . . . Every sin the oftner it is committed, the more it acquireth in the quality of evil; as it succeeds in time, so it proceeds in degrees of badness . . . like figures in Arithmetick, the last stands for more than all that went before it.

Against the foreknowledge of its madness, and against the madness too, senex consciousness builds its establishment of order, system, knowledge, and justice, which again and again breaks down in actuality, for it too is a fantasy of the complex against its accumulating twisted "incurvature." Puer consciousness does not see the madness of the archetype. It moves among the gods like beautiful Ganymede, serving ambrosia, carrying their messages but not reading the horror between the lines. (How long it takes the puer in us to learn to suffer, to stink and shrivel, to find his acid, salt, lye, lead, and dung.) The prophet in senex consciousness, and the measurer, does know what proportions the gods can take and to what madness the archetype can lead with its excess and its infirmity. The establishment is refuge: the realm of ego, of Caesar and senex consciousness, a keep of sanity, and sanity too is a fantasy. The only protection is the dissolution of this fantasy of sanity, and in Joseph Conrad's language the recipe is "immersion in the destructive element" and knowledge of the "horror, the horror," which in this case is Saturn's own special madness, his melancholy. To penetrate the riddle of senex destruction means to go to the heart of darkness.   ("Negative Senex," 85–86)

FATHERS AND DAUGHTERS

Dr. Gene Inborn shall be the patient's name, and we shall analyze from my notes his dream of incest with his daughter. "He felt appalled: shame and horror. No memory of any scene of sexual act or its details [although he was] sure it occurred, [and therefore he] believes on waking that the details had been repressed." To my question where did it happen, he said it wasn't any place specific. About the time, he said, she seemed young, maybe around eleven or twelve, or fourteen. Also, during the dream and while waking from it, he was troubled by the to-him appalling question as to whether he had committed incest actually years ago and had no memory of it.

He worried these questions before, during and after the hour: should he check the facts with her? Would she remember what he didn't; would she want to remember? If he did ask her for corroborating evidence, would this be a seduction, even a compulsion to repeat, as if to make actual in the present what the dream had raised as a possibility in the past? Had he a "faulty" memory? And was the memory trouble a sign of aging, as the incest dream (the first reported in this case) a beginning sign of a senile man's crazy sexual fantasies about young girls? Was the absence of the sexual in the dream a disguise for the absence of sexuality, i.e., impotence? Perhaps the dream was so appalling because he was "losing it"?

Dr. Inborn presented the image of a heavyset, big-footed, slow and reflective man of depressive nature and rather obsessive. He had already been analyzed twice, as a young medical resident and again in a training program. I was now his third or fourth analyst, and he was psychologically intelligent. He carried over into dreams the kinds of interpretative reflections that obsessed his clinical work. The daughter in this case had children of her own, a family he saw once a year at most. He felt fondly attached to her; and his dreams, where she appeared occasionally, showed her image to be a major soul carrier. According to his imagination of her, she read novels, went to lots of movies, wore all sorts of funny shoes, and there was always "music in her house."

The following associations also belong to the case. He remonstrated with himself for having been an "absent father." He never changed her diapers, never bathed her or spanked her, was usually preoccupied at her bedtime, though he sometimes said prayers with her in the dark. He did drive her to school for a while; they did play roughhouse when she had been in a tomboy stage, and earlier when she was small he had pushed her on the playground swings. He had few images of her, more generalized abstractions regarding her. He never had a sexual fantasy of her during those years nor later when she began to go out. He just shoved that out of his mind, or maybe thoughts of her with boyfriends never got into his mind.

Particularly this absence now bothered him. He worried that his having been an absent father was counterphobic to an incest wish or, worse, to a forgotten incest act. Maybe he was "wrong" about the memories of how he was and what he did when she was a child; maybe these memories were "just a reconstruction without a basis in fact." The dream worked in him obsessively as a trauma, even as it made him feel "somehow more alive." His sense of what was real, now and in the past, had been upset radically. . . .

To speak of incest as *archetypal* raises its value to a universal desire, recurrent, ubiquitous, emotionally laden, richly symbolized and inherently shameful as are all desires. *Archetypal* also affirms incest to be eternally present, always there (much as Dr. Inborn believes incest is there even when it is not actually presented in the dream). Its origin lies not in family or tribe; kinship structures may release or ritualize incest, but they do not originate it. Kinship structures and emotions may occur in biological, sociological and psychological families, and so incest may be released or ritualized in many sorts of kinship arrangements. What we see first in fact (kinship) does not mean prior in logic, for *archetypal* also claims that something can be logically prior to the conditions in which it appears even if it never appears apart from those conditions. Incest as *archetypal* can therefore be regarded as sui generis, irreducible, requiring its proper archetypal location in imagination apart from kinship libido, endogamy, regression and the Lung-Layard hypothesis of individuation as internalization through sacrifice (*CW* 16 & 5). Incest as *archetypal* prevents us from assigning it a purpose before we have bracketed out the various purposes incest and its taboo may serve in the humanistic contexts of biology, sociology, anthropology, etc. We need to locate incest first in the imagination of its own appropriate sphere, that is, in the mythical context of divinities where it appears appropriate, even conventional, without the compulsion of desire or the frustration of taboo. . . .

The mythologizing propensity of the psyche "is often pursued far into adulthood" because mythologizing is a basic psychological activity that, try as we will, is never overcome; the psyche never fully yields to the delusion of an only literal, only factual reality. Myth-making, like dreaming, is always going on. The anthropomorphizing of reality, in this case, focused on Dr. Inborn's daughter: the archetypal incest imagined in the guise of a historical human. But daughter and father, too, form a "divine syzygy" that lies embedded within Dr. Inborn and his daughter, emerging in great strength with radical upsetting effects where consciousness is most restricted. What is this restriction? What is the condition of consciousness that calls forth the incest archetype?

We come to a conclusion beyond psychology, at that margin where depth psychology drifts into depth sociology, even world history. Jung says: "When a situation occurs which corresponds to a given archetype, that archetype becomes activated and a compulsiveness appears, which, like an instinctual drive, gains its way against all reason and will . . ." (*CW* 9, i, §99). We saw in the case of Dr. Inborn an obsessively compelling set of worries that would not let him go and a conviction "against all reason and will." To my imagination this case mirrors the effect of the incest archetype in our time, our society and our psychoanalytic theory. We are being abused by incest, in society, and in mind, body, and soul. Then, where is the weakness in the present "situation . . . which corresponds to [the] given archetype"?

The mythical and Neoplatonic settings for incest sketched above present its transgressive nature. That commingling and co-generation become merely ambiguity and dilemma within the restrictive psychology of humanism. Since the essential desire of incest is ever-widening and ever-intensifying erotic connections, making intimate and familiar by mixing souls that prohibit each other, then the restriction of incest to a sheerly human understanding will only invite its abusive incursion. A world limited by the only human constellates what is beyond the human.

("Incest Dream," 66–67, 70, 74)

Returning now to the emptiness of the anima-type woman, we may remember that hitherto her relationship to the anima archetype has had by definition to come through a man. But now we may no longer regard her psychology in this way. The emptiness is no mere void for catching a projection from the opposite sex. Nor may we account for this emptiness through the notions of an unconscious shadow or an undeveloped animus. To derive it from a father complex again puts the origin onto man, leaving the woman only a daughter, only an object created by projection, an Eve born out of Adam's sleep, without independent soul, fate, and individuality.

Rather this emptiness would be considered an authentic archetypal manifestation of the anima in one of her classical forms, maiden, nymph, Kore, which Jung so well describes, and where he also states that "she often appears in woman." Even should we relate this maiden to the daughter, it may remain within the anima constellation. There is no need to search outside for origins in a father.

We all know that fathers create daughters; but daughters create fathers too. The enactment of the maiden-daughter in all her receptive charm, shy availability, and masochistic wiliness draws down a fathering spirit. But its appearance and her victimization are her creation. Even the idea that she is all a result of the father (or the absent or bad father) is part of the father-fantasy of the anima archetype. And so, she must be "so attached" to father because anima is reflection of an attachment. She creates the figurative father and the belief in its responsibility which serves to confirm the archetypal metaphor of Daughter that owes its source, not to the father, but to the anima inherent in a woman's psyche, too.

Moreover, the muse, to whom the nymph has a special connection and toward whom her consciousness is intending, if we follow W. F. Otto, belongs also authentically to the potential of women's psychology in its own right and is not only in reflection to men. It is not *man's* anima, and so it is not a man's inner life that the nymph, hetaera, or muse is reflecting but anima as archetype, which by other names is psyche or soul.   (*Anima*, 63–65)

FATHERS AND SONS

This desire in the father to kill the child we ignore to our peril, especially since psychoanalysis descends from fathers. If this myth is foundational to depth psychology, then infanticide is basic to our practice and our thought. Our practice and our thought recognize infanticide in the archetypal mother, its desire to smother, dissolve, mourn, bewitch, poison and petrify. We are aware that inherent to mothering is "bad" mothering. Fathering too is impelled by its archetypal necessity to isolate, ignore, neglect, abandon, expose, disavow, devour, enslave, sell, maim, betray the son—motives we find in biblical and Hellenic myths as well as folklore, fairy tales and cultural history. The murderous father is essential to fathering, as Adolf Guggenbühl has written. The cry to be fathered so common in psychological practice, as well as the resentment against the cruel or insufficient father so common in feminism—whether as cruel or insufficient ruler, teacher, analyst, institution, program, corporation, patriarchy, or God—idealize the archetype. The cry and the resentment fail to recognize that these shadow traits against which one so protests are precisely those that initiate fathering.

This because: first, they kill idealization. The destructive father destroys the idealized image of himself. He smashes the son's idolatry. Whenever, wherever we idealize the father, we remain in sonship, in the false security of a good ideal. A good model, whether kind analyst, wise guru, generous teacher, honest chief, holds these virtues of kindness, wisdom, generosity, and honesty fixed in another, projected outside. Then, instead of initiation, imitation. Then the son remains tied to the person of the idealized figure.

Second, the terrible traits in the father also initiate the son into the hard lines of his own shadow. The pain of his father's failings teaches him that failing belongs to fathering. The very failure fathers the son's failings. The son does not have to hide his share of darkness. He grows up under a broken roof which nonetheless shelters his own failings, inviting him, forcing him, to be dark himself in order to survive. The commonality—and commonness—of shared shadow can bond father and son in dark and silent empathy as deep as any idealized companionship.

Third, the terrible traits in the father provide a countereducation. How better bring home a true appreciation of decency, loyalty, generosity, succor, and straightness of heart than by their absence or perversion? How more effectively awaken moral resolve than by provoking moral outrage at the father's bad example?

("Oedipus," 277–280)

The union of opposites—male with female—is not the only union for which we long and is not the only union which redeems. There is also the union of sames, the reunion of the vertical axis which would heal the split spirit. Adam must reunite with Eve, but there still remains his reunion with God. Still remains the union of the first Adam at the beginning with the second Adam at the end of history. This division, experienced as the ego-self split and the chasm between consciousness and the unconscious, is in us each at the unhealed heart of the process of individuation. No wonder that our theme is so charged, that we cannot take hold of the senex-puer problem anywhere without getting burned; no wonder that it cannot be fully circumscribed and contained. It cannot become clarified, for we stand in the midst of its smoke. Its split is our pain. This split of spirit is reflected in the senescence and renewal of God and of civilization. It is behind the fascination with *Lebensphilosophie* and the comforting aphorisms of stages of life, which by taking the polarity as its starting point can offer no healing. This split gives us the aches of the father-son problem and the silent distance between generations, the search of the son for his father and the longing of the father for his son, which is the search and longing for one's own meaning; and the theological riddles of The Father and The Son. It tells us that we are split from our own likeness and have turned our sameness with this likeness into difference. And the same split is in the feminine as the spirit is represented in her by the animus, its poles that divide her and cause her to divide others, leading her into the either/or clarifications of the animus that but further new divisions such as love versus loyalty, principle versus abandon, or find her mothering the inspired puer or being the inspired daughter of the senex. The same split gives the frustrations of homosexual eros, the search for angelic beauty, the fear of aging, the longing for the union of sames. We find it too in the insoluble difficulties of the master-pupil transference, the senex-teacher who must have a disciple and the puer-pupil who must have his image of the old wise man carried for him. This is the traditional way the spirit is transferred. Yet just this outer constellation reflects the inner division within each. Owing to the split archetype, a negative polarity is inevitably con-stellated. This leads to the curse of generations, betrayals, to kings and powers not sages and wisdom, and the inability of the master to recognize his pupil and give him blessing. The pupil then "slays the old king" in order to come into his own kingdom, only to become an old king himself in the course of time.

What might this union of sames feel like? How would it be were the polarity healed? We have only hints: some in concepts, some in images.

A primary image of the union of sames is given in that "most widely cherished Renaissance maxim" *festina lente* ("make haste slowly"). Holding the opposites together in a balanced tension was represented in countless emblematic variations summarized by E. Wind. The *puer-senex* or *paedogeron* was one major example of *festina lente*. Maturity in this ideal was not a negation of the puer aspect since the puer was an essential face of "twofold truth."

Festina lente, in other words, presents an ego-ideal based on the two-faced archetype. It is an ideal that may be achieved however only by remaining consequently true to the puer aspect. To be true to one's puer nature means to admit one's puer past—all its gambols and gestures and sunstruck aspirations. From this history we draw consequences. By standing for these consequences, we let history catch up with us and thus is our haste slowed. History is the senex shadow of the puer, giving him substance. Through our individual histories, puer merges with senex, the eternal comes back into time, the falcon returns to the falconer's arm.   ("Senex and Puer," 34–35)

MOTHERS

Here we shall note an essential contrast between mothering and nursing. In their early discoveries, Freudian and Jungian psychologies both were dominated by parental archetypes, especially the mother, so that behavior and imagery were mainly interpreted through this maternal perspective: the oedipal mother, the positive and negative mother, the castrating and devouring mother, the battle with the mother and the incestuous return. The unconscious and the realm of "The Mothers" were often an identity. Through this one archetypal hermeneutic, female figures and receptive passive objects were indiscriminately made into mother symbols. What was not mother! Mountains, trees, oceans, animals, the body and time cycles, receptacles and containers, wisdom and love, cities and fields, witches and death—and a great deal more lost specificity during this period of psychology so devoted to the Great Mother and her son, the Hero. Jung took us a step forward by elaborating other archetypal feminine forms, the anima, and I have tried in several lectures here to continue in Jung's direction by remembering that breasts and milk do not belong only to mothers, that other divine figures besides Maria, Demeter and Kybele have equally important things to say to the psyche, and, that the women attendant on Dionysus were not turned into mothers but nurses. Like those frescoes of the madonna Church which conceals a congregation under her billowed blue skirts, the Great Mother has hidden a pantheon of other feminine modes for enacting life. . . .

For the mothering attitude, it is always a matter of life and death; we are obsessed with how things will turn out; we ask what happened and what will happen. The mother makes things "great," exaggerates, enthuses, infuses the power of life and death into each detail, because the mother's relation to the child is personal, not personal as related and particular, but *archetypally personal* in the sense that the child's fate is delivered through the personal matrix of her fate, becoming fate in general which she then is called. The mother archetype gives the personalistic illusion to fate. Whatever she has to do with takes on overwhelming personal importance which actually is general and altogether impersonal: the desires and loathing of the mother-son relation so intimately personal become suprapersonal enormities, just as the experiences of despair, renewal, continuity and mystery of the mother-daughter relation that seem so fatefully personal become impersonal eternal events.

The growth she furthers is all-out and passionate, the death overwhelming, *mater dolorosa,* for the mother is always too much: goodness and support, concern for weakness, or interest in ambition. Her too-muchness makes the child into hero and rebel, into princess and prostitute, for her passion converts our hurt derelict conditions into archetypal importance.

As Jung spontaneously remarks in that famous passage in his essay on the mother archetype (*CW* 9, 1, §172): "Mother is mother-love, *my* experience and *my* secret." Although the mother experience is archetypal, "strange like nature," "cruel like fate," yet it is so acutely personal that, as Jung observes, we tend to "load that enormous burden of meaning, responsibility, duty, heaven and hell, on to the shoulders of one frail and fallible human being . . . who was our mother" (Ibid.). "This figure of the personal mother looms so large in all personalistic psychologies that, as we know, they never got beyond it . . ." (§159). In other words, the mother archetype itself is responsible for personalistic psychology and for loading the burdens of the archetypal upon personal figures, personal relations and personal solutions, and for taking oneself so personally, one's problems and fate always as "mine." Consequently the mother-complex does show in the too-much and too-little of personal life, flight into impersonal distance coupled with personal fascination and intensity.

("Abandoning," 35-37)

MOTHERS AND SONS

The ecstatic aspect in a man carried by the conjoined archetype of mother-son takes him yet further from the father's inhibitions of order and limit. Ecstasy is one of the goddess's ways of seducing the puer from its senex connection. By overcoming limit, puer consciousness feels itself overcoming fate which sets and is limit. Rather than loving fate or being driven by it, ascending like Horus to redeem the father, there is escape from fate in magical ecstatic flight. Puer aspirations are fed with new fuel: the potent combustible of sexual and power drives whose source is in the instinctual domain of the great goddess. These exaggerations of the puer impulse set him afire. He is the torch, the arrow, and the wing, Aphrodite's son Eros. He seems able to realize in his sexual life and his career every wish of his childhood's omnipotence fantasies. It's all coming true. His being is a magic phallus, glowing and strong, every act inspired, every word pregnant with deep natural wisdom. The great goddess behind the scenes has handed him this ecstatic wand. She governs both the animal desire and the horizontal world of matter over which she offers promise of conquest.

Owing to the emotionality of the Great Mother, the dynamus of the son is unusually labile, unusually dependent upon emotion. Inspiration can no longer be differentiated from enthusiasm, the correct and necessary ascension from ecstasy. The fire flares up and then all but goes out, damp and smoky, clouding vision and afflicting others with the noxious air of bad moods. The dependence of spirit upon mood described in vertical language (heights and depths, glory and despair) has its archetypal counterpart in the festivals for Attis, Cybele's son, which were called *bilaria* and *tristia*.

When the vertical direction toward transcendence is misdirected through the Great Mother, the puer is no longer authentic. He takes his role now from the relationship with the feminine. Ecstasy and guilt are two parts of the pattern of sonship. Even more important is heroism. Whether as hero-lover, or hero-hermit denying matter but with an ear to nature's breast, or hero-conquerer who slays some slimy dragon of public evil, or as Balder, so perfect and so unable to stanch the bleeding from his beautiful wounds, puer has lost its freedom. Direct access to the spirit is no longer there; it requires drama, tragedy, heroics. Life becomes a performance acted out through a role in the relationship with the eternal feminine who stands behind every such son: martyr, messiah, devotee, hero, lover. By playing these roles, we are part of the cult of the great goddess. Our identities are given by the enactment of these roles and thus we become her sons, since our life depends on the roles she gives. She thus can affect even the way that the puer seeks the senex: exaggerating the discipleship of the student to his master, the swagger of the battler with the old order, the exclusivity of the messiah whose new truth refuses everything that has gone before. The mother complex dulls *the precision of the spirit;* issues become quickly either/or, since the great goddess does not have much comprehension of the spirit. She only grasps it in relationship to her; that is, the mother-complex must make of spirit something *related.* It must have effects in the realm of matter: life, world, people. This sounds "only human" and full of "common sense," again terms too often expressing the sentimentalism of the mother complex. Even should a man recognize the mother in his actions and take flight from her relatedness into lofty abstraction and vast impersonal fantasy, he is still the son filled with the animus of the goddess, her pneuma, her breath and wind. And he serves her best by making such divisions between his light and her darkness, his spirit and her matter, between his world and hers.

("Great Mother," 86–87)

PUER

Unlike the term *senex,* our psychology uses the concept of the *puer eternus* widely and freely. It appears early in Jung's work (1912) and has been elaborated in various aspects by him and by many since then. Especially to Marie-Louise von Franz are we indebted for her work on this figure and the problem. Her original and profound writings preclude the necessity to attack the problem in extenso here—and fortunately, because the puer problem is no easy one, even if the term is easily bandied as a neurotic epithet. The single archetype tends to merge in one: the Hero, the Divine Child, the figures of Eros, the King's Son, the Son of the Great Mother, the Psychopompos, Mercury-Hermes, Trickster, and the Messiah. In him we see a mercurial range of these "personalities": narcissistic, inspired, effeminate, phallic, inquisitive, inventive, pensive, passive, fiery, and capricious.

Furthermore, a description of the puer will be complicated because archetypal background and neurotic foreground, positive and negative, are not clearly distinguished. Let us nevertheless sketch some main lines of a psychological phenomenology.

The concept *puer eternus* refers to that archetypal dominant which personifies or is in special relation with the transcendent spiritual powers of the collective unconscious. Puer figures can be regarded as avatars of the self's spiritual aspect, and puer impulses as messages from the spirit or as calls to the spirit. When the collective unconscious in an individual life is represented mainly by parental figures, then puer attitudes and impulses will show personal taints of the mother's boy or *fils du papa*, the perennial adolescence of the provisional life. Then the neurotic foreground obscures the archetypal background. One assumes that the negative and irksome adolescence, the lack of progress and reality, is all a puer problem, whereas it is the personal and parental in the neurotic foreground that is distorting the necessary connection to the spirit. Then the transcendent call is lived within the family complex, distorted into a transcendent function of the family problem, as an attempt to redeem the parents or be their Messiah. The true call does not come through, or is possible only through technical breakthroughs: drugs. But the parental complex is not alone responsible for the crippling, laming, or castration of the archetypal puer figures. This laming refers to the especial weakness and helplessness at the beginning of any enterprise. This is inherent in the one-sided vertical direction, its Icarus-Ganymede propensity of flying and falling. It must be weak on earth, because it is not at home on earth. Its direction is vertical. The beginnings of things are *Einfälle;* they fall in on one from above as gifts of the puer, or sprout up out of the ground as dactyls, as flowers. But there is difficulty at the beginning; the child is in danger, easily gives up. The horizontal world, the space-time continuum which we call "reality," is not its world. So the new dies easily because it is not born in the *Diesseits,* and this death confirms it in eternity. Death does not matter because the puer gives the feeling that it can come again another time, make another start. Mortality points to immortality; danger only heightens the unreality of "reality" and intensifies the vertical connection. Because of this vertical *direct* access to the spirit, this immediacy where vision of goal and goal itself are one, winged speed, haste—even the short cut—are imperative. The puer cannot do with indirection, with timing and patience. It knows little of the seasons and of waiting. And when it must rest or withdraw from the scene, then it seems to be stuck in a timeless state, innocent of the passing years, out of tune with time. Its wandering is as the spirit wanders, without attachment and not as an odyssey of experience. It wanders to spend or to capture, and to ignite, to try its luck, but not with the aim of going home. No wife waits; it has no son in Ithaca. Like the senex, it cannot hear, does not learn. The puer therefore understands little of what is gained by repetition and consistency, that is, by work, or of the moving back and forth, left and right, in and out, which makes for subtlety in proceeding step by step through the labyrinthine complexity of the horizontal world. These teachings but cripple its winged heels, for there, from below and behind, it is particularly vulnerable. It is anyway not meant to walk, but to fly.

But the direct connection to the spirit can be indirect or, rather, can be misdirected through or by the Great Mother. Puer figures often have a special relationship with the Great Mother, who is in love with them as carriers of the spirit; incest with them inspires her—and them—to ecstatic excess and destruction. She feeds their fire with animal desire and fans their flame with promise of scope and conquest over the horizontal world, her world of matter. Whether as her hero-lover or hero-slayer, the puer impulse is reinforced by this entanglement with the Great Mother archetype, leading to those spiritual exaggerations we call neurotic. Primary among these exaggerations is the labile mood and the dependency of the spirit upon moods. Again, they are described in vertical language (heights and depths, glory and despair) and we hear echoes of the festivals for Attis called *tristia* and *hilaria*.

The eternal spirit is sufficient unto itself and contains all possibilities. As the senex is perfected through time, the puer is primordially perfect. Therefore there is no development; development means devolution, a loss and fall and restriction of possibilities. So for all its changeability the puer, like the senex, at core resists development. This self-perfection, this aura of knowing all and needing nothing, is the true background of the self-containment and isolation of any complex, reflected for instance in the ego's narcissistic attitudes, that angelic hermaphroditic quality where masculine and feminine are so perfectly joined that nothing else is needed. There is therefore no need for relationship or woman, unless it be some magical puella or some mother-figure who can admiringly reflect and not disturb this exclusive hermaphroditic unity of oneself with one's archetypal essence. The feeling of distance and coldness, of impermanence, of Don Juan's ithyphallic sexuality, of homosexuality, can all be seen as derivatives of this privileged archetypal connection with the spirit, which may burn with a blue and ideal fire but in a human relationship may show the icy penis and chilling seed of a satanic incubus.

Because eternity is changeless, that which is governed only by the puer does not age. So, too, it has no maturing organic face that shows the bite of time. Its face is universal, given by the archetype, and so it cannot be faced, confronted in personal *Auseinandersetzung*. It has a pose—phallic warrior, pensive poet, messenger—but not a persona of adaptation. The revelations of the spirit have no personal locus in personality; they are eternally valid statements, good forever.

Yet in this faceless form it captures psyche. It is to the puer that psyche succumbs, and just because it is psyche's opposite; the puer spirit is the least psychological, has the least soul. Its "sensitive soulfulness" is rather pseudopsychological, and a derivative of the hermaphroditic effeminacy. It can search and risk; it has insight, aesthetic intuition, spiritual ambition—all, but not psychology, for psychology requires time, femininity of soul, and the entanglement of relationships. Instead of psychology, the puer attitude displays an aesthetic point of view: the world as beautiful images or as vast scenario. Life becomes literature, an adventure of intellect or science, or of religion or action, but always unreflected and unrelated and therefore unpsychological. It is the puer in a complex that "unrelates" it, that volatizes it out of the vessel—that would act it out, call it off and away from the psychological—and thus is the principle that uncoagulates and disintegrates. What is unreflected tends to become compulsive, or greedy. The puer in any complex gives it its drive and drivenness, makes it move too fast, want too much, go too far, not only because of the oral hunger and omnipotence fantasies of the childish, but archetypally because the world can never satisfy the demands of the spirit or match its beauty. Hungering for eternal experience makes one a consumer of profane events. Thus when the puer spirit falls into the public arena it hurries history along.

And finally, as Henry Corbin has often pointed out, the puer eternus figure is the vision of our own first nature, our primordial golden shadow, our affinity to beauty, our angelic essence as messenger of the divine, as divine message. From the puer we are given our sense of destiny and mission, of having a message and being meant as eternal cupbearer to the divine, that our sap and overflow, our enthusiastic wetness of soul, is in service to the gods, bringing eternal refreshment to the archetypal background of the universe.

("Senex and Puer," 23–26)

The way to "solve the mother complex" would be not to cut from Mom, but to cut the antagonism that makes me heroic and her negative. To "solve the mother complex" of the puer means to remove the puer phenomena from the mother, no longer viewing puer problems as mother caused and mother bound. (For in our civilization what cannot be blamed on the mother?) Rather than separate man and mother, we need to separate the archetypal necessity of their association, and to consider puer phenomena in their own right. Then one can turn to each puer aspect and ask it where it belongs, in accordance with the procedure in ancient Greece when consulting an oracle. "To what god or hero must I pray or sacrifice to achieve such and such a purpose?" To what archetypal pattern do I relate my problem? Within which fantasy can I insight my complex? Once the problem has been placed upon a relevant altar, one can connect with it according to its own needs and connect to the God through it. (Had Freud and Neumann followed this method they would not have placed Leonardo's genius on the altar of the mothers by mistaking the kite for a vulture and then retaining the mistake in order to fit theory.)

By taking for granted that puer phenomena belong to the great mother, analytical psychology has given the puer a mother complex. Puer phenomena have received an inauthentic cast for which the epithet "neurotic" feels justified. By laying the complex on the altar of the great mother, rather than maintaining its connection with the *senex-et-puer* unity, we consume our own spiritual ground, giving over to the goddess our eros, ideals, and inspirations, believing they are ultimately rooted in the maternal, either as my personal mother, or matter, or as a causally conditioned worldly field called society, economics, the family, etc. By making spirit her son, we make spirit itself neurotic. By taking the frailties and youthful follies necessary to all spiritual beginnings merely as infantilisms of the mother complex, we nip in the bud the possibility of renewal in ourselves and our culture. This view of things serves only to perpetuate the neurosis, preventing the reunion of senex and puer. Puer then seems opposite and enemy of senex, and the age seems rightly characterized by what Freud suggested, a universal Oedipus complex, son against father because of the mother.

In individuals, these distortions of the puer show themselves in the personal mother complex. In society, there are distortions of spiritual goals and meanings, because an ambitiously heroic ego-development has been the recipe for resolution of the puer syndrome. To assume that the puer is primarily the same as the son of the Great Mother is to confirm the pathological distortions as an authentic state of being. The distortion of puer into son is perpetuated by the mother archetype which prefers the hero myth as the model for ego-development since that model depicts the ego to be primarily and necessarily embroiled with her. Our main Western psychological theories rest on a model which more or less declares the dynamics of the psyche to be derivatives of the family and society, which are the preserve of the mother. Psychology itself is her victim, not only in its therapeutics of ego development, but more fundamentally: the spirit of psychology is lamed by materialism, literalism, and a genetic viewpoint towards its own subject matter, the psyche. The spiritual nature and purposes of psychology never emerge because the puer never emerges from the mother. Or it emerges still bound with a navel cord, psychology as a heroic mission of the priest son whose urge is either to spread self through the world or to become self in disdain of the world.

Psychology, as Jung insisted, always reflects our psychic condition. A psychology that sees mother everywhere is a statement about the psyche of the psychologist and not only a statement based on empirical evidence. To advance the psyche through its collective mother complex, psychology itself must advance in its self-reflection so that its subject, the soul, is no longer dominated by naturalism and materialism, and the goals for that soul no longer formulated via the mother archetype as "growth," "social adaptation," "human related-ness," "natural wholeness," etc.   ("Great Mother," 98–100)

CHILD

Though you and I once were children and may now be parents, and may even be dedicating our working lives to the care and coun-seling of children, we hardly know them. What really is a child, this state called childhood, or adolescence, and who is this particular child now in my charge? Why do children seem a people apart—as we say "men, women, and children"? Why so fascinating, enraging, wondrous, and imcomprehensible?

The smaller the child, the more this is the case. The Platonists, and the romantics who followed them, had a theory to account for our feelings of the child's strangeness, its peculiar terrors and plea-sures. The child's soul descends, they said, from another archetypal world, entering this world trailing clouds of glory as it comes (Wordsworth). A being close to angels, it arrives knowing every-thing essential. Or, as we would say: its collective unconscious is replete with primordial awareness. This angelic guise was demon-strated by pointing at the child's skin when a baby, its face when asleep, its smile, its startling inventive freedom. The angelic guise became a standard icon in graveyard stone and nursery-book litho-graph during the last century especially. Only in this century of our Western history has the child been overburdened with carrying the "bad seed" of our civilization's disorder. Today, children every-where are worried about and need "help," from infant massage to play therapy to corrective lessons. Something is always "wrong" with them.

The soul's difficulties with its descent into the world show up in counseling as "adjustment disorders" or, worse, as autism, mu-tism, attention deficit, antisocial behavior, and the other ills cataloged in our textbooks of abnormal psychology. From the romantic perspective, the counselor serves as a midwife to the psyche—a role Socrates imagined for his work, guiding the child into the world without too much loss of its remnants of mythic memory. Or, to use another simile from classical Greece, the counselor is like a *paedogogos*, a slave or servant who walks along with a child to school.

School tries to put the child's psyche within the mind of practical reason: clocktime, factual truth, and a Xerox notion of images, i.e., accurate reproduction. What you draw is what you see. School defines *realism* as photographic realism and tests the child's sense of reality in the hard schoolyard of competition. Coping before hoping. *Realism*, however, ever since Plato and still in philosophy today, refers to realities of invisible forms that are innate and pattern the actual world. A classical realist would say the child brings reality with him or her, a reality which today we call fantasy. . . .

The daily pressures of work make us forget that the child as symbol, and actual children too, always evokes the twin possibilities of terror and joy, extremes at the outer edges of the curve of normality. The child enters the world still open to emotional intensities beyond the usual. This confronts the therapist often with emotions long dormant, even extinct, in his or her own soul. Those who have most to do with children seem to have lost the feeling for the child's terror and fascination with terror and, even more, to have lost the child's extraordinary possibility for joy. Instead, we meet children with worried concern, therapeutic goodwill and professional smiles, but few laughs. We would bring the child under the normalizing shelter of the bell curve: nothing to extremes. Keats and Blake and Whitman, however, insist on the wildest joy.

Freud did too. He saw the child's sensuous delight in all things as a polymorphous sexual libido. The child enters the world packed with the pleasure principle, a roly-poly of desires for what the world offers. Like a goat's kid, the child dances with surplus exuberance; like a kitten it explores everywhere and takes sudden fright; and like a piglet, how good it all tastes! The world is a good place to be—when, and only when, the imagination with which the child descends is still alive enough to imbue the things of the world with the child's vision of beauty.

Not its innocence makes the child's psyche so susceptible to corruption of its desire, but its attachment to beauty. Eating disorders, media addiction, hyperactivity and victimization by exploiters are based in the child's native desire for beauty in this world comparable to the richness of its fantasy in the unconscious soul. Exploitation could not occur if a child entered the world a mere *tabula rasa* void of any prior delight in and recognition of sensate images. So, the disorders of sensationalism reveal the child's innate aesthetic response to the world as a place of pleasure, in which all things are desirable. *Schlaraffenland* and Paradise are where we begin, and the child will live in a cargo cult of consumerism when the fantasies of the extraordinary that fill its soul are not given imaginary and imaginative response by its adult guides.

But many adult guides who meet the disturbed child are themselves disturbed by their training. We have been initiated into the myth of developmental psychology: that all life moves in one direction starting in infancy (but not before, not beyond). Moreover, the simplistics of our myth say that this one-way direction in time is causal: a person is caused by history, and the earlier the history the more powerful the cause. So, childhood has been declared the source of all our disaffected behavior. This tale told by dynamic and developmental psychology says childhood is basically miserable. Every therapy session searches memory for traces of unhappiness. We do not turn there for beauty and joy, but to uncover the curses of abuse, shame, and fixation on that abuse and shame. Bad mothers, absent fathers and envious siblings are the demons and ogres in psychology's fairy tale. This script curses the family with a psychology of blame instead of honor. It also curses the pleasurable world and the origins of the libido in sensuous joy. No wonder that actual children become so anesthetized that they are content with the pseudostimuli of television, so that by adolescence they have to shoot up to feel. They sit in classes without motivation, walk the streets in sullen rage, and seek desperately for sensuous transcendence in sounds, speeds and sex for an altered state of mind as an alternative script to the soulless and joyless dealing, handling, coping, managing life as a program of practical reason. Unconsciously, they recollect something else, something more, which they would find again, sometimes by suicide. ("Foreword to *Inscapes*," xiii–xvi)

Freud gave the child *primacy:* nothing was more important in our lives than those early years and that style of thought and emotion of imaginal existence called *childhood*. Second, Freud gave the child *body:* it had passions, sexual desires, lusts to kill; it feared, sacrificed, rejected; it hated and longed and it was composed of erogenous zones, preoccupied with feces, genitals, and deserved the name polymorphous perverse. Third, Freud gave the child *pathology:* it lived in our repressions and fixations; it was at the bottom of our psychic disorders (*CP* II, p. 188); it was our suffering. . . .

Jung elaborates these general and special features: futurity, divine heroic invincibility, hermaphroditism, beginning and end, and the motif of abandonment from which my theme is drawn. Jung's elaborations of 1940 should be taken as an addition to those in his previous works where the child motif is related to archaic mythical thinking and the mother archetype (*CW* 5, *passim*) and to paradisiacal blissfulness (*CW* 6, §§422f, 442). Some of the aspects which Jung discusses Freud had already described in his language style. The idea of the creative child occurs in Freud's equation child = penis, and the rejected child in his equation child = feces. " 'Feces,' 'child,' and 'penis' thus form a unity, an unconscious concept (*sit venia verbo*)—the concept, namely, of a little thing that can become separated from one's body." "From the history of an infantile neurosis" (1918), *CP* III, p. 562f.

To these features I would add two others from our Western tradition, the first specifically Christian, the second specifically classical. In the Christian tradition (Légasse) *child* refers also to the simple, the naive, the poor and the common—the orphan—of society and of the psyche, as it did in the language of the Gospels, where *child* meant outcast, the precondition for salvation, and was later placed in association with the feelings of the heart opposed to the learning of the mind. . . .

A purpose of marriage has been defined in terms of procreating and caring for children. But there is also the archetypal child who is constellated by marriage and whose need for care would wreck the actual marriage by insisting that it rehearse archetypal patterns that are *pre* marital (uninitiated, infantile, incestuous). Then there occur those struggles between the actual children and the psychic child of the parents as to whom will be abandoned. Then divorce threatens not only the actual children, but the abandoned child of the parents that found containment in marriage.

The concentration of abandonment in marriage because there is no other home for it, makes marriage the principal scene for enacting the child archetype (not the conjunctio). In marriage we find the idealizations of the child: marriage as alpha and omega of life, hermaphroditism lived as "role sharing," futurity lived as the planning of hopes and fears, and defensive vulnerability. The couple's attempts to contain the child (not each other) produce a familiar pattern alternating between emotionalism and none at all, marriage stiffened into a social norm. Lost in the oscillation is the imagination which the child can bring. Imagination is blown off in affects or concretizes into plans and habits that keep the child cribbed. If we may speak of a "marriage therapy" then it would be based, not on the "neurotic interaction" of the *couple*, but on the child as central factor in marriage, and the child's imagination, i.e., the cultivation of the imaginal psyche, the peculiar fantasy life that plays between your child and mine.

Usually we feel something fundamentally wrong in regard to the child, which wrong we then place into or onto the child. Societies have to do something with children in order to make right this wrong. We do not take children as they are given; they must be removed out of childhood. We initiate, educate, circumcise, innoculate, baptize. And if in the romantic manner we idealize the child— and idealizations are always a sign of distance—calling the child a *speculum naturae*, we do not altogether trust this nature.

With the child's return comes childhood, both kinds: actual with its memories and imaginal with its reminiscences. We have come to call this memorial factor with its two kinds of remembrances "the unconscious," personal and collective. But this term, *the unconscious*, only adds to the burden of differentiating the complexity of psychic life. It might be more beneficial to separate the child (as the reminiscent factor which returns a person to the primordially repressed of nonactual substructures) from a category so indefinite as the unconscious. Then we would be in a better position to free *childhood* as an imaginal mode of perceiving and feeling from its identification with actual childhood which usually had less freedom and joy, less fantasy and magic and amorality than we sentimentally attribute to it. *Our cult of childhood is a sentimental disguise for true homage to the imaginal.* Could childhood be called by its true name— the realm of archetypal reminiscence—then we would not have to become unconscious to find the mythical. We have psychologically confused the "coming up" of events from "the unconscious" with the "coming back" of reminiscence.

Psychology has taken the repressed child to be an axiomatic metaphor of psychic structure. Psychology assumes the repressed is less developed than the repressor, that consciousness is topographically, historically and morally superior to the unconscious, characterized by primitive, amoral and infantile impulses. *Our notion of consciousness inherently necessitates repression of the child.* This constellates our main fear: the return of the inferiority, the child, who also means the return of the realm of archetypal reminiscence. Archetypal fantasy is the most threatening activity of the human soul as we now conceive it, for our Western rational tradition has placed this activity in the ontologically inferior, the primitive amoral realm of actual childhood.

Thus a restoration of the mythical, the imaginal and the archetypal implies a collapse into the infantile realm of the child. Our strong ego-centered consciousness fears nothing more than just such collapse. The worst insult is to be called "childish," "infantile," "immature." So we have devised every sort of measure for defending ourselves against the child—and against archetypal fantasy. These defenses we call the consciousness of the strong, mature and developed ego.

Abortion echoes the older practice of child exposure *(apothesis),* abandoning the unwanted child to its death. As an interior drama the aborted child is the miscarriage of the archetypal qualities we have presented: hope for the future, the sense of conquest, the new start and fulfilled end. The dead child is our lost hope and failed spark, our creative disappointment and stricken imagination that can point no way forward, spontaneity, openness, movement gone. No wonder that grief and mourning may continue many years after an actual abortion since the abortion theme expresses the psychic condition of dead childhood. . . .

The dead child may also be an image for the soul's child, performing the role of *psychopompos* which, like the image and emotion of a classical funerary stele leads the psyche to reflections about all that belongs to the child archetype but from a wholly psychic viewpoint. The dead child then makes possible an interiorization of the futurity and growth fantasies, and independence reverses its meaning to express independence from the values of life. Death itself then is no longer viewed through the eyes of life, but, in being led by the dead child, one may regard death in its own terms as a specifically psychic condition, i.e., the condition where there is nothing else but psyche. Although this motif has been saccharinely sentimentalized—but walk through a Victorian graveyard for its statuary of dead angelic children as emissaries of the beyond—the psychic content concretized in the marble is nonetheless valid. This image uniquely unites eros and Thanatos whose conjunction, although understood in Neoplatonism, was conceptually riven by Freud's rationalism. The dead child may offer healing to what the mind has torn apart and placed in opposition.

("Abandoning," 10–12, 15–16, 22–23, 38–39)

10

Dreams and
the Blood Soul

A persistent message comes through again and again in James Hillman's approach to dreams: draw near to the dream with respect and attention, enter its culture like a foreigner open to new ways. He urges us to "befriend" the dream, getting to know it the way we might get to know a person. The dream then becomes the occasion for learning about the inner worlds; the people who wander the soul; the landscapes of imagination; the stories and themes that are the cycles of fate, mood, and experience.

Hillman does not recommend bringing a dream up into the light and air of conscious life for interpretation, translation, and application. Rather, he suggests that we stay with the dream, letting it take us to places rarely glimpsed, except perhaps in complexes and compulsions. If, as many dreams show, there is an elevator or escalator between consciousness and the lower world of dream, Hillman's advice is always to press the down button.

Befriending a dream requires time, no quick and clever solutions, as though the dream were a puzzle to be solved. The analysis of a dream, therefore, never ends; it goes on and on. Analysis essentially means to "loosen up." In imagination, in reflection, and in conversation, perhaps over years, a dream may loosen somewhat, and we might catch something of its mood and setting, its people and its action. It is as though the atmosphere of the dream, like the tone of a good story, draws us into itself, coloring our very reflection on it.

Avoiding interpretation does not mean leaving the dream untouched. Much work can be done without translating the dream into concepts or taking a lesson which is then applied directly to life. A dreamer or analyst can draw on a wealth of knowledge, on imagina-

239

tion and feeling, and on various traditional sources such as astrology or folktales or painting and work the dream without abusing it.

Hillman offers a way into the dream other than taking up the club of Hercules and heroically getting the dream under conscious submission. Dante and Odysseus offer a different approach: look around, observe every detail, and get to know the locals.

Perhaps because we live in such an extroverted world, surrounded by literalistic readings of life, it is difficult to maintain the underworld point of view. Yet, this is Hillman's charge. Perhaps, he has written, the point of dreaming is to soak the ego over a long period of time in this world of death—death to our usual, conventional sense of life. An ego pickled in the dream juices of death might then be ready for a soulful life.

Hillman has a special interest in dream animals. He takes his clue from religions in which the gods and goddesses are pictured as animals or part animals, or closely associated with animals, and he concludes that rather than being lower on the scale than humans, animals are higher, close to the divine. If the Greek god of healing, Asklepiós, appeared as a snake, if the Native American holy person sought his special animal identity, then it is not so strange to regard the animals of dream as special guides and guardians of the soul.

Hillman's love for the animal, so apparent in many lectures and writings, is an aspect of his sense of community transcending the limits of ordinary personal commerce. We are always in relation to our ancestors; we have nature within as well as without. It stands to reason that the animals would enjoy a special place in this community of the soul.

The dream is the ark of Noah where the many animals, says Hillman, abide with us during a time of blindness, when we fail to see the invisible within a world taken literally. The animals point to other meanings and mysteries that have something to do with our perception of beauty, with being in life with the full sensuousness of the imagination. The dream animal guides us away from the confines of personalism and schools us in that special vision that glimpses epiphanies when they occur in the most ordinary times and places.

Living with dreams saturates consciousness with the mysterious laws and customs of a dark and impenetrable underworld. Hillman's dream book, The Dream and the Underworld, presents a tightly reasoned theory of dream work and suggestions for understanding dream images as being in the service of death. Once again *he eludes our expectations of making sense of the soul or helping make life more successful through dream analysis. Instead he uses dream as the occasion to turn our heads completely around, like Eurydice mesmerized by the underworld, to face this phantasmic, unredeemable, elusive realm of the soul's interior.*

WORK WITH DREAMS

The classical Jungian attitude toward the dream is expressed very well by a term I would borrow from existential analysis. . . . This term is: to *befriend* the dream. To participate in it, to enter into its imagery and mood, to want to know more about it, to understand, play with, live with, carry, and become familiar with—as one would do with a friend. As I grow familiar with my dreams I grow familiar with my inner world. Who lives in me? What inscapes are mine? What is recurrent and therefore what keeps coming back to reside in me? These are the animals and people, places and concerns, that want me to pay attention to them, to become friendly and familiar with them. They want to be known as a friend would. They want to be cared for and cared about. This familiarity after some time produces in one a sense of at-homeness and at-oneness with an inner family which is nothing else than kinship and community with oneself, a deep level of what can also be called *the blood soul.* In other words, the inner connection to the unconscious again leads to a sense of soul, an experience of an inner life, a place where meanings home. . . .

Friendship wants to keep the connection open and flowing. The first thing, then, in this noninterpretive approach to the dream is that we give time and patience to it, jumping to no conclusions, fixing it in no solutions. Befriending the dream begins with a plain attempt to listen to the dream, to set down on paper or in a dream diary in its own words just what it says. One takes especial note of the feeling tone of the dream, the mood upon waking, the emotional reactions of the dreamer in the dream, the delight or fear or surprise. Befriending is the feeling approach to the dream, and so one takes care receiving the dream's feelings, as with a living person with whom we begin a relationship. (*Insearch,* 57–60)

An imaginal ego is at home in the dark, moving among images as one of them. Often there are inklings of this ego in those dreams where we are quite comfortable with absurdities and horrors that would shock the daylight out of waking consciousness. The imaginal ego realizes that the images are not his own and that even his ego-body and ego-feeling and ego-action in a dream belong to the dream image. So the first move in teaching ego how to dream is to teach it about itself, that it too is an image.

An imaginal ego is further built by voiding its old ground, the attitudes mentioned above—moralism, personalism, naturalism, literalism—deriving from the corporal perspective. The old heroic ego loses its stuffing and returns to a two-dimensional shade. Then it is able to reflect its deeds metaphorically. Then it may realize that the ego in the dream is also a wholly subjective figure, or shade, who is now voided of the I who lay himself down to sleep. Ego-behavior in the dream reflects the pattern of the image and the relations within the image, rather than the patterns and relations of the dayworld.

Admittedly, the dream-ego and the waking-ego have a special "twin" relationship; they are shadows of each other, as Hades is the brother of Zeus. But the *I* in the dream is no secret stage director (Schopenhauer) who wrote the play he acts in, no self-portrait photographer taking his own snapshot from below, nor are the wants fulfilled in a dream the ego's wishes. The dream is not "mine," but the psyche's, and the dream-ego merely plays one of the roles in the theater, subjected to what the "others" want, subject to the necessities staged by the dream.

The work on dreams follows the work of dreams. We work on the dream, not to unravel it as Freud said, to undo the dream work's undoing, but to respond to its work with the likeness of our work, all the while aiming to speak like the dream, imagine like the dream. Work on dreams does not forego analysis, but the analysis is in service of another archetypal principle and carried out in another attitude than the usual one. Analysis of course means making separations and differentiations. A dream is pulled apart, even violated, and this is indeed the necessary destructive work of intellect and of discriminating feeling. But now, the archetype served by a dream analysis is not only making conscious where consciousness means sunlight; we may place this destructive analytical work now in connection with Hades, who would take the life out of all our natural assumptions, all our futuristic previews, or with the *bricoleur* and his hermetic sleight of hand that steals what we want to hold fast.

Analytical tearing apart is one thing, and conceptual interpretation another. We can have analysis without interpretation. Interpretation turns the dream into its meaning. Dream is replaced with translation. But dissection cuts into the flesh and bone of the image, examining the tissue of its internal connections, and moves around among its bits, though the body of the dream is still on the table. We haven't asked what does it mean, but who and what and how it is.

We may also understand our resistance to dreaming as a resistance in our "natural" nature to Hades. We "can't remember," go vague, forget to jot it down, or scribble it beyond deciphering, and excuse ourselves by pointing to the obvious slipperiness of dreams. Yet if each dream is a step into the underworld, then remembering a dream is a recollection of death and opens a frightening crevice under our feet. The other alternative—loving one's dreams, not being able to wait for the next one, such as we find in enthusiastic *puer* psychology, shows to what extent this archetype is in love with easeful death and blind to what is below.

Again, a duplicity. This time the experience is fear and desire. Like Persephone, we are both repelled and attracted, sometimes seizing only half the experience, struggling like her against being carried down by the dream, other times in its embrace and ruling from its throne. Beyond Hades as destroyer and lover, however, there is Hades of incomparable intelligence. Work with dreams is to get at this hidden intelligence, to communicate with the god in the dream. Because the dream is both black and white, its intelligence is neither altogether obscure nor altogether clear. . . .

Because of this individuality of the dream, conceptual generalities about dreams must fail. As Heraclitus (frg. 113, Freeman) said: "The thinking faculty is common to all," but (frg. 115, Freeman), "The soul has its own *logos*, which grows according to its needs." By digesting and transforming the day's remainders, according to the logos (intelligence) of the soul rather than to the laws of common thought, the dream work makes an individualized soul. This cannot be made only in the day world where, as Heraclitus says: "One day is like any other." The deformative, transformative work in dreams constructs the house of Hades, one's individual death. Each dream builds upon that house. Each dream is practice in entering the underworld, a preparation of the psyche for death.

If we think back on any dream that has been important to us, as time passes and the more we reflect on it, the more we discover in it, and the more varied the directions that lead out of it. Whatever certainty it once might have given, shifts into complexities beyond clear formulations each time the dream is studied anew. The depth of even the simplest image is truly fathomless. This unending, embracing depth is one way that dreams show their love.

(*Dream and the Underworld*, 102–103, 130–131, 133, 200)

We can also make the dream matter by analogies. Analogy follows another notion of matter, that of extension. By spreading the dream out, disclosing connections all over the place, an image takes on weight and can even make me feel that I am walking on its ground, that I am everywhere in the dream rather than it in me.

Analogy is a word used in comparative anatomy for referring to a relation where there is likeness in *function* but not in *origin*. For instance, there are analogies between the [dream] hag with the box of shit and images of crones in legends, witches in fairytales, the goddess Kali, putrefying corpses in coffins, even memory images of my grandmother, or a smelly old schoolteacher: they look alike; function alike; feel alike. But we do not have to go one step further and claim the hag is an image of the Great Mother archetype; for this relation expressed by the genitive *of*, would then be one of origin: the mother archetype generates hag (and other images) *of* the archetype. Analogies keep us in the functional operation of the image, in the patterns of similarities, without positing a common origin for these similarities. The operative term is *like*. This is like that. A dream:

There is a black dog, with a long tail, that shows its teeth at me. I am terribly afraid.

Analogizing is quite an easy procedure. We simply ask the dreamer, "What is this dog, this scene, this fear, like?" Then we get: It's like when there is sudden sound and I jump with fright; like coming to analysis and expecting you to pounce on everything I say; like anger—sometimes I get so angry (or hungry) that I could savage anyone who gets near me; like my ulcer that gets angry and hungry at the same time; like my mother used to look—her teeth; like going home after work in the dark and being afraid my wife will bark at me, jump at me; it's like dying—I'm so afraid—it's so vicious and low and degrading; it's like a film I saw when I was little with black dogs in it and I had to leave the movie theater I was so terrified; like the jackal god, Anubis; like Mephistopheles in *Faust;* like when I get sexy—I want to tear into the meat and just eat and screw like a dog in the street, anywhere; it's like the dog was a snake with a long tail. And so on.

Here we see a main difference between analogizing and interpreting. Should any one of the above analogies be taken as the meaning of the image, I would lose the others. I would have narrowed the image down to only one place where it matters. Analogies are multiple and don't lose the others; they don't lose the dog either. They keep the image there, alive and well, returning to it each time for a fresh sense of it. Interpretation transforms it into a meaning.

Analogizing is like my fantasy of Zen, where the dream is the teacher. Each time you say what an image means, you get your face slapped. The dream becomes a koan when we approach it by means of analogy. If you can literalize a meaning, *interpret* a dream, you are off the track, lost your koan. (For the dream is the thing, not what it means.) Then you must be slapped to bring you back to the image. A good dream analysis is one in which one gets more and more slaps, more and more analogies, the dream exposing your entire unconsciousness, the basic matters of your psychic life.

("Inquiry into Image," 86–87)

She mounted the stairs to my third-floor office, resentful over the climb. She wore a hat and bright clothes. She had a dumpy body, good facial features and large clear eyes. She had lots to say, mainly about previous failed analyses, and what was wrong everywhere. Then she told her dream (of two days previous): it was simply an image of a barren tree made only of fingernails. In telling it, she stretched out her fingers and clawed the air. To her, it was the image of her cold and bleak existence. To me, it was a meeting with the aggressive, clutching, taloned Mother. She accused me of "freezing her out"—and I did. But were that all, nothing would have happened, for within the cold distance that often constellated between us there was an archetypal pattern. Once she dreamed of my image as a totem pole; my normal head up high and a Chinese figure, both baboon and buddha, in the stomach region. This image was the analysis, I carrying her severance between head reactions and stomach reactions. And the analysis was a ritual activity, its dimension mainly vertical (spiritual, heights-depths, ancestral) in which the real action was taking place through the totemic power of projected images.

The tree presented both demands she put on others and also demands put upon her by the tree of life, or perhaps her family tree. It craved, and until she could nourish it, it would claw the world like a harpy or other mythical being with long nails. By emphasizing the archetypal nature of the images she was more able to take them without personal guilt.

Images provided the main place of connection between us. Rather than premature attempts at personal relatedness (which tended each time to develop into paranoid accusations and defensive denials—her usual pattern with others), feeling was given to the products of her soul. Our connection was below our disparities and was less in terms of the fluctuations of personal feelings toward each other, than it was valuing the impersonal psychic movements that went on at the common collective level. These needed recognition with both thought and feeling. By my passionate concern with them she could appreciate their importance and feel their intimate connection to her as well. In this way analyst is bridge, midwife, partner, and the feeling, by finding archetypal backing, is both deeply personal and impersonal at the same time.

❧

Her dreams were few, short and to the point, as if bringing focus to the spread-out confusion of her conscious life. The job during the first months was to receive this *massa confusa* into the analysis by listening to it (the past, ideas she could take back to America and capitalize on, what was wrong with Jung, with me and with analysis, her daily ailments and conflicts). I felt the job was less to analyze these contents than to let them be, meanwhile selectively turning toward dreams. During this period she began staying more in her room, recording dreams and "working on her material," an alchemical "closing of the vessel" to consolidate her psychic matter.

She dreamed: "I am in the office of an older doctor (now dead). He was our family friend when I was a girl. He is trying to water plants all over the place with a hose. He puts the hose in my hands and tells me to do the job. There is no way to shut off the hose and I am trying to water without spilling a drop on the desk, furniture or floor. I am having an awful time with the hose."

The effect of handling the tremendous surge of libidinal pressures that would further the growth of healing was now in her hands. The doctor isn't going to do it, but she can't quite manage it, partly because she is trying to be faultless. Of course there is a spillover, wetting not only the interior growth (plants) but also the civilized area of daily living (furnishings). Analysis is still under the aegis of the *old doctor,* a cure from above by senior superior wisdom which puts her into the role of *little girl.* The caution I drew from the dream was: Don't seek for the source of the flow or try to shut it off. She has a phallus too. Let her point the hose even if she sloshes about. She'll get the hang of it.

In the fourth month she began a consecutive active imagination with little Annie (herself as a child, and as her granddaughter whom she raises and loves). The first figure encountered through her meetings with Annie is her father. This brings up fear, and a heavy sullen hatred. She could make no peace with him and she devised all sorts of tortures for him. In a painting she made of her "situation," she was a tiny stick figure under a dark sky god. She wrote out long arguments with her children, but did not send them as letters, internalizing, or putting this material back in the vessel.

The grandmother-granddaughter relationship is of archetypal significance. It moves the family problem out of the immediate recollections of actual parents toward a more symbolic situation connecting both backward and forward. At one and the same time she was working on her own past and revising her relationships to her children and their children. This is her first movement into the archetypal mother-daughter mystery, which returns later.

Next she dreamed: "In a steam room, as if fainting or in a trance! I feel at last I am doing what is wanted of me." Three days later: "I am lying on a cot at the end of a corridor. I hear two women whispering in the middle of this long passage some distance away. The hall is black. I hear the clicking of a barber's scissors from behind a door, and a chink of light comes through it."

These dreams place her in an archetypal healing situation away from *old doctor.* The steam room is the alchemical bath, where the substances of personality are dissolved for change. There is intense inner heat, pressure, clouding of normal consciousness, melting of defense formations, weakening of ego, will and habit. The water pressure and the hose (directed by the ego) is relaxing and heating and contained now in an appropriate chamber. The dark passage is both the place of transition and refers back to the antechamber or waiting room and cot *(kline)* of the Greek incubation healing ritual. She is in the dark, waiting, outside where the light is. The barber (once bloodletter and healer) trims the hair of men (her active masculine head products that need clipping and shaping). It is precisely in this situation of "being in the dark" that her paranoid fantasies (whispering women) appear, representing the knowledge that she does not yet directly have access to but is present in their whispering and received through her paranoid fantasies.

At this point she had a delusional attack. She suspected that I was planning to send her to an asylum. (Her husband had often threatened her with this.) I had asked about her delinquent bills and her health, which meant I did not like her; she was ugly, and so I was planning to put her away. She asked, "What is the diagnosis?" I had been gathering information all these months as evidence against her. Moreover, she said that I now found her worse off than at the beginning of the treatment.

I confirmed her feeling of worsening, not literally but in terms of the dreams—the panic belongs to the state of the steam room and darkness in the corridor. Her questions and challenges are attempts to strike conflict and bring light. My answers could help clip her head. Her sense of being bad, ugly and disliked belonged to the ugliness of the primal material that now was being cooked, causing the pressure she felt. After forty-five minutes she left, saying: "I feel like a child after a nightmare when the lights are turned on."

A source of the delusional tendency now showed up in the active imagination. She relived a scene with her father in which he put her in a corner with strong soap in her mouth for having said bad words. She was neither allowed to cry nor let saliva out. Instead, she (little Annie) "made up a story for herself: a little soap bubble comes from her mouth and she climbs into it and floats over the head of her father."

Overwhelming insights derived from this image. For the first time she saw her delusional formations as defenses against her father; but I pointed out as well their value, that the soap bubbles were also her way of surpassing her father through imagination. It was not fantasy that was wrong but its defensive misuse. This led to a dream in which she was wearing a bizarre bright jacket for public perform-ances. She then was making a journey through various ups and downs and peculiar turns and through tunnels. She comes out wear-ing the same jacket now faded, less striking, more presentable.

The peculiar twists of landscape and dark tunnels were experi-enced as another two months of sufferings and disorientation. She felt herself bleeding internally (inward draining of the life force as part of a new circulation within herself). She feared returning to America without her bright persona, in her "faded jacket," her aging, her common mortality.

Dream: "My cousin Arthur is making love to me. He kisses my mouth, my face, and then, lightning fast, kisses me through my clothes on my labia, worshipping me there. A woman figure in gray is standing by. I feel both spiritual exaltation and physical orgasm. I am turning from ice to water. April! I want to have intercourse with him at once but he is gone. My labia have the abstract shape of a triangle pointing down."

Cousin Arthur was a tricky black sheep, but he bore the name of Britain's hero-king. He does not stay for intercourse; his trickster magic is only to melt and open her by bringing love to her genitals, which are not the actual ones, but clothed and abstracted into the downward pointing triangle, an ancient sign of female and matter and what her saintly mother had denied. That it was her cousin refers both to the psychic incest of loving her own kind, her own family and blood, and to an archaic ritual taboo.

Mrs. Carson felt I did not get the huge importance of the dream, indicating that a piece of her was skeptical. The paranoid doubt was both a complex, the partial personality that did not want to yield, and that which kept her from identification with the dream as a resolution through sexual eros. Arthur was an opening of the way, not the ending of an analysis. Arthur was Eros awakening Psyche, the erotic personification that stirs the psyche into life, giving Mrs. Carson too a new sense of importance.

The unknown woman who stood by in the Arthur dream now began to appear in others. As this "woman in the gray dress" grew in importance giving a new sense of stolid ancestral support, Mrs. Carson could now take on the shadow side and pathology of her mother without idealizing. Twice she dreamed of bleeding inwardly and she understood why her mother just gave up and died.

The upper-level defenses of course continued even during the "bleeding." She went on pastry binges, then vegetarian cures. She made appointments with "important people" who could advance her educational career. She thought of adding another analyst, or of bringing in other expert opinions on her case. Perhaps she had an internal disease?

The blood images continued and partly answered her medical fear. She saw in a dream menstrual pads wrapped in gold string. Then: "Blood dream—the picture is all red. Red rain coming down, blood coming down like rain. The blood is in some way going out of people's skins and into other people. People's blood was actually being exchanged. I had no horror or feeling of faintness at the sight of all this blood. I accepted it factually."

The very sanguine approach shows how already she has been transfused with new emotional reactions. The long-drawn experience with pain and suffering through the last six months had actually resulted in a new vital connection among the personified parts of the psyche which was at the same time "rain."

Now many things came together. She felt she was no longer little Annie but an adolescent girl. Our personal battles subsided and she wrote me a list of things she liked about me. She dreamed of a bouquet of old-fashioned flowers, and of a black psychological counselor. She found a place of retreat inside herself. Then came this dream: "My father is sitting in an armchair. The mood is different from anything ever previous. There is a homey, comfortable atmosphere in the room. Is it a library or living-room? My father wears a maroon smoking-jacket, and he is placidly smoking a pipe and carrying on pleasant conversations. He seems a man of education and culture who would be pleasant to know, not a man to be afraid of."

With this almost too good movement within the father complex, there next came a new and most difficult phase.

❧

Mrs. Carson dreamed: "In bed with Binzie (her daughter) about six years old. The child calls, 'Mom.' I was sleepy and didn't want to wake up. I wanted to sleep and not be bothered and I felt guilty and I didn't answer."

Motherhood and guilt were so tied in one complex that to be free of guilt she had to refuse the call of the child. Facing this meant waking up to the archetypally shadow side of mothering. It meant "being a bad mother," which her saintly mother image had made impossible, and thus had made her unconsciously live out. It also meant facing the idea that "remedial education" (which, by the way, she had internalized and practiced on herself with little Annie) had it roots partly in the guilt over bad mothering. She was unable to distinguish between the guilt to her actual children of the past and the internal younger personality, the daughter now calling.

The mother-daughter myth (Persephone-Demeter-Hecate) was the myth now constellating. This was the central religious and sexual mystery of Greek psychology, an initiation into the archetypal feminine cycle from maidenhood to old witchery and death. As a mystery it had to be "undergone" and not "explained," especially not by reductions to personal life.

Next she dreamed: "Women. All young women, mothers about twenty-five to thirty years old. All are playing with dolls, very seriously like little girls do." I took this dream too as a put-down, considering her attitude toward her children to have been one which treated them like dolls imbued only with the life of mother's wishful projecting psyche.

She left on "holiday" and did not come back when expected. A month passed since the last hour. She called to say she was ill again. She had refused my remark that she was partly responsible for "bewitching her daughter" (Binzie) who treated her so badly. And she had refused my view of the dolls. "You are just like all the other analysts; you don't understand."

I hadn't; she was right. I had interpreted personalistically from my mother complex countertransference and thus done injustice to the archetypal nature of the process and its images. I had lost touch with the myth. We managed to make one meeting to talk about it again. This time we decided that the dolls were an imaginative way into mother, much as her imagination with little Annie. The circle of women were her young motherhood imagining how to mother, an attempt of the psyche to redeem the past within herself. She had indeed awakened from her sleep.

The hours during the last two months were scattered, partly she was away, partly I. The regularity and intensity of the first six months was over. She was secretly making plans to go back to America, but held this from me because "You would not let me go." Her desire to stay in Zurich had been put on to me, and split off from her. "Zurich was like a pilgrimage for me, like what old people do in the East." But she did not get what she came for. "Maybe what I got was more important?" "I feel I have been uncursed, but not redeemed."

One part of the personality wanted to leave, and to leave in thanks. Another part was afraid to leave, and yet another could leave only by cutting. The ending of the analysis as much as the beginning's *massa confusa* shows the multiplicity of personality, that a whole is made of many coexisting parts; pathologizing belongs. Unity of opposites means ambivalence. The paranoid fantasies were not gone, nor was the tree of clawing fingernails turned to sweet green leaves. But now, more or less, she was aware of the delusional tendency and the demands and could see through them by herself more readily. She had had practice, too short perhaps, in looking for the fantasy images within the emotional obsessions.

The indecision about return continued. She phoned, asking to see me at once. She came with a large paper sack and wanted all her dreams, all her drawings and letters back. She felt I was now bad for her: I had cooked her too long in the alchemical stove. "Who do you think you are to be so responsible for me!" She would not even sit down. I had the happy insight that this new wave of personal attack was the psyche's attempt to free herself from the transference dependency. And I told her so. She relaxed, and told me a new dream image: She saw Helen Hayes in a gray dress on the center of the stage in the play *Our Town*. Home it was, and the gray lady was still there, but now in the center of the stage.

She came to say good-bye. No hat, little makeup, but not altogether the gray lady: she had adjusted to this internal archetypal figure, but not identified with her. She had one more dream. "A baby about nine months old, in a high chair, about to be fed." She complimented me and even one of her former analysts. She had written to one of her children and apologized for an old score.

Some months later she wrote from Florida. Her children were adding to her monthly income, and one had let her visit for a long while. She mentioned a dream of a child with a mouth full of teeth, and cared for by two other women besides herself.

("Archetypal Theory," 90–97)

ANIMALS

Since I prefer not to consider animal images as instincts inside us, I do not use the hermeneutics of vitality for responding to their appearance in dreams. Here, I am trying to move away from the view that animals bring us life or show our power, ambition, sexual energy, endurance, or any of the other *rajas*, the hungry demands and compulsive sins and vices that have been put off upon animals in our culture and continue to be projected there in our dream interpretations. To look at them from an underworld perspective means to regard them as carriers of soul, perhaps totem carriers of our own free soul or death soul, there to help us see in the dark. To find out who they are and what they are doing there in the dream, we must first of all watch the image and pay less attention to our own reactions to it. As from a duck blind or when downwind stalking a deer, our focus is on the image, acute to its appearance, ourselves abashed, eclipsed in that intensity in order to follow the precise movements of its spontaneity. Then we might be able to understand what it means with us in the dream. But no animal ever means one thing only, and no animal simply means death.

In our tradition of underworld myth and folklore, only a few kinds of animal crop up regularly: The *dog* of Hecate, Cerberus of Hades, and the blue-black dog-jackal, Anubis; the *horse* of Hades's chariot, the horsemen of death, and the nightmare images in horse form; little *birds* are souls and large ones are winged-death daimones; the serpent as chthonic side of the god, the part that slips away into invisibility through holes in the ground and embodies the soul of the dead person. Then we also find special animals sacred to gods and goddesses who have strong underworld affiliations: pregnant cows to Tellus; pigs to Demeter; dogs to Hecate. In some fairy tales, death comes as a fish, as a wolf, as a fox. An unspecific, black, horned animal is frequently an animal image of death. Sometimes this figure is imagined as a black goat. Goats, says Farnell, were never loved by heroes. Especially in the classical world, black animals were sacrificed to the chthonic powers. . . .

The main point here is that there are many animal ways into the underworld. We may be led or chased down by dogs and meet the dog of fear, who bars the way to going deeper. We may be driven down by the energetic rapture of hard-riding horsepower; go down through the air like a bird in its many modes—twittering, sailing, diving—a sudden seizure of the spirit, the impulse suicide of a quick mental move. We may descend by means of our own piggishness, which has a hidden holiness, too, in its depths. Again, the descent and death that the animal constellates is not necessarily of our physical being because an animal is a physical being. This would be to take the animal image literally. Rather, the animal presents a *familiaris*, a dumb soul brother at our side, or a soul doctor, who understands psychic laws other than those of the day-world ego and which are a death for that world. . . .

A preparation for the underworld may be initiated by an animal sacrifice in a dream. It would not be right to take this only from the day-world view of giving up a piece of one's vital desire. For example, a woman began an analysis with a dream of "having to put her dog away." It was her old family German shepherd, now owned by her daughter. In the dream, she takes it to the animal doctor who "puts it to sleep." This dream combined the Demeter-Persephone motif, the family spirit of protectiveness and guardian watchfulness that kept her sheepish and in the flock, and the dog as guiding spirit into the realm of the dead. The dog went to Sleep and Death, and she was led there too by feelings of loss, lethargy, and aloneness. The animal doctor is also a doctor-animal or one who has animal wisdom, able to perform the death rites of therapy in regard to the animal. After this dream, there followed encounters with many family ghosts, dead relatives, perverse desires, ancient sins. She was no longer protected by the dog from the dog. The dog was now ruling her land of sleep, her sleeping earth, digging up all sorts of bones and dirt. A *nekyia* had begun.   (*Dream and the Underworld*, 148–151)

D uring one of my itinerant teaching seminars on animal images in dreams, a woman handed me this dream:

I was flying in an airplane piloted by my husband. As he was flying, I was looking at the scenery below. Then I told him, Look, I see a polar bear under some water down there. My husband kept on with his flying. Then I looked at his radar screen and the polar bear had registered on it along with something else as two X's. Then my husband said, I think I'll take a look, and turned the plane around until we saw the polar bear again, still sitting under water.

When the dreamer is flying and piloted by her husband—what she is coupled with, to, by in that syzygy—then she looks down on the world as scenery. The scenery consists in the waters below in which is a living animal. At first the animal appears in the flying plane on the radar screen—an abstract kind of awareness of the bear in the flying, looking-down, screening mind, which makes the husband say "I think," and to re-spect, that is, look again, by turning the plane around, reversing his forward direction. The polar bear registers as an X, an unknown quantity, in fact as two Xs, for the dream says: "The polar bear had registered on the radar screen along with something else as two X's." The bear is qualified by the number two; something else is with it, something more to it, a second bear, a ghost bear, a resonance registering only abstractly. What is this double bear still sitting, sitting still under water. A Jewish legend says that each animal species has a corresponding one in the water. Is this bear in the water the bear that did not get into the ark? Why does this bear sit there in the waters below? Who is this bear? Why must they see it?

Another polar bear dream from a woman in her thirties:

A polar bear is after me. I am terrified and try to close a door to keep him out. A man goes after him, and then I see the bear come back, hurt. He has been hit by a car and his shoulder is all torn and bloody and he keeps looking at it confused. I feel sorry, anguished that this happened. I didn't want him hurt, I just didn't want him to hurt me.

The dream exhibits the familiar motif of pursuit by the animal. But does the bear pursue her because it comes "after her," that is, because she stays ahead of it, counterphobic to it, closing doors against the white animal that comes for her? An anonymous man goes after the bear, resulting in its being hit and bloodied and confused by a car—such is the strength of the "man" in this woman's dream and the vehicle of her drive. It can confuse the animal. But now there is reconciliation through pain: as the bear is wounded, she is anguished—a relationship conceived in terms of hurt. Perhaps hurt has opened the door between them.

A third polar dream comes from a woman of fifty-two:

I see a large huge strong Polar Bear—gleaming white and standing on the very far edge of his earth—a point of ice and snow at the top of the Pole, and facing blue icy water. He stands on his hind legs, upright, and his head is thrown back, nose pointing to heaven, and he bellows, rends the air with anguish. Watching, I recognize he is at the end of his rope from searching for his mate and child, and calls out in terrible agony and helpless power.

Gleaming white, at the farthest edge of earth, at the end of his rope, at the top of the pole, upright and pointing to heaven, this bear—for all his power at that place—is in agony. Not because he is hunted or wounded, but because in this extreme vertical northernmost pointedness, he cannot find his mate and child; alone. Large, huge and strong, yet helpless. What terrible anguish is rending the air of her dream? What must be heard? Witnessing this bear, to what is the woman bearing witness?

And now a fourth dream of a polar bear, this time from a man:

I am hunting a white polar bear in very cold wilderness, making every effort to kill it. After several vain attempts, the white polar bear and I become friendly. It should be noted that although the atmosphere was a pure, clear cold, I was not wearing heavy clothing. Suddenly, I am drowning in the middle of a lake as my brother and the polar bear watch from the shore. Somehow, the white bear swims out and saves my life.

Not the brother "swims out and saves my life," but the white bear, paired with "my brother" and perhaps more than a brother at least in the capacity of saving his life. The bear he has been trying to kill by making every effort (for so is how he tries to kill the bear: "by making every effort") saves his life. The vanity of attempting to kill the bear, yet the pursuit of it, has brought him into friendly affinity of hunter with the hunted. And, "it should be noted" that this dreamer is not wearing protective clothing. He has his own inner heat now that he and the bear are friendly. Yet again: who, what is the bear that "saves my life?"

These four dreamers are modern Americans. I vouch they have no empirical relations with polar bears: they are not hunters, explorers, zoologists, Eskimos. I am rather certain they have not read the *Kalevala*, been to the Drachenloch, or studied Shamanism. Nor do I believe they know about the holy nature of the white animal in folklore. I strongly doubt that the woman in whose dream the white bear howled for its mate and child has read Thomas Bewick's illustrated eighteenth-century *History of Quadrupeds* where it states that among polar bears "fondness for offspring is so great that they embrace their cubs to the last, and bemoan them with the most piteous cries."

Within this condensed context of a lecture I cannot pretend to deal adequately with dreams, but were we anthropologists among the peoples of the north polar circle, we would recognize in this polar bear what is called the "animal guardian," master of animals who is himself an animal, and who, more than protector of the hunt, more than totemic ancestor—the great white bear as grandfather or grandmother—is, as Ivar Paulson says, the supreme being in phenomenal form, "among the oldest theophanies in the religious life of mankind."

These white bears could be theophanies, displays of divinities, presenting the dilemmas, the agonies, the potentialities in precise detail of what Jung called the "religious instinct." In each case we read how the dreamer deals with the white animal: behaves toward it, feels in regard to it, and where he or she encounters it. Yet a bear is more than, other than a religious instinct. An unknown quantity is left over from the reduction, the image of the polar bear itself, the other bear in the water, and we turn to animal dreams also for the animal's sake.

The dreams were given to me as an animal-dream collector to be used as I see fit, and I am grateful to all dreamers whose dreams I shall be recounting for their generosity. The dreams form part of a collection I began at the Jung Institute in Zurich in 1959 for a study group to inquire into animal motifs in dreams. The collection has grown over the years. I should hasten to add that though the material is honestly empirical, handed me in written form by the dreamers and usually with no comment, or by analysts, the method of working these dreams is not empirical in the usual sense. No statistical frequencies, no correlations between dreams and the condition of the dreamers as in the fashion of the old dream books: when you see a polar bear in your dream, then you will catch cold, or be lonely, find your life threatened, or saved, and so on. We soon gave up adducing the significance of this or that animal in direct relation with diagnosis and prognosis. Too simple. There is a strange gap between dream research and dream interpretation, between a scientific explanatory psychology and an understanding imaginative psychology. It is like the gap between the day world of nomothetic norms, inducing laws from many cases, and the night world of idiographic descriptions: how the dream animal appears in an image, and what it "means." Yet not "means to the dreamer," because we did not have the dreamers. We thus were attempting to understand the dream animals as dream naturalists. What is the animal kingdom in the human dream: how does it behave; what does it want; what is the relation between dream animal and dream human?

I am suggesting that we read the animal and not only about the animal. I am suggesting that the dream animal can be amplified as well by a visit to the zoo as by a symbol dictionary, and I am suggesting that we dream interpreters not reduce the dream to the symbol, but reduce ourselves, that is, our own vision to that of the animal, a reduction which may be an extension, an amplification, of our vision so as to see the animal with an animal eye.

What does the animal recognize when it comes upon another animal? Without benefit of a bestiary, its text is the living form. The reading of living form, the self-expressive metaphors that animals present, is what is meant by the legends that saints and shamans understand the language of animals, not in the literal speech of words as much as psychically, animal soul to animal image, speaking with animals as they come in dreams.

("Animal Kingdom," 279–282, 302–303)

A young man dreams:

(24) Green caterpillar on my leg in a garden restaurant. I lit a match and held it under the creature and it became like charcoal.

Right thereafter he dreams:

(25) Lying on my bed, I see insects on the ceiling. One was green and the other was blue. They seemed to be dancing or fighting. I took a broom and crushed them and wiped away the spot so that the ceiling looked all right again.

(26) Beetles and roaches come into the room where we are. It is the upstairs family room. My father, brother and I fight the beetles with lots of powders on the floor and make a very irregular mess. They don't seem to die. Probably takes time. My mother and sister interfere with our work. It is hard to work with them around.

A woman reports this dream:

(27) I'm gardening out in the backyard with my husband and children. A few limp damp weeds get pulled, dragged up, and I track a few into the

kitchen on my shoe. One weed I pick up and it reveals itself as a bee and I stalk it, trying first to kill it with a brush and then I get a large kitchen knife and cut it in half, after which I feel safe.

Let us note the different sorts of extermination: fire, crushing, powders, knife. Dreamers defend against the insects in different ways. For example, the kitchen knife that cuts the bee in two: better and worse or an upper and a lower, so that she feels safe when she can dissect problems with sharp practical distinctions.

The insects crushed against the ceiling are swept out of the young man's uplooking attitude, restoring it to the *status quo ante* of blankness. Jung calls this move "the regressive restoration of the persona" (*CW* 7, §§254–59). By crushing the insect, we exercise the will and strengthen the heroic stance. By setting fire to the bug, the dreamer cruelly tortures what tortures him. Here, we see an answer to Jung's question about torture in the alchemical work (*CW* 13, §§439–40). Jung asks, is the subject the torturer or the victim of it? In dream (24) the source of the suffering lies in the means the dreamer uses to rid himself of the bug in the garden. Yet, this same torture ignites the alchemical process, that "work in fire," that *opus contra naturam*, which turns sheer green nature into the nigredo of ignorance of mind, powerlessness of will, and darkness of heart. Nonetheless, the caterpillar, symbol of transformation par excellence, releases in the imaginal ego of the dream the transformational reaction of fire, the Promethean act. To side with the dreamer against the invasive caterpillar for the sake of igniting the ego into action or to side with the poor caterpillar against the cruel dream-I misses the complexity of the alchemical process. Or, in Berry's language, there is always a telos in a defense, and a defense woven into every aim.   ("Going Bugs," 56–57)

MOTIFS

Concerning black in dreams, I would like to bypass both the richness of color symbolism, and the many notions already explored in religious mysticism about darkness and alchemical symbolism about the nigredo, in order to restrict myself to *black persons in dreams.*

It is a Jungian convention to take these blacks as shadows, a convention to which there can be no objection. However, analytical psychology has tended to see these black shadows as earthy in the Ge or Demeter senses and thus as potentials of vitality (sexuality, fertility, aggressivity, strength, emotionality). Moreover, the content of the black shadow has been further determined by sociological overtones. Personal associations to blacks in the culture affect the interpretation of the image. The black shadow today supposedly brings spontaneity, revolution, warmth, or music—or frightening criminality. In other eras, black figures in whites' dreams might have been loyalty, or apelikeness, or lethargy, servility, and stupidity, or been translated into superb force and wholeness, the Anthropos or "original man." Blacks have had to carry every sort of sociological shadow, from true religion and faithfulness, to cowardice and evil. The sociological vogues all have forgotten that The Black Man is also Thanatos.

As we saw above, the inhabitants of the netherworld in Egypt were black, and in Rome they were called *inferi* and *umbrae.* Cumont *(After Life in Roman Paganism)* says this "term implies, besides the idea of a subtle essence, the notion that the inhabitants of the dusky spaces underground were black, and this is in fact the colour often given to them. It is also the colour of the victims offered them and of the mourning garments worn in their honour."

I think it would be archetypally more correct, and so more psychological, to consider black persons in dreams in terms of their resemblance with this underworld context. Their concealed and raping attributes belong to the "violating" phenomenology of Hades, of which we have already spoken, just as their pursuit resembles the hounding by the death demons. They are returning ghosts from the repressed netherworld—not merely from the repressed ghetto. Their message is psychic before it is vital. They bring one down and steal one's "goods" and menace the ego behind its locked doors.

In other words, their terrifying aspect might be where their true dynamic lies, although our sociological prejudice will not allow this possibility. Coming from death's kingdom as creepers in the night, of course they frighten. But anxiety, as we have known ever since Freud, signals the return of the repressed, and the repressed nowadays, goodness knows, is certainly not sexuality, not criminality, not brutality—all those things we say that black figures "represent." They present death; the repressed is death. And death dignifies them.

Following this through then, black persons in dreams would no longer have to carry the sociological shadow of primitivity (for the developmental fantasy of the ego), vitality (for the ego's heroic strength), or inferiority (for the ego's moral or political fantasy). In other words, we would move away from a pseudo negro-psychology to a genuine shadowpsychology, an attempt to restore to the black figures "the idea of a subtle essence."

When images of ice appear in dreams, one is likely to imagine that they refer to regions of the spirit: high mountains, remote polar purity, and the thin splendor of the clean. There is another realm of ice—deep, deep down. Below the water, the hellfires, and the mud, there is the ninth circle of the Inferno that is all ice. According to Dante, this is the place of Cain, Judas, and Lucifer. Gnostic writings also describe a snow-and-ice region of the underworld. This frozen *topos* is another way of imaging psychopathy. But there is more to it.

The descent to the underworld can be distinguished from the night sea journey of the hero in many ways. We have already noticed the main distinction: the hero returns from the night sea journey in better shape for the tasks of life, whereas the *nekyia* takes the soul into a depth for its own sake so that there is no "return." The night sea journey is further marked by building interior heat (*tapas*), whereas the *nekyia* goes below that pressured containment, that tempering in the fires of passion, to a zone of utter coldness.

Therapeutic analysis remains incomplete if it is satisfied with bringing balm to burning problems. It has still to venture into the frozen depths that have so fascinated poets and explorers and that in depth psychology are the areas of our archetypal crystallizations, the immovable depressions and the mutisms of catatonia.

Here we are numb, chilled. All our reactions are in cold storage. This is a psychic place of dread and of a terror so deep that it comes in uncanny experiences, such as voodoo death and the *totstell* reflex. A killer lives in the ice. Or, this ice may be experienced as a paranoiac distance, such as Nietzsche describes in "Zarathustra's Night Song": "Light am I . . . this is my loneliness to be begirt with light. . . . Alas, there is ice around me, my hand burneth touching iciness."

We may recall here that the Styx is a river of icy hatred that protects the underworld and is holy and eternal as are the god's oaths that they swear by that frigid river. If the ice serves a function in the underworld, then the icy area of our nature serves a function in the soul. Glacial cold—psychopathic, paranoiac, catatonic—is not absent feeling or bad feeling, but a kind of feeling of its own. Cain, Judas, and Lucifer are beyond human warmth and psychology's techniques of sharing the heart, as if humanism would reconstruct the globe so that all humanity lived in the tepid balance of the temperate zones. Cain, Judas, and Lucifer are not tepid, not temperate; they have another kind of heart. The icy chasm of Christianism's shadow is a realm of radical importance that cannot be reached with Christianism's bleeding heart. An archetypal approach to this zone follows the homeopathic maxim: like cures like. The *nekyia* into hell's ice requires coldness. If any connection is to be made, we must be able to work with the cruel extremities of ice itself. We can meet Cain, Judas, and Lucifer by being aware of our own desires to be false and to betray, to kill our brother and to kill ourselves, that our kiss has death in it and that there is a piece of the soul that would live forever cast out from both human and heavenly company. These desires that seek no redemption and have abandoned all hope also move in the therapist's heart—not only his charity and faith. These desires of the Ninth Circle give that cold psychological eye that sees all things from below, as images caught in their circles, an eye that glitters with the inhuman insight of Lucifer, light bearer.

The heart has a coldness, a place of reserve like the refrigerator that preserves, holds, protects, isolates, suspends animation and circulation, an alchemical congelation of substance. The cruelty and mean despising are the surroundings of a private sense of ultimate deepening. Maybe in my ice is my fairy-tale princess, whom ego psychology wants to kiss into life; but maybe she is otherwise engaged in her frigid stillness, deepening toward the Ninth Circle, below everything moving; a detachment and stability reminding of the cold body of death. Here is a soul figure who is neither flighty, nor sensuously rippling, nor brooding moods and emotions. Instead the glitter of ice reflects perfection; nothing but crystallized insights and sharp-edged truths are good enough. Desire for absolutism, absolution in perfection. The ice maiden is a terrible taskmaster, frigid and unresponsive; but since her region is on the map of psychic geography, polar coldness is also a place one can be. Therefore the urge to warm the cold and melt the ice (oppositionalism again) reflects a therapeutic effort that has not been able to meet the ice at its own level. The curative urge conceals the fear of the Ninth Circle, of going all the way down to those depths that are so quickly and surely called psychotic.

Pagan and early Christian tomb inscriptions speak of the dead soul as refrigerated: *in refrigeratio anima tua; deus te refrigeret; in refrigerio et in pace.* The literary tradition also used *refrigerium* and *refrigerare* for the condition of the released soul after death. The source of this convention is supposedly the translation into Latin of Greek words akin to psyche that mean "cool." (*Psykter* = "wine cooler"; *psychos* = "wintertime, cold weather"; *psychros* = "cold, unreal, cold hearted, frigid.") The basic form, *psychō*, means something like "blowing cold" or "cooling breath." Indeed there is an ancient connection between the dimension of coldness and the soul *(anima, psyche).*

Psyche not only was in a cold place or was a place of coldness in various senses of the word. It was also given a cooling drink of sweet psychic refreshment, for instance, by Osiris. These cold drinks return in our dreams. Are we supposed to understand Cokes, ice cream, Kool-Aid against this antique background? The problem here is the literalization of sweetness into sugar (or its synthetics), i.e., the problem of the naive, naturalistic attitude of the child, to whom, if something is sweet, it must taste sweet, and if it is cold, it must be sensed concretely as cold. When the place of ice is also the place of sugar, there is a confusion between the psychic needs of the underworld and the emotional needs of the child. The dream image shows them concocted together. (The problem will be given a clue by the color and name of the drink, as well as by the location of the image.) The dream-ego, sipping its chocolate ice-cream soda, is one that has to take its dark ice with a creamy sweetener, but at least the dream-ego is imbibing the cold drink of death.

(*Dream and the Underworld*, 144–146, 168–171)

W hen we take the dream as a corrective to the leftovers of yesterday or as instruction for tomorrow, we are using it for the old ego. Freud said the dream is the guardian of sleep. And indeed the dream ego belongs to the family of Night (Nyx), serves there regularly, and takes its instruction in terms of its own "family," from its mother and its brother and sister phenomena. Perhaps the point of dreams is that, night after night, year after year, they prepare the imaginal ego for old age, death, and fate by soaking it through and through in *memoria*. Perhaps the point of dreams has very little to do with our daily concerns, and their purpose is the soul-making of the imaginal ego. (*Myth of Analysis*, 187)

11

Love's Torturous
Enchantments

If each god has his own logos, then Eros, too, has his special logic and necessities. In art he has often been pictured as a handsome adolescent, and in the story of Eros and Psyche, which James Hillman takes as his primary myth of psychoanalysis, he is the wild son of Aphrodite, easy to love and difficult to abide with. He brings the psyche promises of pleasure and many occasions for suffering. He pleases without measure, and he tortures without any apparent misgiving.

Rather than present a program of painless love, the aim of many psychologies, Hillman explores the betrayals and impossibilities of love as valuable initiatory moments of the soul. Initiation is a rite of soul-making. Innocence may have to be punctured. Idealized notions of self, other, and love may have to earn their ripening shadows. A third element may have to appear to keep the two in love from closing their world in on themselves. Primal, Eden-like trust may have to mature so that one doesn't go about life with an innocence frequently shocked and undone by disappointment and betrayal.

Hillman speaks for love that is soulful, rounded with psychological reflection, and he speaks for psychological life that honors love as its principle. Eros always leads to psyche. Even, and perhaps especially, impossible loves invite interiorizing. As the ancient tale spells out, the soul tortured by love is in an ordeal in which specific initiations are carried out. The psyche's attachment to the love that is so difficult keeps it within the work of initiation. Its leaning toward death echoes the subtle relationship between eros and death, both enticing consciousness away from the logic of reason and pragmatics.

The centering of psychology on love, affirmed as a fundamental principle in Sigmund Freud and Carl Jung, and made into a primary motive in humanistic psychologies, in Hillman is absolute. In this he follows his romantic ancestors, William Blake for example, for whom desire far outweighed reason as a measure of wisdom and ethics. Desire, longing, attachment, intensity, endurance, receptivity—these qualities of soul in league with erotic demands of fate are prized in Hillman's writings.

As a naturalist of the phenomenon of love, Hillman studies betrayal, one of love's specific tortures. But he doesn't intend to correct betrayal. Indeed, generally Hillman consciously avoids psychological moralisms, the subtle "shoulds" and "oughts" that infest psychoanalysis. He inquires into the innocence that invites betrayal and the atonement necessary for forgiveness. On both sides, he sees signs of the initiatory role of love.

Finally, Hillman depicts the human person as Transparent Man, made visible to himself through the torments of love. In love, the person is always the fool, emptied of prudence, his desires evident to the world, his transgressions revealed to all, especially to himself. But this transparency, created by the departure of innocence, is the occasion for involvement, another of those amorous words suggesting that the soul is always attached to life. Erasmus said that it is one's foolishness that allows for intimacy. Hillman places this foolish logic of love over the logics of health, normalcy, adjustment, success, happiness, and good communication. He recommends a therapy of love.

Because archetypal psychology gives subjectivity back to the figures of the psyche and to the world, love moves in several directions. It is not only the ego that loves, but other figures, images, and dreams love and desire us. Dreams also suggest that figures love each other. All of this love in the soul offers a way beyond the will to love or the commandment to love. The heroics of love give way to a gracious receiving of love.

It is easy to miss the radical positioning of love in Hillman's psychology. Everyone would say that love is important. But Hillman's approach to the psyche is in every instance rooted in a love of whatever he finds. This absolute love is the basis for keeping clear of strong-willed acts in the name of health that, however well meant, are antagonistic to the soul. Psychological love does not require an understanding of the processes and mysteries that are presented for reflection. It is a love that requires unlimited faith in expressions of soul. It is a love that inspires interest in all kinds of emotional suffering, crazy fantasies, absurd symptoms, and repeated mistakes. On the other hand, it engenders passionate anger in the face of soullessness and inhumanity, irreverence, cruelty to nature and animal life, and, above all, puritanical oppressions of the vibrant springs of life that want to burst forth where they will.

Love that leads to psyche is not bound by human concerns and conditions. It is both active and receptive. It comes into life as a grace, so that, like Psyche of the tale, one has a relationship to love itself.

LOVE'S TORTURE

Torment of the soul in its relationship to eros is a major theme in the tale of Eros and Psyche.

From the mid-fourth century before our era until the sixth century, when it was absorbed by Christian allegory, the collective witness of terra cotta, sculpture, engraved gems, and bas reliefs attests to the popularity of this tale, in its *fabula* form as *Märchen* or folktale. These figurative works . . . state . . . that the psyche is tortured by love. We find Psyche sad, kneeling, weeping; Psyche, the begging suppliant, prostrate at the feet of Eros; Psyche chained or bound to the chariot of love; Eros shooting and wounding Psyche; Psyche's wings burned, or the burned moth or butterfly, whose name in Greek gives them symbolic identity. (The same motifs occur in dreams today. A woman dreams that she tries to burn a wormlike insect in a bonfire; but it proves indestructible, and out comes a winged butterfly. A young man dreams of crushing green winged creatures on his ceiling and whitewashing over the spot, or of ridding himself of a caterpillar by setting fire to it; but in a later dream a crowned and winged frog-insect appears.) The insistence upon this aspect of the Psyche-Eros tale became redoubled in the Renaissance representations, where Psyche is tied in cruel knots, crushed in the press, burned at the stake—in an extraordinary mixture of Christian metaphors with the pagan tale of love and torture.

The torture of the soul seems unavoidable in every close involvement, of which the transference of an analysis is one example.

Despite all one does to avoid and to alleviate suffering, it would seem that the process in which the people find themselves arranges it, as if we were driven by a mythical necessity to enact Psyche and Eros. Jung (*CW* 13, §439f) has discussed the motif of torture, raising the questions: What is tortured? What does the torturing? Our myth tells us that psyche suffers from love; a girl is tortured into womanhood, as a man's anima is awakened through torment into psyche, a torment which, as Neumann observes, transforms eros as well. Eros is tortured by its own principle, fire. It burns others; and it burns alone when cut off from psyche, that is, when it is without psychological insight and reflection. Psyche pursues its tasks, without hope or energy, loveless, inconsolable. Their separation is the split we experience: while eros burns, psyche figures out, does its duties, depressed.

Before connection is possible, psyche goes through the dark night of the soul (the burned wings of the night moth), that *mortificatio* in which it feels the paradoxical agony of a pregnant potential within itself and a sense of guilty, cut-off separateness. The torment continues until the soul-work (Psyche's tasks) is completed and the psyche is reunited with a transformed eros. Eros needs to regress, it would seem, into a state of burning unrest and agitation, dominated by the mother, by Penia or deprivation, in order to realize that he has himself been felled by his arrow and has found his mate, Psyche. He gains psychic consciousness. Only then does the union take place, and for it the sanctification of the gods is required.

Their long separation, Psyche's tasks, and their mutual torments—being burned, chained, dragged—present the images of erotic obsession complete even to its sadomasochistic aspects. Without wings the soul cannot soar above its immediate compulsions, can gain no perspective. For our psyche to unite legitimately with the creative and bring to sanctified birth what it carries, we evidently need to realize both our loss of primordial love through betrayal and separation and also our wrong relation to eros—the enthrallment, servility, pain, sadness, longing: all aspects of erotic *mania.* As Jung says, ". . . for always the ardour of love transmutes fear and compulsion into a higher free type of feeling." Seen against the oedipal background, these torments cannot redeem, since in that myth compulsion overcomes love; in our tale, despite the same phenomena of torment, love—because it finds soul—overcomes compulsion.

The myth of the process "arranges" suffering; yet this suffering is neither blind and tragic, as with Oedipus, nor is it the endurance of the hero in the belly of the whale. The suffering in our tale has something to do with initiation, with changing the structure of consciousness. The tale itself has deep roots in ancient Isis mysteries; as Merkelbach says, "Initiation rites are a symbol of a whole life." As such, the ordeals of Psyche and Eros are initiatory; they are symbolic of the psychological and erotic ordeals to which we are put. This gives us a wholly different view, not only of transference and analytical suffering, but of the ground of neurosis in our time. Neurosis becomes initiation, analysis the ritual, and our developmental process in psyche and in eros, leading to their union, becomes the mystery.

We must have a new way of grasping what goes on in our lives and in our practices, another view of the women who leave their children for a lover; the women who fall in love with youth, as the men do with beauty; the insupportable triangles and jealousies we suffer; the repetitive erotic entanglements which, because they are soulless and without psychological reflection, lead only to more despair; the divorces that become the necessary path for psychic development when there is no possibility for eros in a marriage; the marriages that need to be held together if only for the sake of the psychic suffering, which then may constellate eros in a new way; the analyses that are haunted by images of former loves, going back sometimes fifty years, and how these become the redeemed and redeeming figures; or the fact that failed love often means failure as a person and leads to suicide, and why the worst of all betrayals are those of love. These situations, and the intense emotions flowing from them, feel central to a person's being and may mean more to working out his fate than the family problem and his conscious development as a heroic course. These events create consciousness in men and women, initiating us into life as a personal-impersonal mystery beyond problems that can be analyzed.

When these events are told through this tale, portraying "an Odyssey of the human soul"—a tale of union, separation, and suffering and an eventual reunion of love and soul blessed by the archetypal powers—they can be handled in another spirit: one of confirmation and encouragement. *For whatever the disguise, what is taking place is the creative eros connecting with an awakening psyche.* All the turns and torments are part of—shall we say bhakti yoga?—a psychological discipline of eros development, or an erotic discipline of psychological development, aiming toward psychic integration and erotic identity. Without this devotional discipline we have the easy playboy's pairings of Alcibiades, anima and sex, ending in power, not love. Thus we can understand why we meet so much "impossible love": the dead lover or bride, unrequited and humiliating love, the love choice of the "wrong" person (who is married, or cannot divorce, or is the analyst, or is homosexual, or is in a distant land or ill). The arrow falls where it will; we can only follow.

Of all forms of impossibility, the arrow strikes us into triangles to such an extraordinary extent that this phenomenon must be examined for its creative role in soul-making. The sudden dynamic effect on the psyche of jealousy and other triangular fears and fantasies hints that this constellation of "impossibility" bears as much significance as does the conjunction. To explain it oedipally or through the anima/animus, to see it morally and negatively, does not allow it objective necessity. So necessary is the triangular pattern that, even where two exist only for each other, a third will be imagined. In the fantasies of analysis, when there is no third, the two collude for one; or the analyst is the third in the patient's life, while the patient is the third in the analyst's; or the previous patient is the third. The constructive-destructive aspect of eros creativity intervenes like a daimon to prevent the *hieros gamos* by insisting upon "the other," who becomes the catalyst of impossibility. We witness the same Eros which joins two now breaking the reciprocity of the couple by striking his arrow into a third. The stage is set for tragedy and for every extreme sort of psychic and erotic aberration. Perhaps this is its necessity: the triangles of eros educate the psyche out of its girlish goodness, showing it the extent of its fantasies and testing its capacity. The triangle presents eros as the transcendent function creating out of two a third, which, like all impossible love, cannot be lived fully in actuality, so that the third comes as imaginal reality. But it comes not as imagery in meditation but through violence and pain and in the shape of actual persons, teaching the psyche by means of the triangle that the imaginal is most actual and the actual symbolic. We say, at one and the same time: "It's nonsense, a projection, all in my imagination" and "I can't go on without the actual you."

All impossible love forces upon us a discipline of interiorizing. Anima becomes psyche as the image of the impossibly loved person who tends to represent the daimon that, by inhibiting compulsion, fosters new dimensions of psychic awareness. These experiences show most transparently eros actually making soul. They also show the countereffects of the soul upon eros. The psyche acts as a *causa formalis*, making qualitative changes possible in eros. This maturing process provides the basic pattern described in so many fictional "love stories." The effect of psyche upon eros is primarily one of a process character, a change in timing, yielding qualities of subtlety, awareness, and indirection within involvement. These qualitative changes come about when one accepts as *necessary for the soul* all the desires, impulses, attachments, and needs of eros; these form the primary material for the transformation. Similarly, the effect of eros on psyche is characterized by what we have already described as an awakening and engendering. And this too has a prerequisite: bringing eros to *all psychic contents whatsoever*—symptoms, moods, images, habits—and finding them fundamentally lovable and desirable.

The idealizations which eros tends always to constellate can be counterbalanced: creativity expresses itself also as destruction. Love's torture may not always lead to the happy ending of our tale. The idealizations may be further weighted by recalling the connections in Hesiod, the Orphics, and Renaissance Neoplatonism between eros and chaos.

Eros is born of chaos, implying that out of every chaotic moment the creativity of which we have been speaking can be born. Furthermore, eros will always hearken back to its origins in chaos and will seek it for its revivification. Aristophanes writes even of their mating. Eros will attempt again and again to create those dark nights and confusions which are its nest. It renews itself in affective attacks, jealousies, fulminations, and turmoils. It thrives close to the dragon.

The voice of order in us will have none of this. Eros, yes; but chaos, never. In a passage from the taxonomist Simpson, quoted by Lévi-Strauss, we hear this voice of Apollonian reason and its enmity to chaos: "Scientists do tolerate uncertainty and frustration, because they must. The one thing that they do not and must not tolerate is disorder. The whole aim of theoretical science is to carry to the highest possible and conscious degree the perceptual reduction of chaos." By refusing chaos, its consequent, eros, may also be lost to science, which may or may not damage science in its quest for order. But it will damage the scientist's soul-making and creativity. The mythic relation of eros and chaos states what academic studies of creativity have long said, that chaos and creativeness are inseparable.

Since chaos is also a gap, an emptiness or lacuna, eros has a predeliction for the psychopathic holes in the psyche, for its form-lessness, its not-yetness and hopelessness. (Psyche is always depicted as a young girl, which has less to do with youth than with the lacunae of the anima, its emptiness, which we feel as despair, a wound, and as an aesthetic vagueness, especially when touched by eros.) To call this unformed void of psychopathic darkness in one's nature the shadow does it only partial justice, because shadow tends to mean moral evil as seen from ego. But chaos refers to a *prima materia,* indicating a peculiar inherent connection between the worst inert sludge of human nature, its inchoate *increatum,* and the attractions of eros. This alone gives some account of the peculiar and "impossi-ble" fixations in our lives between the erotic and the psychopathic, between the idealizations of eros and its affinity for chaos. Thus, behind the idealizations of Othello's eros for Desdemona lies the lacuna of his psychopathy, so that he is compelled to say: ". . . and when I love thee not, Chaos is come again" (*Othello* III, iii).

At first the entanglements which Eros constellates seem per-sonal, as if all of love hung on the right word or move at the magical right time, as if it were a matter of effort and doing. But then the entanglements become reflections of archetypal patterns, patterns that appear in everyone's life. The images *(eidola)* are what everyone has experienced in his psyche through loving. In this way Eros leads to the archetypes behind the patterns, and we are played into myth after myth: now a hero, now a virgin running, now a satyr who must clutch, now blind, now soaring. Precisely this mythical awareness and enactment result from psychological creativity.

Thus we begin to recognize in ourselves that *eros* and *psyche* are not mere figures in a tale, not merely configurations of archetypal components, but are two ends of every psychic process. They always imply and require each other. We cannot view anything psychologi-cally without an involvement with it: we cannot be involved with anything without its entering our soul. By experiencing an event psychologically, we tend to feel a connection with it; in feeling and desire we tend to realize the importance of something for the soul. *Desire is holy,* as D. H. Lawrence, the romantics, and the Neoplato-nists insisted, because it touches and moves the soul. Reflection is never enough.   (*Myth of Analysis,* 92–100, 105–106)

Emotion always has some survival value and reveals some truth about reality, but this truth is symbolic, not merely sociological or biological. We cannot therefore condemn an emotion without giving it full hearing, without trying to grasp the transformation as symbolic. The peculiar emotional behavior of our time may perhaps be an adaptation to reality and have survival value, if not only for the individual, perhaps also for the collective psyche of the species. How often are neuroses—abortive emotion from many points of view—also creative adaptations. . . . Too often the therapist with too narrow a view of emotion sees it as an abortive transformation and rushes in with relief. One could expect Job's friends or the companions of Jesus in Gethsemane today to step forward with a tranquilizer. In short, emotion, no matter how bizarre, must be taken in awful earnest before diagnosing it abortive.

This refusal to meet the challenge of emotion, this *mauvaise foi* of consciousness is fundamental to our "age of anxiety." It is characteristic of—even instrumental in—what has been called "the contemporary failure of nerve." We do not face emotion in honesty and live it consciously. Instead emotion hangs as a negative background shadowing our age with anxiety and erupting in violence. A "therapy" of this condition depends altogether upon a change in the attitude of consciousness toward emotion—a change for which this work attempts to provide a ground. If there is anything novel in this synthesis of final causes it is this: *emotion is always to be valued more highly than the conscious system alone.* This tends to run counter to the mainstream of thinking about emotion in the psychology, philosophy, physiology and therapy of today.

Behind the difficulty of affirmation lies the healthy, natural tendency to avoid the numinous and demonic, that dark unruly horse of the Phaedrus myth, violent yet harnessed to the chariot in which we sit and which we try to manage. What to do about this horse has occupied the great philosophers and religious teachers for thousands of years. Many alternatives have been formulated. The ancients spoke of *mediopatheia, apatheia, ataraxia* and *catharsis*. Some church fathers suggested governing, while sectarians have offered on the one hand a radical, disciplined annihilation of the horse, or on the other, an enthusiastic loss of identity in favor of the animal in Dionysian orgy. More recently, methods of "abreaction," "acting out," or mechanical and chemical therapy have been put forward. All of these we have refused in favor of the notion of development. But by development we do not mean a progressive climb away from the dark beast so as to escape it. Nor do we mean a dropping of the reins in favor of the whip such as the charioteer does in a scene of such blood and cruelty (*Phaedrus*, 254), that it serves to indicate how subtly the dark horse can creep under the human skin of the charioteer who believes himself superior. No, this is not the way; but Plato himself gives us another image—the reins. We are reined to the horse, it to us. This is emotional existence, driving and being driven, the true image of *homo patiens*. Here we come close to the image of the centaur which Benoit proposes as the Zen image for solving emotional states. These passionate mythological monsters, one of whom was the wise instructor of such culture heroes as Achilles, Hercules and Aesculapius, represent a humanization of emotional driving power. Centaurs were said to be able to capture wild bulls which expresses the idea that wilder emotion can be tamed by conscious emotion, or as was said above, "only through emotion can emotion be cured." And it was a centaur, mythology tells us, who taught mankind something of the arts of music and medicine—as if to say the origins of healing our emotional malaise are to be found in the union of mind with flesh, of wisdom with passion.

(*Emotion*, 282–283, 285, 288–289)

Why do we focus so intensely on our problems? What draws us to them? Why are they so attractive? They have the magnet power of love: somehow we desire our problems; we are in love with them much as we want to get rid of them, and they seem there before a relationship begins, before an analysis begins. Now, if the problem contains some strange compelling fascinating third, then it is a love object or is a place where love itself is hiding, right in the problem. This means that problems are secret blessings or, let's say, they are not so much problems as they are emblems—like Renaissance *emblemata* showing a terrible impossible group of intertwined images that don't make sense and yet are the motto, the coat of arms, the basic family raised to the dignity of an emblem which sustains. . . . Problems sustain us—maybe that's why they don't go away. What would a life be without them? Completely tranquilized and loveless, too. There is a secret love hiding in each problem. . . .

Oh, I think analysis is a big improvement over that [nineteenth-century] literature. The novelists put first value on the emotions, exploring them, analyzing them. What I try to do is not to put the feelings first but the images, that is not to call something miserable because your feeling is miserable, but to examine the misery in terms of the image. That gives a new handle on it. What is the precise image of the misery? It may be yourself, chained, unable to move. Or yourself like Cinderella, sitting by the fire and deserted, or yourself thrown into a ditch or hated, paranoid, everybody laughing at you and betraying you. Or your misery may be screaming and calling and burning for the other person—in a particular place or scene. I remember once my own misery showed in a dream as a leopard that was on fire inside my bloodstream. You'd be amazed at the images that lie inside the feelings—but one thing is sure, there always will be some revelatory image. Once a woman patient was tortured by a lover who left her—and what was this torture, really, in her imagination? It was a tall erect phallus, and she was bowing, and it just stood there imperious, impervious, and she was groveling . . . now that was a revelatory image. And it gave her something to work with. When you see the image, then you can begin to see the archetypal structures and the myths that are going on in the various feelings you have, and then the feelings become a kind of necessary quality of the image, rather than being obsessive in themselves. The image gives you an imagination of the feeling. The image frees you from your obsession with feelings. As the images change, the feelings change. Unfortunately most psychology has been emphasizing feeling all the time and then reducing these feelings back to parental feelings or sexual feelings rather than imagining the feelings through in detail or mythologizing them. It can help to play your love against the rich background of suffering offered by myths, by literature and drama: then what's going on not only begins to make new sense, but also cultures you.   (*Inter Views*, 180–181, 187)

BETRAYAL

The need for security within which one can expose one's primal world, where one can deliver oneself up and not be destroyed, is basic and evident in analysis. This need for security may reflect needs for mothering, but from the paternal pattern within which we are talking, the need is for closeness with God, as Adam, Abraham, Moses, and the patriarchs knew.

What one longs for is not only to be contained in perfection by another who can never let one down. It goes beyond trust and betrayal by the other in a relationship. What one longs for is a situation where one is *protected from one's OWN* treachery and am-bivalence, one's own Eve. In other words, primal trust in the pater-nal world means being in that garden with God and all things *but Eve*. The primeval world is pre-Eve'l, as it is also pre-evil. To be one with God in primal trust offers protection from one's own am-bivalence. One cannot ruin things, desire, deceive, seduce, tempt, cheat, blame, confuse, hide, flee, steal, lie, spoil the creation oneself through one's own feminine nature, betray through one's own left-handed unconsciousness in the treachery of the anima who is that source of evil in Eden and of ambivalence in every Adam since. We want a logos security where the word is *Truth* and it cannot be shaken. . . .

This way of understanding the tale implies that the situation of primal trust is not viable for life. God and the creation were not enough for Adam; Eve was required, which means that betrayal is required. It would seem that the only way out of that garden was through betrayal and expulsion, as if the vessel of trust cannot be altered in any way except through betrayal. We are led to an essential truth about both trust and betrayal: they contain each other. You cannot have trust without the possibility of betrayal. It is the wife who betrays her husband, and the husband who cheats his wife; partners and friends deceive, the mistress uses her lover for power, the analyst discloses his patient's secrets, the father lets his son fall. The promise made is not kept, the word given is broken, trust becomes treachery.

We are betrayed in the very same close relationships where primal trust is possible. We can be truly betrayed only where we truly trust—by brothers, lovers, wives, husbands, not by enemies, not by strangers. The greater the love and loyalty, the involvement and commitment, the greater the betrayal. Trust has in it the seed of betrayal; the serpent was in the garden from the beginning, just as Eve was pre-formed in the structure around Adam's heart. Trust and the possibility of betrayal come into the world at the same moment. Wherever there is trust in a union, the risk of betrayal becomes a real possibility. And betrayal, as a continual possibility to be lived with, belongs to trust just as doubt belongs to a living faith.

If we take this tale as a model for the advance in life from the "beginning of things," then it may be expected that primal trust will be broken if relationships are to advance; and, moreover, that the primal trust will not just be outgrown. There will be a crisis, a break characterized by betrayal, which according to the tale is the *sine qua non* for the expulsion from Eden into the "real" world of human consciousness and responsibility.

For we must be clear that to live or love only where one can trust, where there is security and containment, where one cannot be hurt or let down, where what is pledged in words is forever binding, means really to be out of harm's way and so to be out of real life. And it does not matter what is this vessel of trust—analysis, marriage, church or law, any human relationship.

One cannot help but remark upon the *accumulation of anima symbolism constellated with the betrayal motif.* As the drama of betrayal unfolds and intensifies, the feminine becomes more and more apparent. Briefly, may I refer to the washing of the feet at the supper and the commandment to love; to the kiss and the silver; to the agony of Gethsemane—a garden, at night, the cup and the salty sweat pouring like drops of blood; to the wounded ear; to the image of the barren women on the way to Golgotha; to the warning from the dream of Pilate's wife; to the degradation and suffering, the gall and bitter sop, the nakedness and weakness; the ninth-hour darkness and the abundance of Marys; and I refer especially to the wound in the side at the helpless moment of death, as Eve was torn from Adam's side. And finally, the discovery of the risen Christ, in white, by women.

It would seem that the message of love, the Eros mission of Jesus, carries its final force only through the betrayal and crucifixion. For at the moment when God lets him down, Jesus becomes truly human, suffering the human tragedy, with his pierced and wounded side from which flows the water and blood, the released fountain of life, feeling, and emotion.

The puer quality, the position of fearless safety of the miracle preacher, is gone. The puer God dies when the primal trust is broken, and the man is born. And the man is born only when the feminine in him is born. God and man, father and son no longer are one. This is a radical change in the masculine cosmos. After Eve was born from sleeping Adam's side, evil becomes possible; after the side of the betrayed and dying Jesus was pierced, love becomes possible. . . .

But before we turn to the possible fruitful outcome of betrayal, let us stay a while with the sterile choices, with the dangers which appear after betrayal.

The first of these dangers is *revenge*. An eye for an eye; evil for evil; pain for pain. . . .

The next of these dangers, these wrong though natural turns, is the defence mechanism of *denial*. If one has been let down in a relationship, one is tempted to deny the value of the other person; to see, sudden and at once, the other's shadow, a vast panoply of vicious daimones which were of course simply not there in primal trust. These ugly sides of the other suddenly revealed are all compensations for, an enantiodromia of, previous idealizations. . . .

More dangerous is *cynicism*. Disappointment in love, with a political cause, an organization, a friend, superior, or analyst often leads to a change of attitude in the betrayed one which not only denies the value of the particular person and the relationship, but all love becomes a Cheat, causes are for Saps, organizations Traps, hierarchies Evil, and analysis nothing but prostitution, brainwashing, and fraud. Keep sharp; watch out. Get the other before he gets you. Go it alone. . . .

Self-betrayal is perhaps what we are really most worried about. And one of the ways it may come about is as a consequence of having been betrayed. In the situation of trust, in the embrace of love, or to a friend, or with a parent, partner, analyst, one lets something open. Something comes out that had been held in: "I never told this before in my whole life." A confession, a poem, a love letter, a fantastic invention or scheme, a secret, a childhood dream or fear— which holds one's deepest values. At the moment of betrayal, these delicate and very sensitive seed pearls become merely grit, grains of dust. The love letter becomes silly sentimental stuff, and the poem, the fear, the dream, the ambition, all reduced to something ridiculous, laughed at boorishly, explained in barnyard language as *merde*, just so much crap. The alchemical process is reversed: the gold turned back into feces. . . . For it was just through this trust in these fundamentals of one's own nature that one was betrayed. So we refuse to be what we are, begin to cheat ourselves with excuses and escapes, and self-betrayal becomes nothing other than Jung's definition of neurosis *uneigentlich leiden*, inauthentic suffering. One no longer lives one's own form of suffering, but through *mauvaise foi*, through lack of courage to be, one betrays oneself.

This is ultimately, I suppose, a religious problem, and we are rather like Judas or Peter in *letting down the essential thing*, the essential important demand to take on and carry one's own suffering and be what one is no matter how it hurts.

Besides revenge, denial, cynicism, and self-betrayal, there is yet one other negative turn, one other danger, which let us call *paranoid*. Again, it is a way of protecting oneself against ever being betrayed again, by building the perfect relationship. Such relationships demand a loyalty oath; they tolerate no security risks. "You must never let me down" is the motto. Treachery must be kept out by affirmations of trust, declarations of everlasting fidelity, proofs of devotion, sworn secrecy. There must be no flaw; betrayal must be excluded.

But if betrayal is given with trust, as the opposite seed buried within it, then this paranoid demand for a relationship without the possibility of betrayal cannot really be based on trust. Rather it is a convention devised to exclude risk. As such it belongs less to love than to power. It is a retreat to a logos relationship, enforced by word, not held by love.

✤

It may well be that betrayal has no other positive outcome but forgiveness, and that the experience of forgiveness is possible only if one has been betrayed. Such forgiveness is a forgiving which is not a forgetting, but *the remembrance of wrong transformed within a wider context*, or as Jung has put it, the salt of bitterness transformed to the salt of wisdom.

This wisdom, as Sophia, is again a feminine contribution to masculinity, and would give the wider context which the will cannot achieve for itself. Wisdom I would here take to be that union of love with necessity where feeling finally flows freely into one's fate, reconciling us with an event.

Just as trust had within it the seed of betrayal, so betrayal has within it the seed of forgiveness. This would be the answer to the last of our original questions: "What place has betrayal in psychological life at all"? *Neither trust nor forgiveness could be fully realized without betrayal.* Betrayal is the dark side of both, giving them both meaning, making them both possible. Perhaps this tells us something about why betrayal is such a strong theme in our religions. It is perhaps the human gate to such higher religious experiences as forgiveness and reconciliation with this silent labyrinth, the creation.

("Betrayal," 65–67, 70–74, 78–79)

IMAGINAL LOVE

In the darkness of this [analytical] initiation, the two people instinctively move nearer to each other. A bond forms, as if an eros between the dying, something that is other than the transference of past emotions, other than love between pupil and guide, between patient and doctor, a quite rare and inexplicable feeling brought by the mystery of the image.

I do not know what this kind of loving is, but it is not reducible to other more familiar forms. Perhaps it is an experience of the eros in Thanatos. Perhaps it is an experience of telestic eros, of which Plato speaks in the *Phaedrus*, the eros of the mysteries and initiations of the soul; or, it may have something to do with the creative eros that always occurs when one is close to soul, the myth of [Eros] and Psyche moving through our emotions. Whatever the nature, there is a loving in dream work. We sense that dreams mean well for us, back us up and urge us on, understand us more deeply than we understand ourselves, expand our sensuousness and spirit, continually make up new things to give us—and this feeling of being loved by the images permeates the analytical relationship. Let us call it *imaginal love*, a love based wholly on relationship with images and through images, a love showing in the imaginative response of the partners to the imagination in the dreams. Is this Platonic love? It is like the love of an old man, the usual personal content of love voided by coming death, yet still intense, playful, and tenderly, carefully close.   (*Dream and the Underworld*, 196–197)

Therefore, therapy is love of soul. The teaching and healing therapist—if we use the Socratic-Platonic model of philosopher who teaches and heals—is on the same plane of being as the lover; both take their origins from the same primordial impulse behind their seeking (*Phaedrus* 248D). Therapy as love of soul is a continual possibility for anyone, waiting upon neither the therapeutic situation nor a special "therapeutic eros," a misnomer which is a construct of reflection. This love would show in therapy through the spirit with which we approach the phenomena of the psyche. No matter how desperate the phenomena, eros would keep connected to the soul and seek a way through. This spirit of resourceful inventiveness and creative intelligence, our tales of Eros tell us, he has inherited from his father, either Poros or Hermes. Love not only finds a way, it also leads the way as psychopompos and is, inherently, the "way" itself. Seeking psychological connections by means of eros is the way of therapy as soul-making. Today this is a way, a *via regia*, to the unconscious psyche as royal as the way through the dream or through the complex.

Creative insights are thus not only the reflective ones; they are those vivencias, those exciting perceptions arising from involvement. Psychological perceptions informed by eros are life-giving, vivifying. Something new comes into being in oneself or the other. Love blinds only the usual outlook; it opens a new way of perceiving, because one can be fully revealed only to the sight of love. Reflective insights may arise like the lotus from the still center of the lake of meditation, while creative insights come at the raw and tender edge of confrontation, at the borderlines where we are most sensitive and exposed—and, curiously, most alone. To meet you, I must risk myself as I am. The naked human is challenged. It would be safer reflecting alone than confronting you. And even the favorite dictum of reflective psychology—a psychology which has consciousness rather than love as its main goal—"Know Thyself," will be insufficient for a creative psychology. Not "Know Thyself" through reflection, but "Reveal Thyself," which is the same as the commandment to love, since nowhere are we more revealed than in our loving.

Nowhere, too, are we more blind. Is love blindfolded, in statuary and painting, only to show us its compulsion, ignorance, and sensuous unconsciousness? Love blinds in order to extinguish the wrong and daily vision so that another eye may be opened that perceives from soul to soul. The habitual perspective cannot see through the dense skin of appearances; how you look, what you wear, how you are. The blind eye of love sees through into the invisible, making the opaque mistake of my loving transparent. I see the symbol you are and what you mean to my death. I can see through the blind and foolish visibility that everyone else sees and into the psychic necessity of my erotic desire. I discover that wherever eros goes, something psychological is happening, and that wherever psyche lives, eros will inevitably constellate. Like the early Eros figures, I am naked: visible, transparent, a child. Like the later Amor figures, I am blind: seeing none of the evident, obvious values of the normal world, open only to the invisible and daimonic.

Now our image of the goal changes: not Enlightened Man, who sees, the seer, but Transparent Man, who is seen and seen through, foolish, who has nothing left to hide, who has become transparent through self-acceptance; his soul is loved, wholly revealed, wholly existential; he is just what he is, freed from paranoid concealment, from the knowledge of his secrets and his secret knowledge; his transparency serves as a prism for the world and the not-world. For it is impossible reflectively to know thyself; only the last reflection of an obituary may tell the truth, and only God knows our real names. We are always behind with our reflections—too late, after the event; or we are in the midst, where we see through a glass darkly.

How can we know ourselves by ourselves? We can be known to ourselves through another, but we cannot go it alone. That is the hero's way, perhaps appropriate during a heroic phase. But if we have learned anything from the rituals of the new life-form of the past seventy years, it is just this: we cannot go it alone. The opus of the soul needs intimate connection, not only to individuate but simply to live. For this we need relationships of the profoundest kind through which we can realize ourselves, where self-revelation is possible, where interest in and love for soul is paramount, and where eros may move freely—whether it be in analysis, in marriage and family, or between lovers or friends.

In a man's dreams the anima is often the image for neurovegetative symptoms and emotional lability; that is, she represents the semisomatic events which are not yet psychic experiences, which have not yet undergone enough psychization. In these dreams she is closed off, under water, "unable to come out"; or she is as magical and incomprehensible as the symptoms themselves; or she may still be a child at the threshold of puberty; sometimes she is drowned, burned, frozen, idiotic, dwarfed, syphilitic—in need of care; sometimes she is part of a mythical inscape where fairies and animals move through the vegetation not yet cut into by human perceptions.

In these dreams a man may attempt to bore through a wall to reach "the girl in the next room," or he may find the line cut on the telephone so that he "can't get through." Sometimes the attractive girl speaks only a foreign tongue, comes from some heathen culture, and draws him back into the historical past; such figures enter, excite the dreamer erotically, and disappear. Or an insect or mouse that he tries to crush reveals itself as a beautiful but tiny girl. Nothing makes sense; seductions abound. Day after day a man is victim to feelings and fantasies that turn his head on every street corner. Just when the sails of fantasy swell and the voyage of imagination is about to get under way, his symptoms lay him low. The classical approaches that he can use for dealing with other archetypal assaults, such as refusing the mother or confronting the shadow, fail utterly. In response to questioning she smiles and fades. He falls asleep or wastes the day in a bad mood. She resists all analytical approaches that would reduce her, interpret her, or explain her. Only one way seems open, a hint of which is given by her easy seductiveness—the erotic way. A man is asked to love his soul.

The conclusions to which we are forced by the empirical data in analytical work are that *anima becomes psyche through love* and that *it is eros which engenders psyche*. Thus we come to one more notion of the creative, this time as perceived through the archetype of the anima. *The creative is an achievement of love*. It is marked by *imagination* and *beauty*, and by connection to *tradition* as a living force and to *nature* as a living body. This perception of the instinct will insist on the importance of love: that nothing can create without love and that love shows itself as the origin and principle of all things as in the Orphic cosmogony. Since this perspective seems the one most in keeping with the intentions of the psyche in its configuration as anima, it is this view of creativity which we shall expand upon in regard to the opus of analytical work.

(Myth of Analysis, 53–55, 90–92)

Let's stay with the word *love* because it is so amazing to realize that love is working toward clarification, that's its intention, and all the ferment, all the seething, is its "increase," becoming clarified like a broth, like a butter, because what happens is transparency. And when we try to "clear things up," go over the past to see it better, or put ourselves through confessions—all that is part of love becoming clarified. We are working at transparency. Impossible dark spots of the interior person get lit up, the shadow, the ugliest man, all the shames and embarrassments regarding the concealed personal tied-up self—well, there they are. "Good morning! How are you! Nice to see you!" They aren't gone away or healed or integrated. Those hysterias you mentioned, those delusions. There they are, but they have become transparent, for a moment at least, like rubies and emeralds. The leopard can't change his spots, but the spots can be gems. I am trying to say that your shadow is your virtue, and that is what love is mostly about. And that's what remains—if anything has to remain—after a person's dead. His faults, his unbearable qualities, or hers, become clarified, and you remember them as virtues. They stand out sharp and clear, like essences. It's amazing how the very thing you couldn't bear in your mother or father, in your wife or husband—they die, and then the rubies show right in the shadow. . . . *(Inter Views, 191–192)*

There are three portions or persons of Eros that have been classically differentiated: *himeros* or physical desire for the immediately present to be grasped in the heat of the moment; *anteros* or answering love; and *pothos*, the longing toward the unattainable, the ungraspable, the incomprehensible, that idealization which is attendant upon all love and which is always beyond capture. If *himeros* is the material and physical desire of eros, and *anteros* the relational mutuality and exchange, *pothos* is love's spiritual portion. *Pothos* here would refer to the spiritual component of love or the erotic component of spirit. When *pothos* is presented on a vase painting (fifth century, British Museum) as drawing Aphrodite's chariot, we see that *pothos* is the motive force that drives desire ever onward, as the portion of love that is never satisfied by actual loving and actual possession of the object. It is the fantasy factor that pulls the chariot beyond immediacy, like the seizures that took Alexander and like Ulysses's desire for "home."

Pothos here is the blue romantic flower of love that idealizes and drives our wandering; or as the romantics put it: we are defined not by what we are or what we do, but by our *Sehnsucht:* Tell me for what you yearn and I shall tell you who you are. We are what we reach for, the idealized image that drives our wandering. *Pothos*, as the wider factor in eros, drives the sailor-wanderer to quest for what cannot be fulfilled and what must be impossible. It is the source of "impossible love," producing the Tristan complex that refuses *himeros* and *anteros* in order to maintain the transcendence of *pothos*. This side of eros makes possible living in the world as a scene of impossible mythical action, mythologizing life. This component of eros is the factor, or the divine figure, within all our senseless individuation adventures, the phallic foolishness that sends us chasing, the mind's mad wanderings after impossibilities, our forever being at sea, and the fictive goals we must set ourselves—all so that we may go on loving.   ("Pothos," 53–54)

When archetypal psychology speaks of love, it proceeds in a mythical manner because it is obliged to recall that love too is not human. Its cosmogonic power in which humans take part is personified by gods and goddesses of love. When cosmogonies about the creation of the world place love at the beginning, they refer to Eros, a daimon or a god, not just to a human feeling. Love's cosmogonic power to structure a world draws humans into it according to styles of the gods of love. . . .

Even if we stay only with Aphrodite, or Venus as she has been called since the Romans, we find her love to be a complicated group of myths, now enmeshed with Ares, now with the heights of Uranus, the waves of Poseidon, the concrete artifacts of Hephaestus; now in opposition to Artemis or to Hera and Athena, now in a triangle with Eros and so an enemy of Psyche. She has remarkable progeny—Priapus with the grand erection is a son of her love (as is Eros himself), and Hermaphroditus—who carry her business into extremes. But she has her own odd sides, sometimes appearing black, bearded, and helmeted, secretly in love with war, and her loving is complicated further by her genealogy, which reveals her deepest kinship connections, what she is truly most "like." There we discover that she is born out of the froth of emotions when the old man Uranus's genitals are cut off (the repressed sexuality of any stern senex attitude); there we see her passion for revenge, her sisters Nemesis and the Furies; there we see too her enactment in the queens of beauty, the Helens of this world, their thousand avenging ships, their wars that drag on for ten years, the rages and treacheries.

To comprehend the logos of love, even if only the one presented through Aphrodite, one must follow the whole course through. The train of her myths tells more of psychic reality than do the defining statements of love in philosophy, theology, and psychology. Love's images are multitudinous and yet precisely characterized by the locations of her temples, by her festivals and her favorite landscapes, localities, animals, plants, and mythical persons. Other languages at least sometimes try to catch some of these differentiations with several terms for love. We have but one. So when we say God is Love, just whom do we mean?

The god within the beautiful illusions of humanistic therapy may well be Aphrodite. Her role in psychotherapeutic thinking has not yet been adequately examined. Let us recall that from the earliest days of depth psychology in Charcot's Parisian clinic the content of the repressed was aphroditic: *la chose génitale.* Freud, who watched these demonstrations of girls in their trance postures, returned to Vienna germinating his erotic theory of the neuroses. The word he chose for the soul's movement and energy, *libido,* comes from the Dionysiac-Aphroditic vocabulary referring originally to *lips,* the downpour of sexual liquids. . . .

Despite the richeries that can be dug out of Aphrodite's myths, neither all of love nor all of therapy can be awarded to one god. Psychotherapy, beginning with Freud's introduction of death into its purview, has come to realize that soul-making leads beyond the pleasure principle and that love is not enough. As Norman Brown *(Life Against Death)* has written, "Love is a little moment in the life of lovers; and love remains an inner subjective experience leaving the macrocosm of history untouched. Human history cannot be grasped as the unfolding of human love." Love develops its own history and counterhistory, in groups, in families, in transference, in the *histoire* of an affair, with dates and keepsakes in its museum of memorabilia. This history stands outside the arena of events and sets up its private, oppositional calendar with anniversaries and festivals, commencing at the hour when love was born.

Love meets the needs of soul only within specific archetypal patterns in particular instances. Then one or another of its mythical fantasies speaks directly to my situation. It could be Hera eternally embraced with Zeus in their marriage bed, or Eros sulking and blind to the soul's actual plight, or Jesus vivid and morbid on the cross. It is love in one or another of these imaginal forms that works on us. But to take love as *the* principle of psychotherapy is again to find a monotheistic panacea for the imaginative complexity of our psychic life. *(Re-Visioning,* 184–186)

12

The Divine
Face of Things

One of the key moves in James Hillman's re-visioning of psychology is to liberate it from its medicine complex. This allows him to honor pathology and depart from salvational fantasies of psychotherapy altogether. This, in turn, leads psychological analysis, whether of an individual life or of culture or ideas, into an unredeemable and inexhaustible depth. Whatever is analyzed becomes more soulful through the exploration of its unending, mysterious images.

If health is the primary value in a psychology informed by the fantasy of medicine, then in a psychology of image and eros the primary value is beauty. What Hillman says over and over is that the soul does not need to be free of symptoms. It doesn't require that life be lived perfectly. Something other than the soul finds virtue in hygienic living and successful relationships and life strategies. What the soul needs and craves is the experience of the world, taking it in as it presents itself.

True to form, Hillman traces the genealogy of the idea of aesthetics and adopts the Greek aisthesis, which connotes perception rather than a refined sense of beauty. Aesthetics in this primordial sense involves sensing the things of the world in their particularity and being affected by the many ways things present themselves.

The unpsychological life, or life in which psyche is not in pursuit of eros and beauty, looks at the world and sees scientific classifications of things, or microscopic structures, or new resources for a consumerist appetite. It does not see things in their sensate, unique bodies. Marsilio Ficino said that the world is an animal. Hillman pursues this idea that in all its variety the world shows itself to us as a living being. Each thing has a face and calls for our attention. The response is aesthetics.

Archetypal psychology recognizes that the soul needs a vital relationship to the gods. The soul thrives when it acknowledges a divine factor in any human endeavor. Hillman's psychology of beauty restores sensitivity to one of the most neglected, and therefore, for human life, most troubling of the gods, Aphrodite. He understands her as the divine figure immanent in the world of sense. Naked, jeweled, alluring Aphrodite is nature and culture exposing itself to the soul with its beauty, ornament, and form. The soul delights and, to use a Renaissance term, feeds on this beauty.

Beauty may not be the primary concern of a literalistic, achieving attitude toward life, but when soul is placed in the center, beauty takes on absolute importance. To the soul, beauty is not accidental or peripheral. Neoplatonic tradition would say that the human soul longs for union with its matrix, the world soul. A vital, sensitive aesthetic sense is the means by which the human soul finds that reunion, that intimacy with the world. When society splits its relationship to the world into functioning on the one hand and entertainment on the other, soulful work and pleasure are lost.

Admittedly, beauty and aesthetics, like everything else, cast a broad, dark shadow. Hillman writes about certain aspects of the shadow of aestheticism. It can have a puer preciousness and shallowness. It can glorify the beautiful to the extent that it represses the hardness and sharpness of life. It is possible to become a monotheist in the religion of Venus.

In spite of these dangers, the aesthetic life is particularly important in our time because it is so overlooked and undervalued. Hillman recommends that to revive this aesthetic sense we might look to the animals and see the beauty they reveal in expressing their own natures so directly. Our proper form of display, he says, is rhetoric, our fantasy-filled capacity to speak, tell stories, paint, dance, sing, make music, build buildings, write letters, make movies, and so on. The beautiful, and therefore the soul, is in the everyday display of our natures.

Narcissus was saved when he saw the beauty of his own face reflected in a pool of water. We are saved from our narcissistic distancing from the world when we see our own beauty in the display of everyday life and in the daily arts of the soul. We find our own face, the unique visage of our soul, in the world's display of itself.

PSYCHIC BEAUTY

While the erotic can be a form of *mania*, as Plato said, it also beautifies. Moreover, beauty is the first attribute which draws Eros to Psyche. "To love," says Diotima, "is to bring forth upon the beautiful." We have had to neglect beauty in our work because, on the Oedipal model, it was regressive, seductively sexual, the attraction of Jocasta. On the heroic model, beauty too often represented the merely aesthetic approach, producing an embellishment rather than a meaning, a *puer* avoidance of the battles of purposeful achievement, and a neglect of the ugly bitterness of the shadow. Perhaps now we may realize that the development of the feminine, of anima into psyche, and of the soul's awakening is a process in beauty. This implies that the criteria of aesthetics—unity, line, rhythm, tension, elegance—may be transposed to the psyche, giving us a new set of qualities for appreciating what is going on in a psychological process. The beauty of soul which alone surpasses the allure of Aphrodite will show in the aesthetic imagination of the psyche and the attractive power of its images. It will show in the ways in which the psyche gives form to its contents—for instance, the manner in which the anima contains the erotic. But mainly the beauty of psyche refers to a sense of the beautiful in connection with psychological events. By being touched, moved, and opened by the experiences of the soul, one discovers that what goes on in the soul is not only interesting and meaningful, necessary and acceptable, but that it is attractive, lovable, and beautiful.

The ultimate beauty of psyche is that which even Aphrodite does not have and which must come from Persephone, who is queen over the dead souls and whose name means "bringer of destruction." The Box of Beauty which Psyche must fetch as her last task refers to an underworld beauty that can never be seen with the senses. It is the beauty of the knowledge of death and of the effects of death upon all other beauty that does not contain this knowledge. Psyche must "die" herself in order to experience the reality of this beauty, a death different from her suicidal attempts. This would be the ultimate task of soul-making and its beauty: the incorporation of destruction into the flesh and skin, embalmed in life, the visible transfigured by the invisibility of Hades's kingdom, anointing the psyche by the killing experience of its personal mortality. The Platonic upward movement toward aestheticism is tempered by the beauty of Persephone. Destruction, death, and Hades are not left out. Moreover, Aphrodite does not have access to this kind of beauty. She can acquire it only through Psyche, for the soul mediates the beauty of the invisible inner world to the world of outer forms.

(Myth of Analysis, 101–102)

ANIMAL BEAUTY

*K*osmos is an aesthetic term which can best be translated as "fitting order." Therefore it is equally a moral term, used for instance by Aeschylus for "good order," "good behavior," "decency," and by Homer, in the negative *kata kosmon* for "bad order," "shamefully." Liddell and Scott give such translations as "becomingly," "duly," "decently"; other connotations are "discipline," "form," "fashion." A second group of meanings refers especially to the world of women, where *kosmos* is used for ornament, decoration, embellishment, dress and is descriptive of sweet songs and ways of speech. The verb *kosmos* means "to arrange, adorn, furnish." Our word *cosmetics* is closer to the original atmosphere of *kosmos* than is the Latinate *universe*.

From the perspective of the Greek word the physical world is an orderly arrangement, a display of palpable things; and so it may be conceived as a whole universe only because of its aesthetic and moral fittingness. Without these sensate echoes, without the aesthetic and moral connotations contained in *kosmos*, the word today refers only to a vast gasbag, outer, empty, spacey and cold, while the *logos* of the cosmic is without sweet song. By this I mean that the mode of adequate response to the world as universe is to seek sufficient explanation, to the world as cosmos to seek sufficient appreciation.

Abandoning idealizations, lifting repression, allowing desire admit the profound attachment of our minds to things, of things to each other and their desire to enter and be held in the mind, to be perceived, named, known and loved, the joy in the animals at Adam's recognition, their ennoblement by being spoken of. Each thing needs other things—once called "the sympathy of all things." Attachment is embedded in the soul of things, like an animal magnetism (Mesmer), a cosmic longing or cosmogonic eros of the Greeks and Freud. The soul's longing does not call for deliverance, rather it reports cosmic dependence, declaring frankly that clutching and clinging are ecological passions of the soul, keeping things in the embrace of each other and maintaining the intercourse of their self-revealing conversations.

When cosmos is understood as the arrangement and expression of things, as the patterning order each event presents, embellishing each event with its own kind of time and fitting space, cosmos becomes the interiority things bring with them rather than the empty universal envelope into which they must be brought. . . .

Cosmos would be the shine in display, the beauty attesting to the presence of soul, the face that claims (Levinas), the form that shapes, the tension that holds, the pathology that limits, and the immediacy afforded by phenomena to one another, their intelligible truth. Here, truth too shifts from noetic and universal coherence to the inherence of behavior: remaining true to itself, true to form, true to its nature, in law abiding—truth and law indistinguishable from beauty.

Here I turn to the work of the late Adolf Portmann, the eminent Basel zoologist and philosopher of nature. He demonstrated that *selbstdarstellung* or display of interiority is as essential to organic life as are the useful behaviors of survival. Animal life is *biologically aesthetic:* each species presents itself in designs, coats, tails, feathers, furs, curls, claws, tusks, horns, hues, sheens, shells, scales, wings, songs, dances. And this display of secondary qualities is primordial.

The aesthetic is rooted in biology. Nothing precedes it genetically. The coat of an animal is phylogenetically prior to the optical structures necessary for seeing the coat. To show is primarily to show— secondarily to be seen. There are creatures in ocean deeps where no light falls which nonetheless have brilliant colors that can never be perceived; and there are symmetrical markings on primitive oceanic organisms that bear no useful purpose, neither for camouflage against enemies, attractions for breeding, signaling, staking territory, lures for prey. *Sheer appearance for its own sake,* or what Portmann also calls "unaddressed phenomena." Sheer appearance as purpose of its own, recalls Kant's notion of the aesthetic as "purposiveness without purpose." And more: sheer appearance as its own purpose recalls the original aesthetic meanings of *kosmos*—"ornament, decoration, embellishment, dress." An animalized cosmology restores the aesthetic to primary place. To restore this aesthetic sense of cosmos therefore requires giving first place to animals.

("Cosmos," 287, 298–299, 294)

W hen patients are urged to wriggle like a snake or hug like a bear, they are encouraged to be as ugly and violent as only humans can be. These therapies do not notice the beauty of actual animals and that reconnecting to the animal means getting to a more sensitive, more artful and humorous place in the psyche. Thus, these therapies I was condemning, in the name of finding the animal soul, actually reenact our Western tradition's contempt.

Besides, giving up on language betrays our own human nature. I think that the human form of display, in the ethologist's sense of "display," is *rhetoric.* Our ability to sing, speak, tell tales, recite, orate is essential to our lovemaking, boasting, fear-inspiring, territory-protecting, surrendering, and offspring-guarding behaviors. Giraffes and tigers have splendid coats; we have splendid speech. Returning to animality, in your sense of "animal," I therefore heartily endorse, as you know, for instance, from my recent seminars with Gary Snyder, Gioia Timpanelli, and Robert Bly, and also from my lectures on the subject going back to the sixties, all of which have been aimed at evoking the animal as psychic presence. I have been trying to foster self-recognition of human being as animal being.

("On Animals," 8)

In fact, says Bachelard, "a need to animalize . . . is at the origins of the imagination," whose first function "is to create animal forms." The complex expressing itself in the animals creates an active and screaming universe in which fear, brutality, and rage shape imagination, a universe in which "energy is an aesthetic."

This obscure phrase—"in this universe the energy is aesthetic"—closes his chapter on muscles and cries. The phrase refers to the human scream which sounds forth the animality of "an angry universe." "All animals, even those least on the offensive, articulate their war cry." In this sounding, the *dynamis* of nature becomes aesthetic. And if we carry this insight further, all aesthetic reactions of our nostrils, muscles, throat and teeth are the force of nature through us, nature acting upon nature, speaking with nature.

The animalizing tendency begins not in a human need; we do not invent animal symbolisms. Imagination itself invents animal forms, even out there in nature; animals themselves, out there in nature, are living symbols. Primordial brutal life is symbolic, aesthetic—and cruel. ("Cruelty must be placed at the origins of instinct; without it *animal behavior* cannot begin.") The universe when perceived via the Lautréamont complex is aesthetic because it is animal. And it is from the animals that we have learned symbolism. Freudian and literary symbolisms are but mutilated examples of the symbolic powers already in action in nature. ("Bachelard," 113)

THE SHADOW OF AESTHETICS

It is said that the bleeding of Christ tells of love, of compassion, of suffering and of the endless flow of the divine essence into the human world, and of the bond through blood kinship and blood mystery of the human world with the divine. The bleeding of Jesus is a transfiguration of a basic puer motif onto a theological plane.

But our job is psychological—an examination of an archetypal motif—so what does this specific form of woundedness [bleeding] say about the psychology of the puer? His bleeding reveals his archetypal structure in several ways. *First*, it is an image for vulnerability in general, the skin too thin for real life, the sensitivity to every pointed instrument of attack, the defenselessness of youngly naive and open truth. The bleeding tells of the puer propensity for victimization, for the constellation around him of the psychopathic attackers: Loki, Hagen, the Roman soldiers, the crowd of arrows into Sebastian. He draws the assassins to himself, a hero-in-reverse, noble for his martyrdom, remembered finally less for what he does than for what is done to him. The bloodthirsty aggression that comes to him from the outside belongs to his fate, but he is unaware that it belongs to his character too. He points up the ancient idea that "character for man is destiny," so that the insights arising from the complexes composing our character also tell us about our fate. (*Amor fati* thus also means loving one's complexes.) To draw blood or to have it drawn is part of the same constellation of bloodletting. As the hero, i.e., puer, cannot stop his manic seizure of slaughter (Achilles abused Hector's corpse for twelve days), so the hero-in-reverse cannot staunch his own bleeding. He has no tourniquet partly because his bleeding is so beauteous. Why stay such blood, a blood that is latent with flowers? Myths tell us again and again that from slain pueri spring wondrous blooms. The puer is transfigured by his wounds into glory. It is as if he does not sense his broken vessels, cannot smell blood, only flowers. Aestheticism can defend one even against pain. Parsifal has only to ask Amfortas "What ails him?" but the question of the wound never occurs to this beautiful young man single-minded on his quest for the grail. So Amfortas's wound continues to suppurate—ailing is all in the king, the senex; there is none in the pure young knight.

There are other wounds, suppurating and bitter, leading neither to death nor cure, serving instead as focus of psychic complexity. Prometheus's liver is always being torn at; Hercules burns in his poisoned shirt; Philoctetes's foot is continually infected. No flowers here, but rather the stuff for reflection for thousands of years in myths, dramas, and poems. These bitter wounds hurt; they stink and give rise to continual complaint, and, in Philoctetes's case, the complaint gives the dignity of an individualized destiny.

("Ulysses' Scar," 110)

Feeling can also become too *aesthetic*, love only for the beautiful, or love only for beautiful women, or the inability to enter into that aspect of feeling where it is harsh and savage. Anima aestheticism cannot shout, yet shouting can belong to appropriate feeling. In Stendhal's *De l'amour* there is a chapter where he speaks of Beauty being dethroned by Love. He refers to that step in the development of the feeling function where the anima complex, as the worship of Beauty, is replaced by the appropriate feelings of love for a woman. From one point of view, the more important a woman's beauty is to a man, the less individual and personal is the relationship. Overfondness for usual beauty, from this point of view, is a sign of anima love rather than an expression of the feeling function. Hence the difficulty a beautiful woman has in finding an individual relationship with a man. She is doomed to catching his anima feeling, and she may be driven to sacrifice her beauty to gain his love. The aesthetic distortion also serves to suppress negative feelings and leaves a man incapable of coping with the tough situations of life where ugliness and plain dirt belong. The aesthetic anima does not like swearing and cursing, suffering dumb animals, the smell of gunpowder, the oppressed poor, the noise of cities and pollution, whereas "her" feelings do go to the beauties of nature, cultured art and religions of incense and song. ("Feeling Function," 124)

THOUGHT OF THE HEART

When Petrarch, age twenty-two, in the Church of Santa Chiara at Avignon, on April 6, 1327, caught sight of a lovely girl, his heart pounded or stopped or leapt into his throat. His soul had been assailed by beauty. Was this when the Renaissance began? Or had it already begun, this *Vita Nuova*, when Dante, in 1274 at the age of nine first saw Beatrice ("she who confers blessing"), crimson-dressed girl-child and anima mundi, awakening his heart to the aesthetic life.

"At that moment," writes Dante, "I say . . . the spirit of life, which hath its dwelling in the secretest chamber of the heart, began to tremble so violently that the least pulses of my body shook; and in trembling it said these words: 'Here is a deity stronger than I; who, coming, shall rule over me' " (*Vita Nuova*, II). From then on he was a devotee of this deity in the shape of his soul figure, dedicated to love, imagination, and poetic beauty, all three inseparably.

These couples, Petrarch and Laura, Dante and Beatrice, had no personal satisfaction, no human relationship. Yet what emerged from these happenings in the heart was the transformation of all Western culture, commencing as an aesthetic transformation; it was generated by Beauty. Was not Psyche in the Apuleius tale singled out by her beauty, and is not Aphrodite, the Beautiful One, the soul of the universe (*psyché tou kosmou* or *anima mundi*) that produces the perceptible world according to Plotinus (III, 5, 4) and also the soul of each of us?

Can we attend to what these figures and tales are saying? Can we realize that we are each, in soul, children of Aphrodite, that the soul is a *therapeutes*, as was Psyche, in the temple of Venus—*that* is where it is in devotion. The soul is born in beauty and feeds on beauty, requires beauty for its life. If we read Plato the way Plotinus did, and understand Psyche the way Apuleius did, and experience soul as did Petrarch and Dante, then *psyche is the life of our aesthetic responses*, that sense of taste in relation with things, that thrill or pain, disgust or expansion of breast, those primordial aesthetic reactions of the heart are soul itself speaking. Psyche's first trait and the way we know her first, is neither by her labors, the *work* of soul-making, nor by her sufferings for love, nor in her oppression in lostness, the absence and deprivation of soul—these in the Apuleian tale all come later. We know her first by her primary characteristic given with her nature: Psyche is beautiful.

How is it possible that beauty has played such a central and obvious part in the history of the soul and its thought, and yet is absent in modern psychology? Imagine—eighty years of depth psychology without a thought to beauty! Even now psychology tends to reduce the aesthetic from its primacy to a diagnostic attribute, "aestheticism." Those tales of Petrarch and Dante become anima fascinations, immature idealizations of repression, unrelated narcissism, typically puer aestheticizing.

We have taken Psyche's beauty only symbolically as meaning something other than itself. We have not read carefully what Apuleius says, nor placed it against his Platonic background. Else we would have understood that Psyche's beauty was visible, sensate, as Laura's was to Petrarch, as Aphrodite shows herself nude. Moreover, in our psychological interpretations of Psyche we have mistaken her beauty as a mere motif to be understood, rather than as the essential characteristic of Psyche's image, a mistake which requires a new reading of the tale in terms of the soul's essentially aesthetic nature.

If beauty is not given full place in our work with psyche, then the soul's essential realization cannot occur. And, a psychology that does not start in aesthetics—as Psyche's tale starts in beauty and as Aphrodite is the *psyché tou kosmou* or soul in all things—cannot claim to be truly psychology since it omits this essential trait of the soul's nature. We are led already to see that a full depth psychology expressing the nature of Psyche must also be a depth aesthetics. Further, if we would recuperate the lost soul, which is after all the main aim of all depth psychologies, we must recover our lost aesthetic reactions, our sense of beauty. . . .

By beauty we do not mean beautifying, adornments, decorations. We do not mean aesthetics as a minor branch of philosophy concerned with taste, form and art criticism. We do not mean "disinterestedness"—the lion asleep. Nor can beauty be held in museums, by maestros at the violin, a profession of artists. Indeed we must cleave beauty altogether away from art, art history, art objects, art appreciation, art therapy. These are each positivisms: that is, they posit beauty into an instance of it: they position *aisthesis* in aesthetic events such as beautiful objects.

In pursuing what we mean by beauty we are obstructed by the

word *beauty* itself. It strikes the ear as so effete, so ineffectual, lovely and etheric, so far removed from the soul's desperate concerns. Again we see how our notions are determined by archetypal patterns, as if beauty had become relegated only to Apollo, the examination of invisible forms like music, belonging to collectors and subject to disputes in journals of aesthetics. Or, beauty has been given over wholly to the soft hands of Adonis and Paris, beauty as violets, mutilation and death. In Plato and Plotinus, however, beauty does not have this glabrous, passive and ungenerative sense at all, and it is rarely brought into relation with art. In fact beauty is not "beautiful" and Socrates's person is witness. Rather, the beautiful in Platonic thought can only be understood if we can enter an Aphroditic cosmos and this in turn means penetrating into the ancient notion of *aisthesis* ("sense perception") from which aesthetics derives.

We must press beyond our usual ideas of beauty that have held the imagination captive to heavenly notions only, Aphrodite Urania, and away from the world of sense in which Aphrodite was always immanent. Hence, her nakedness has been pornographized by denigrating the visibility of physical appearance. As well, these lofty ideas have mystified revelation into an eschatological expectation: revelation comes as an epiphany that must shatter the sensate world only when we cannot sense the revelation in the immediate presentation of things as they are.

As Corbin writes *(Man of Light)*: Beauty is that great category which specifically refers to the *Deus revelatus*, "the supreme theophany, divine self-revelation." As the gods are given with creation so is their beauty in creation, and is the essential condition of *creation as manifestation*. Beauty is the manifest anima mundi—and do notice here it is neither transcendent to the manifest or hiddenly immanent within, but refers to appearances as such, created as they are, in the forms with which they are given, sense data, bare facts, Venus Nudata. Aphrodite's beauty refers to the luster of each particular event; its clarity, its particular brightness; that particular things appear at all and in the form in which they appear.

Beauty as Plato describes it in the *Phaedrus* (250b) is the manifestation, the showing forth of the hidden noumenal gods and imperceptible virtues like temperance and justice. All these are but ideas, archetypes, pure forms, invisible didactic talk unless accompanied by beauty. "For beauty alone," he says, "this has been ordained, to be the most manifest to sense . . ." (250d). Beauty is thus the very sensibility of the cosmos, that it has textures, tones, tastes, that it is attractive. Alchemy might call this cosmic gloss, sulfur. . . .

If beauty is inherent and essential to soul, then beauty appears wherever soul appears. That revelation of soul's essence, the actual showing forth of Aphrodite in psyche, her smile, is called in mortal language, "beauty." All things as they display their innate nature present Aphrodite's goldenness; they shine forth and as such are aesthetic. Here, I am merely restating what Adolf Portmann has elaborated at Eranos for forty years: the idea of *Selbstdarstellung* ("self-presentation") as the revelation to the senses of essential *Innerlichkeit* ("interiority"). Visible form is a show of soul. The being of a thing is revealed in the display of its *Bild* ("image").

Beauty is not an attribute then, something beautiful, like a fine skin wrapped round a virtue; the aesthetic aspect of appearance itself. Were there no beauty, along with the good and the true and the one, we could never sense them, know them. Beauty is an *epistemological* necessity; it is the way in which the gods touch our senses, reach the heart and attract us into life.

As well, beauty is an *ontological* necessity, grounding the sensate particularity of the world. Without Aphrodite, the world of particulars becomes atomic particles. Life's detailed variety is called chaos, multiplicity, amorphous matter, statistical data. Such is the world of sense without Aphrodite. Then sense must be made of appearance by abstract philosophical means—which distorts philosophy itself from its true base.

If, as we said in Part I, philosophy takes rise in *philos*, it also refers to Aphrodite in another way. For *sophia* originally means the skill of the craftsman, the carpenter (*Iliad*: XV, 412), the seafarer (Hesiod, *Works*: 651), the sculptor (Aristotle, *Nichomachean Ethics*, vi: 1141a). Sophia originates in and refers to the aesthetic hands of Daedalus and Hephaestus, who was of course conjoined with Aphrodite and so is inherent to her nature. With Aphrodite informing our philosophy, each event has its own smile on its face and appears in a particular mode, fashion, style. Aphrodite gives an archetypal background to the philosophy of "eachness" and the capacity of the heart to find "intimacy" with each particular event in a pluralistic cosmos (William James).

Now, the organ which perceives these faces is the heart. The thought of the heart is physiognomic. To perceive, it must imagine. It must see shapes, forms, faces—angels, daimones, creatures of every sort in things of any kind; thereby the heart's thought personifies, ensouls, and animates the world. Petrarch sees Laura:

> . . . *in pathless forest shades,*
> *I see the face I fear, upon the bushes*
> *Or on an oaken trunk; or from the stream*
> *she rises; flashes on me from a cloud*
> *Or from clear sky; or issues from a rock, . . .*
>
> (*Metricae* I, 6)

The lines are not *to* Laura, a love lyric, but a description of Laura, the soul personified, the figuration in the heart by means of which aesthetic perception proceeds. It brings to life things as forms that speak. . . .

This link between heart and the organs of sense is not simple mechanical sensationalism; it is aesthetic. That is, the activity of perception or sensation in Greek is *aisthesis* which means at root "taking in" and "breathing in"—a "gasp," that primary aesthetic response.

Translators have turned *aisthesis* into "sense perception," a British empiricist's notion, John Locke's sensation. But Greek "sense perception" cannot be understood without taking into account the Greek goddess of the senses or the organ of Greek sensation, the heart, and the root in the word—that sniffing, gasping, breathing in of the world. . . .

Phenomena need not be saved by grace or faith or all-embracing theory, or by scientific objectiveness or transcendental subjectivity. They are saved by the anima mundi, by their own souls and our simple gasping at this imaginal loveliness. The *ahh* of wonder, of recognition, or the Japanese *shee-e* through the teeth. The aesthetic response saves the phenomenon, the phenomenon which is the face of the world. "Everything shall perish except His face," says the Koran (xxxviii: 88) which Corbin (*Creative Imagination*) can understand to mean "Every thing . . . except the Face of that thing." God, the world, everything can pass into nothingness, victims of nihilistic constructions, metaphysical doubts, despairs of every sort. What remains when all perishes is the face of things as they are. When there is nowhere to turn, turn back to the face before you, face the world. Here is the goddess who gives a sense to the world that is neither myth nor meaning; instead that immediate thing as image, its smile, a joy, a joy that makes "forever."

❀

So, the question of evil, like the question of ugliness, refers primarily to the anesthetized heart, the heart that has no reaction to what it faces, thereby turning the variegated sensuous face of the world into monotony, sameness, oneness. The desert of modernity.

Surprisingly, this desert is not heartless, because the desert is where the lion lives. There is a long-standing association of desert and lion in the same image, so that if we wish to find the responsive heart again we must go where it seems to be least present.

According to *Physiologus* (the traditional lore of animal psychology), the lion's cubs are stillborn. They must be awakened into life by a roar. That is why the lion has such a roar: to awaken the young lions asleep, as they sleep in our hearts. Evidently, the thought of the heart is not simply given, a native spontaneous reaction, always ready and always there. Rather, the heart must be provoked, called forth, which is precisely Marsilio Ficino's etymology of beauty; *kallos*, he says, comes from *kaleo*, "provoke." "The beautiful fathers the good" (Plato, *Hippias Major*, 297b). Beauty must be raged, or outraged into life, for the lion's cubs are stillborn, like our lazy political compliance, our meat-eating stupor before the television set, the paralysis for which the lion's own metal, gold, was the Paracelsian *pharmakon*. What is passive, immobile, asleep in the heart creates a desert which can only be cured by its own parenting principle that shows its awakening care by roaring. "The lion roars at the enraging desert," wrote Wallace Stevens. "Heart, instinct, principle," again Pascal. . . .

The more our desert the more we must rage, which rage is love.

The passions of the soul make the desert habitable. One inhabits, not a cave of rock, but the heart within the lion. The desert is not in Egypt; it is anywhere once we desert the heart. The saints are not dead; they live in the leonine passions of the soul, in the tempting images, the sulfuric fantasies and mirages: love's road. Our way through the desert of life or any moment in life is the awakening to it as a desert, the awakening of the beast, that vigil of desire, its greedy paw, hot and sleepless as the sun, fulminating as sulfur, setting the soul on fire. Like cures like: the desert beast is our guardian in the desert of modern bureaucracy, ugly urbanism, academic trivialities, professional official soullessness, the desert of our ignoble condition. . . .

We fear that rage. We dare not roar. With Auschwitz behind us and the bomb over the horizon, we let the little lions sleep in front of the television, the heart, stuffed full of its own coagulated sulfur, now become a beast in a lair readying its attack, the infarct.

Psychologically, we subdue our rage with negative euphemistic concepts: aggression, hostility, power complex, terrorism, ambition, the problem of violence. Psychology analyzes the lion. Perhaps Konrad Lorenz was wrong, and the counselors wrong too, who seek to find a way beyond aggression. Is it "aggression," or is it the lion roaring at the enraging desert? Has psychology not missed the native sulfur, neglected Mars who rides a lion, Mars, beloved of Aphrodite?

(*Thought of the Heart*, 24–33, 41–44)

SOURCES

In order to present an unencumbered text, footnotes and references have to a large extent been removed. For full references consult the original sources mentioned in the excerpts. For the bibliography of James Hillman's works, see "The Complete Checklist of Works by James Hillman" in *Archetypal Psychology: A Brief Account,* 3rd ed., Dallas: Spring Publications, 1988. (Unless otherwise noted, James Hillman is the author or editor of the works cited.)

BOOKS

Anima

Anima: An Anatomy of a Personified Notion. Dallas: Spring Publications, 1985.

City and Soul

City and Soul. Irving, Texas: Center for Civic Leadership, University of Dallas, 1978.

Cookbook

Freud's Own Cookbook [with Charles Boer]. New York: Harper & Row, 1985.

CP

Sigmund Freud. *Collected Papers.* Translation supervised by Joan Riviere. London: Hogarth Press.

CW

H. Read, M. Fordham, G. Adler, and W. McGuire, eds. *The Collected Works of C. G. Jung.* Bollingen Series XX. Translated by R. F. C. Hull. Princeton, N.J.: Princeton University Press and London: Routledge and Kegan Paul, 1970.

Dream and the Underworld

The Dream and the Underworld. New York: Harper & Row, 1979.

Emotion

Emotion: A Comprehensive Phenomenology of Theories and Their Meanings for Therapy. London: Routledge & Kegan Paul, 1960.

Healing Fiction

Healing Fiction. Barrytown, N.Y.: Station Hill Press, 1983.

Insearch

Insearch: Psychology and Religion. London: Hodder and Stoughton; New York: Charles Scribner's Sons, 1967; Irving, Texas: Spring Publications, 1979.

Inter Views

Inter Views: Conversations Between James Hillman and Laura Pozzo on Therapy, Biography, Love, Soul, Dreams, Work, Imagination and the State of the Culture. New York: Harper & Row, 1983.

Myth of Analysis

The Myth of Analysis: Three Essays in Archetypal Psychology. Evanston, Ill.: Northwestern University Press, 1972; Harper Colophon edition, New York: Harper & Row, 1978.

Paranoia

On Paranoia. Eranos Lectures Series 8. Dallas: Spring Publications, 1988.

Re-Visioning

Re-Visioning Psychology. New York: Harper & Row, 1975.

Spr

James Hillman, ed. *Spring: An Annual of Archetypal Psychology and Jungian Thought.* Zurich and Dallas: Spring Publications.

Suicide

Suicide and the Soul. London: Hodder and Stoughton; New York: Harper & Row, 1964; Dallas: Spring Publications, 1976.

Thought of the Heart

The Thought of the Heart. Eranos Lectures Series 2. Dallas: Spring Publications, 1984.

Transportation

Psychological Fantasies in Transportation Problems. Irving, Tex.: Center for Civic Leadership, University of Dallas, 1979.

Typologies

Egalitarian Typologies versus the Perception of the Unique. Eranos Lectures Series 4. Dallas: Spring Publications, 1986.

ARTICLES

"Abandoning"

"Abandoning the Child." *Eranos Jahrbuch* 40 (1971): 358–406 (Leiden: E. J. Brill, 1973; revised in *Loose Ends: Primary Papers in Archetypal Psychology.* New York and Zurich: Spring Publications, 1975, 5–48.)

"Abnormal Psychology"

"On the Necessity of Abnormal Psychology." *Eranos Jahrbuch* 43 (19/4): 91–135 (Leiden: E. J. Brill, 1977; reprinted in *Facing the Gods*, edited by James Hillman. Dallas: Spring Publications, 1980), 1–38.

"Animal Kingdom"

"The Animal Kingdom in the Human Dream." *Eranos Jahrbuch* 51 (1982): 279–334. (Frankfurt a/M: Insel Verlag, 1983.)

"Anima Mundi"

"Anima Mundi: The Return of the Soul to the World." *Spring* (1982): 71–93.

"Archetypal Theory"

"Archetypal Theory: C. G. Jung." In *Operational Theories of Personality*, edited by A. Burton, 65–98. New York: Brunner/Mazel, 1974.

"Bachelard"

"Bachelard's Lautréamont, or Psychoanalysis Without a Patient." Afterword essay. In *Lautréamont*, Gaston Bachelard, translated by Robert S. Dupree, 103–123. Dallas: The Dallas Institute Publications, 1986.

"Bad Mother"

"The Bad Mother: An Archetypal Approach." *Spring* (1983): 165–181.

"Betrayal"

"Betrayal." Lecture 128, London: Guild of Pastoral Psychology, 1964. (Reprinted in *Spring* (1965): 57–76, and in *Loose Ends: Primary Papers in Archetypal Psychology*. New York and Zurich: Spring Publications, 1975, 63–81.)

"Blue"

"Alchemical Blue and the Unio Mentalis." *Sulfur: A Literary Tri-Quarterly of the Whole Art* I (1981): 33–50.

"Ceiling"

"Interiors in the Design of the City: The Ceiling." *The Institute Newsletter* (The Dallas Institute of Humanities and Culture) 2/1 (1983): 11–18. (Reprinted in *Stirrings of Culture*, edited by R. Sardello and G. Thomas. Dallas: The Dallas Institute Publications, 1986, 78–84.)

"Chronic Disorder"

"On Culture and Chronic Disorder." *The Institute Newsletter* (The Dallas Institute of Humanities and Culture) 1/2 (1982): 12–17. (Reprinted in *Stirrings of Culture*, edited by R. Sardello and G. Thomas. Dallas: The Dallas Institute Publications, 1986, 15–21).

"Cosmos"

"Cosmology for Soul." In *Cosmos-Life-Religion: Beyond Humanism*, 280–301. Nara, Pakistan: Tenri University Press, 1988.

"Extending the Family"

"Extending the Family: From Entrapment to Embrace." *The Texas Humanist* 7/4 (1985): 6–11.

"Feeling Function"

"The Feeling Function." In *Lectures on Jung's Typology* (with "The Inferior Function," by Marie-Louise von Franz), 74–150. New York and Zurich: Spring Publications, 1971.

"Foreword to Inscapes"

Foreword. In *Inscapes of the Child's World*, John Allan, xiii–xx. Dallas: Spring Publications, 1988.

"Going Bugs"

"Going Bugs." *Spring* (1988): 40–72.

"Great Mother"

"The Great Mother, Her Son, Her Hero, and the Puer." In *Fathers and Mothers: Five Papers on the Archetypal Background of Family Psychology*, edited by P. Berry, 75–127. New York and Zurich: Spring Publications, 1973.

"Image-Sense"

"Image-Sense." *Spring* (1979): 130–143.

"Incest Dream"

"A Psychology of Transgression Drawn from an Incest Dream: Imagining the Case." *Spring* (1987): 66–76.

"Inquiry into Image"

"An Inquiry into Image." *Spring* (1977): 62–88.

"Mars"

"Mars, Arms, Rams, Wars: On the Love of War." In *Facing Apocalypse*, edited by V. Andrews, R. Bosnak, and K. W. Goodwin, 118–136. Dallas: Spring Publications, 1987.

"Moisture"

"Souls Take Pleasure in Moisture." In *Stirrings of Culture*, edited by R. Sardello and A. Thomas. Dallas: The Dallas Institute Publications, 1986, 203–205.

"Monotheistic or Polytheistic?"

"Psychology: Monotheistic or Polytheistic?" *Spring* (1971): 193–208, 230–232. (Expanded in appendix to *The New Polytheism*, by David Miller, 109–142. Dallas: Spring Publications, 1981.)

"Natural Beauty"

"Natural Beauty Without Nature." *Spring* (1985): 50–55.

"Negative Senex"

"The 'Negative' Senex and a Renaissance Solution." *Spring* (1975): 77–109.

"Oedipus"

"Oedipus Revisited." In *Eranos Jahrbuch* 56 (1987). (Frankfurt a/M: Insel Verlag, 1987): 261–307.

"On Animals"

"James Hillman on Animals: A Correspondence with John Stockwell." *Between the Species* 1/2 (1985): 4–8.

"On Senex Consciousness"

"On Senex Consciousness." *Spring* (1970): 146–165.

"On Soul and Spirit"

"James Hillman on Soul and Spirit: An Interview with Barbara Dunn." *The Common Boundary* 6/4 (1988): 5–11.

"Pan"

"An Essay on Pan." In *Pan and the Nightmare*, 3–65 and 156. New York and Zurich: Spring Publications, 1972.

"Peaks and Vales"

"Peaks and Vales: The Soul/Spirit Distinction as Basis for the Differences Between Psychotherapy and Spiritual Discipline." In *On the Way to Self-Knowledge*, edited by J. Needleman and D. Lewis, 114–147. New York: Knopf, 1976. (Collected in *Puer Papers*, 54–74. Dallas: Spring Publications, 1979.)

"Pothos"

"Pothos: The Nostalgia of the Puer Eternus." In *Loose Ends: Primary Papers in Archetypal Psychology*. New York and Zurich: Spring Publications, 1975, 49–62.

"Right to Remain Silent"

"The Right to Remain Silent." *Journal of Humanistic Education and Development* 26/4 (1988): 141–153.

"Salt"

"Salt: A Chapter in Alchemical Psychology." In *Images of the Untouched*, edited by J. Stroud and G. Thomas, 111–137. Dallas: Spring Publications, 1981.

"Senex and Puer"

"Senex and Puer: An Aspect of the Historical and Psychological Present." *Eranos Jahrbuch* 36 (1967): 301–360. (Zurich: Rhein, 1970; revised in *Puer Papers*, 3–53. Dallas: Spring Publications, 1979.)

"Sex Talk"

"Sex Talk: Imagining a New Male Sexuality." *Utne Reader* 29 (1988): 76.

"Silver (I)"

"Silver and the White Earth." *Spring* (1980): 21–48, 111–137.

"Silver (II)"

"Silver and the White Earth (Part Two)." *Spring* (1981): 21–66.

"Soul and Money"

"A Contribution to Soul and Money." In *Soul and Money*, by Russell A. Lockhart, James Hillman et al., 31–43. Dallas: Spring Publications, 1982.

"Ulysses' Scar"

"Puer's Wound and Ulysses' Scar." In *Puer Papers*, 100–128. Dallas: Spring Publications, 1979.

"Walking"

"Walking." In *The City as Dwelling*, 1–7. Irving, Tex.: Center for Civic Leadership, University of Dallas, 1980.

INDEX

abandoned child, 159–60
abandonment, in marriage, 236
abortion, 238
acedia, 153
action, 72; and ideation, 52
active imagination, 57–58
Adam, 277
Aeschylus, 293
aesthetics, 57, 290–96, 300–303;
  shadow of, 297–98
affliction, 146–49, 161–62
agitated depression, 158
albedo, 64–67
Albertus Magnus, 210
alchemical psychology, 125–29
alchemy, 8, 19, 35
allegory, 24–25
America, and war, 182
analogy, and dreams, 244–45
analysis, 10, 16, 77, 79–81, 87, 290;
  of dreams, 242–43, 245, 246–53
angel, 64, 65, 69–70
anima, 21, 36, 85–91, 116, 119,
  218–20; and animus, 40, 41, 90;
  and beauty, 292, 298; and
  betrayal, 278–79; consciousness
  and, 31, 33–34, 89–91; depression,
  156; impossible love, 271; and
  psyche, 285; senex, 212–13
animals, 68–69, 293–96; in dreams,
  240, 253–60

anima mundi, 95–96, 99–102
animation, 99
anima women, 16
animism, 98
animus, 36, 40, 41, 90
Anteros, 286
anxiety, 262, 274
Aphrodite, 39, 181, 211, 213,
  287–88, 291, 293, 299, 301–2
apocalypse, 184
Apollo, 39, 206
appearance, 302
Apuleius, 299–300
archai, 15–16
archetypal psychology, 2–3, 10, 11,
  15–17, 22, 26–27, 50, 95–96, 291;
  depression, 155; image, 25; and
  love, 267, 287; and pathologizing,
  146–48; therapy, 73
archetypes, 23–24, 26–27, 59–60;
  beauty, 301–3; child, 236–37;
  father, 220–21; incest as, 218–19;
  and meaning, 117–18; parental,
  223; and pathologizing, 145; *puer
  eternus*, 227–30; senex, 208–16;
  sickness in, 151–52
Aristophanes, 272
Aristotle, catharsis, 82
art, 42, 299–300
Asklepiós, 71
Athena, 39, 184

315